CLAIMING BELONGING

CLAIMING BELONGING

Muslim American Advocacy in an Era of Islamophobia

Emily Cury

CORNELL UNIVERSITY PRESS   ITHACA AND LONDON

First published 2021 by Cornell University Press

Library of Congress Cataloging-in-Publication Data

Names: Cury, Emily, author.
Title: Claiming Belonging : Muslim American Advocacy in an Era
   of Islamophobia / Emily Cury.
Description: Ithaca : Cornell University Press, 2021. | Includes bibliographical
   references and index.
Identifiers: LCCN 2020013038 (print) | LCCN 2020013039 (ebook) |
   ISBN 9781501753596 (hardcover) | ISBN 9781501754005 (paperback) |
   ISBN 9781501753602 (ebook) | ISBN 9781501753619 (pdf)
Subjects: LCSH: Muslims—Political activity—United States. | Islam and politics—
   United States. | Muslims—United States—Social conditions—21st century. |
   Islamophobia—United States. | Islam and state—United States.
Classification: LCC E184.M88 C89 2021 (print) | LCC E184.M88 (ebook) |
   DDC 305.6/970973—dc23
LC record available at https://lccn.loc.gov/2020013038
LC ebook record available at https://lccn.loc.gov/2020013039

For my father

Contents

Acknowledgments

This book went under contract when my firstborn daughter was two months old. Every major step in the writing process was intrinsically linked to her early milestones. She started crawling just as I finished writing a particularly challenging chapter. The day she uttered her first word was the same day I heard back from an interviewee, finally agreeing to speak with me. And so on. Writing a book while caring for a newborn was challenging at times, exasperating at others, and downright depressing on more than a few occasions. But it was also elucidating. A young child puts things in perspective like few things can. My daughter reminds me that change is intrinsic to life, and that so much of what makes us human is shared. I must have spoken to more strangers in the past year and a half than I have my entire adult life. In the first few months, people routinely stopped us with greetings of "congratulations" and "welcome to the world." They genuinely wanted to "see the baby," to say hello, to ask how I was feeling. Maybe I live around a lot of nice people, or maybe we are all just eager to connect. I don't know. What I do know is that her presence has made me see everything and everyone around me with a keener set of eyes, and, for that, I am grateful.

I have a long list of people to thank, as anyone who has worked on a project for almost a decade might. First and foremost, I am forever indebted to the American Muslims whose voices are featured in these pages and who gave me so much of their time and energy, even when I knew they had little of either to spare. I hope I have done your work justice. Scholars at the City University of New York's Graduate Center helped shape so much of my early thinking on the subject in these pages. I am deeply and tremendously grateful to my former mentor (and now dear friend) Dov Waxman, who, over the years, read and commented on multiple versions of what became this manuscript. No one has had more of an influence on my thinking, work habits, and writing than he has. I first met Dov in 2009, when I took his seminar on the Arab-Israeli conflict. He has been a constant presence in my life since then. I am forever thankful for all the hours, the coffees, the e-mails checking in. And I am particularly thankful for the friendship we—along with our beautiful spouses and children—have built. Thanks to Susan Woodward for scaring the bejesus out of me in her class—surviving it gave me the confidence I needed to survive early academic life and taught me how much I was indeed capable of accomplishing. Thank you to Anny Bakalian and Mehdi Bozorgmehr for the many hours we spent talking about Muslim and Arab American mobilization. Their support and kindness sustained me during those early years.

I have been fortunate enough to find friends and colleagues that, for one reason or another, believed in me and took it upon themselves to support me. When I joined Northeastern University in 2015, Valentine Moghadam took me under her wings, enveloping me with her intellect and graciousness. My office was right next door to hers, and we spent a lot of "in-between" time talking about our research, current events, and developments in the Middle East—the region we both hail from. Those conversations kindled my spirit. I thank my lucky stars that, even after I left Northeastern for a new job, our tête-à-têtes continue. Thank you to Denis Sullivan for teaching me so much about what being an academic entails, which we should be taught, but too often aren't. I offer a very special thanks to my dear friend, Sarah A. Tobin, for her intellectual generosity, care, and guidance through the years. I have never met anyone more supportive than Sarah. She demystified what academic publishing entailed, gave me the confidence I desperately needed to pursue this undertaking, and was there for me every step of the process. I am thankful for her every day.

I owe a special debt of gratitude to my editor at Cornell University Press, Emily Andrew, for her stewardship and guidance. Emily understood what it meant to write this book while caring for a young child, and never once made me feel inadequate for it. She gave me the space I needed to focus on the work, provided constant support and advice, and was a true ally in this process. I would also like to recognize Alexis Siemon and the entire team at Cornell University Press who worked very hard to bring this book to fruition. Thank you to Jaime Jarvis for meticulously reading through the manuscript and providing me with her keen editorial eye. I am deeply appreciative to the anonymous readers for their exhaustive and excellent feedback and for investing their time to help me improve the manuscript.

In 2016, I was invited to participate in a workshop on Muslim American politics organized by Melissa Michelson, Nazita Lajevardi, and Brian Calfano. The event, held at Menlo College, was nothing short of exhilarating—as was the follow-up workshop held at UCLA the following year. I am grateful to the organizers and to my fellow workshop participants for sharing so much of their knowledge and expertise. One of the many outcomes of our workshop includes a symposium on Muslim American politics, published in 2019 in the *Journal of Politics and Religion*. Portions of chapter 5 previously appeared in that symposium in an article titled "Contesting Islamophobia and Securing Collective Rights: Muslim American Advocacy in the 2016 Elections." Portions of chapter 6 were published in the same journal in 2017 as "Muslim American Policy Advocacy and the Palestinian Israeli Conflict: Claims-Making and the Pursuit of Group Rights." Portions of chapter 2 appeared in the *Journal of Diaspora Studies* in 2016 as "Muslim American Integration and Interest Group Formation: A Historical Narrative." These articles were the seeds for this book.

Thank you to my students at Northeastern University and Pine Manor College, where I now teach, for being an unending source of inspiration. Anyone who complains about Millennials and Generation Z must not spend a lot of time around these age cohorts. Teaching them is the greatest honor of my life. Thank you to my family and friends for giving me so much. To my mother, whose love and struggles have made me a better person; to my dear aunt and uncle, Nadia and William, for bringing me to this country and giving me a new life; and to Roula, Hussam, and Lynne for being more than siblings.

My final and deepest gratitude goes to my husband, Ziad, for his patience, encouragement, and unwavering belief in me. Thank you for prioritizing my goals and tolerating years of missed dinners, nights out, and social commitments without complaining. Thank you for brainstorming with me, for always asking the right questions, and for never tiring of talking about the subject in these pages. Your care and love sustained me and made this project possible. When the task of writing another sentence seemed intolerable, your calm and steady presence propelled me forward. Your positivity and joyfulness make everything shine a little brighter. Thank you for being on this journey with me.

CLAIMING BELONGING

MAKING MUSLIM CONSTITUENTS VISIBLE

It was an early spring morning in Washington, DC, and I had just arrived to attend the 2017 Annual Muslim American National Advocacy Day on Capitol Hill, an event that in recent years had become a political pilgrimage of sorts for hundreds of Muslims from across the United States. The city was in full bloom, bursting with life and color. It was even more beautiful than I remembered it from my visit a few years earlier. Feeling invigorated by my surroundings and the morning sunshine, and with plenty of time before the event started, I decided to walk. The scenery was familiar: tourists and tour buses lining the streets, young children trailing their parents, hurried young professionals tugging at their phones. But it felt different. After a short stroll from Union Station, I found myself outside the United States Supreme Court, that imposing neoclassical structure, with its wide staircase and tall Corinthian columns, where so much of who we are and what we are as a nation has been argued and decided. I paused to admire the two marble statues looming over me—*Contemplation of Justice* to my left, *Authority of Law* to my right. I thought of the past few months and of how much our national politics had changed since I last stood there. For someone who came of age in New York City in the late 1990s and knew Donald Trump primarily as the über-wealthy owner of Trump Tower—an extravagant stop on the "Fifth Avenue Tour" I gave to family and friends visiting from overseas—the idea that he was president was still surreal.

I checked my phone and, realizing time had flown faster than I'd thought, sped my pace toward the Capitol building. As I made my way to the Welcome Center, I surveyed my surroundings. I was looking forward to the next two days, but I was also checking to see whether any Islamophobic protesters had arrived before me, as I had been warned they might during a webinar earlier that week. (Thankfully, they had not.) I was eager to meet the Muslim leaders, activists, and community organizers who were already in the building, and to interact with the individuals who had come to lobby their members of Congress and make themselves seen and their demands known. I was less ready to confront the disgruntled hecklers who often showed up to these events. Just in case, I rehearsed what I had been told to say and do—or, rather, refrain from doing—in an encounter: *Don't engage them, don't agree to any interviews, don't touch them or their equipment.* Simple enough. If anyone went as far as to approach and try to provoke an interaction, we had been advised to smile, give a thumbs-up, and say, "Beautiful day to be on Capitol Hill"[1]—in other words, to deny them any opportunity for a confrontation. I was relieved to be left wondering whether this tactic would have worked.

Once inside the building, a group of young volunteers greeted me and guided me to the auditorium, where the opening session was about to begin. I was surprised to see so many people in the audience; I counted roughly three hundred individuals in the room. The crowd was ethnically diverse, reflecting the diversity of the American Muslim community. The majority were Southeast Asians and Arabs, and there were significant numbers of African Americans, as well as a few white and Latinx individuals, who, based on the recent demographic trends I was familiar with, I assumed were converts to Islam. My interactions with the attendees later that day would confirm these observations; indeed, I was thrilled to meet members from the IslamInSpanish mosque in Houston, the only Latino-led Islamic center in the United States. I was also heartened to find so many children and young adolescents in that auditorium, many volunteering at the event—the next generation of Muslim American activists in the making.

As participants studied the day's agenda and prepared to meet with their elected officials, the speakers encouraged them to share personal stories of how specific bills would affect them and their loved ones, putting a human face on the legislative issues. The organizers also reminded participants to use social media, including the hashtag #MuslimHillDay, to document and amplify their advocacy efforts, and to take and share photos with members of Congress—but only after asking for permission. Many of the elected officials consented to being photographed that day, but not all. Some, particularly Republicans from conservative districts, were worried the photos would be taken out of context and used to score political points against them. No matter: delegates were advised to keep their spirits high and to remember that change happens incrementally. The day's goal was to make their voices heard and begin cultivating lasting relationships with elected officials. These seemingly modest expectations, alongside the ambivalence of the officials, are largely reflective of the Muslim American political experience. In representing just 1 percent of the total US population, Muslim advocacy groups know that exerting enough pressure on elected officials to become an influential political force is unlikely, at least in the short term. Their primary goal, one that is reflected in events such as these, is not to effect policy change but to make Muslim constituents visible.

Nonetheless, there was a sense of excitement in the room, an air of anticipation. People were in good spirits, despite the fact that this was the first Muslim Hill Day, as the organizers dubbed the event, held since Donald J. Trump had become president. The Muslim community, along with other minority communities and communities of color across the country, was feeling targeted—and rightly so. Anti-Muslim rhetoric, which had been a feature of the 2016 campaign (although many pundits discounted it as campaign talk), did not abate after the elections. Instead, it intensified and was translated into specific policies, as Muslims and other targeted communities had feared all along. On January 27, 2017, a mere seven days after his inauguration, President Trump signed the first iteration of the executive order known as the "Muslim ban," which barred people from seven Muslim-majority countries from entering the United States.[2]

Faced with legal challenges and mass protests at airports all across the country, the administration then turned its attention to other ways of inhibiting Muslims from migrating to the United States. Along with continuing to adjust the Muslim ban to withstand legal scrutiny, the Trump administration implemented a policy of "extreme vetting" that, according to the Cato Institute, a libertarian think tank, significantly decreased the number of immigrants coming to the United States from Muslim-majority countries. According to a Cato Institute report published in December 2018, "all the major categories of entries to the United States—refugees, immigrants, and visitors—[were] significantly down under the Trump administration for Muslims or applicants from Muslim majority countries. The number of Muslim refugees decreased by 91 percent from 2016 to 2018 and the number of Muslim immigrants saw a 30 percent decline during the same period."[3] In this policy environment, anti-Muslim incidents increased to the highest point since the immediate aftermath of the attacks of September 11, 2001, and continued to rise in the coming years. Not surprisingly, these themes dominated the 2017 Muslim Hill Day, foreshadowing Muslim American policy engagement in the Trump era.

Muslim Americans Have Arrived!

Muslim organizations in the United States have been holding national advocacy days since the mid-2000s, when the Council on American-Islamic Relations

(CAIR), the nation's largest Muslim advocacy group, began organizing these events. Despite their modest size and their being largely ineffectual in actually influencing decision makers, as Muslim leaders themselves are quick to point out, these lobbying days are far from insignificant. First, they make Muslim citizens more visible as constituents and raise awareness about issues important to Muslim American communities. They also encourage American Muslims to engage in politics—an important feat for a community whose political participation is still relatively anemic. And they confer a degree of national visibility and legitimacy to the organizations and leaders that claim to represent Muslims in America. In other words, events such as these provide Muslim organizations with an important national stage for communicating who Muslim Americans are and what they stand for—helping, in the process, to construct a sense of collective identity among Muslims in the United States.

Walking the halls of Congress and engaging policymakers also highlights U.S. Muslims' commitment to American democracy and to an institutional, gradualist approach to change making; an approach not all U.S. Muslims agree with. Robert McCaw, director of government affairs at CAIR, explained it this way:

> As a community under attack, we need to ask ourselves: "how can we move the narrative forward?" American Muslims didn't ask to be thrust into the highlight of the election, especially with this hateful rhetoric. But we are using this as an opportunity to ensure that the values of America—freedom, equality—are respected. American Muslims are the most diverse ethnic and racial community in the U.S., so when you force politicians to respect the rights of American Muslims, you force them to respect the rights of *everyone* . . . We're in it for the long haul. Change is not going to happen overnight. We know that. All we can do is try to move the needle forward, just like so many other discriminated against communities have done in the past. This way, other groups who come after us won't have to start from scratch.[4]

CAIR and the other Muslim advocacy groups at the center of this book view themselves as the newest (and most vilified) members of a long lineage in the American movement for the civil rights of minority groups. Almost without exception, all the individuals I interviewed made some reference to this point. Some, like CAIR's former communications director Corey Saylor, did so with confidence: "We have been called to take the torch from those who have struggled and made gains before us, push it forward, and pass it on to the next group of Americans who will be targeted."[5] Others were more self-reflective, judging that Muslim organizations "still had much to learn from other groups about how to mobilize their communities for the long term."[6] All, however, agreed that the struggles Muslims face are not unique but rather part of a broader history of structural discrimination and racism toward American minority groups. The specific group under attack might change, but the experiences they endure are similar, as are the ways they should go about responding, particularly after the achievements of the Civil Rights Movement of the 1960s.

Islamophobia was the term most of the people I interviewed used to describe their experience with individual and structural, state-sanctioned discrimination. Indeed, it is the term the vast majority of Muslim leaders, activists, and victims of anti-Muslim bias use. National surveys by the Pew Research Center, Gallup, and the Institute for Social Policy and Understanding commonly employ the term, and media coverage of *Islamophobia* has risen sharply, particularly since the 2016 presidential election. A simple Google Trends search shows that the number of people searching the term has increased since 2015, reflecting a growing familiarity with and interest in it. As ubiquitous as the term is, however, its meaning is still being conceptualized by scholars and activists alike. In fact, there is an important debate regarding whether *Islamophobia* is an accurate descriptor for anti-Muslim bias. After all, people have phobias to many things. Should the discrimination and targeting facing Muslims in the United States and around the world be seen as resulting from fear? According to Maha Hilal, a scholar-activist, community organizer, and steering committee member of the DC Justice for Muslims Coalition, the answer is a resounding no: "People have phobias to spiders, or heights, or closed spaces. Not to other people. That is called discrimination. That is called racism. We should call anti-Muslim bigotry what it is. Not a 'phobia,' but deep seated, structurally based prejudice."[7]

Although I agree with Hilal's critique, I employ the term intentionally, and for several reasons. First, it came up often, and forcefully, during my research. Many of the people I interviewed understood and described their individual and collective experiences as instances of Islamophobia. The term is also widely used by Muslim advocacy organizations and community leaders—a usage that both reflects and helps frame and interpret the Muslim American experience. To use any other term would diminish the voices of the people at the center of this story. Finally, scholarship on Islamophobia has grown and become more theoretically developed in recent years. As a result, many of the polling and research institutes from which I draw data have become increasingly rigorous in terms of operationalizing and measuring Islamophobia.

I use this term with the understanding that Islamophobia is not a fear but a structural system of oppression. It is pervasive and deeply rooted in American history, manifested through state laws and policies as well as individual acts of aggression and microaggression. Khaled Beydoun, one of the leading scholars of the American Muslim experience, explains Islamophobia as "the presumption that

Islam is inherently violent, alien, and inassimilable, a presumption driven by the belief that expressions of Muslim identity correlate with a propensity for terrorism. Islamophobia is the modern progeny of Orientalism. A worldview that casts Islam as the civilizational antithesis of the West and that is built upon the core stereotype and baseline distortions of Islam and Muslims embedded in American institutions and the popular imagination by Orientalist theory, narrative and law."[8] What is crucial, in Beydoun's analysis, is the dialectic between private and public expressions of Islamophobia. Individual acts of bias or aggression toward Muslims are made possible, sanctioned, and legitimized by state laws and policies that might seem impartial on the surface but disproportionally target Muslims. As Beydoun explains, "If the law is laden with damaging stereotypes of Islam and Muslims, and American citizens are expected and instructed to obey the law, the dialectic between the state and the citizen—and the hostility the state authorizes—is made clear."[9] This dialectic, he goes on to argue, is contingent on media representations that recycle Orientalist tropes, state policies and laws that criminalize an entire faith group, and political rhetoric that fuels hatred and suspicion toward millions of Americans.[10] Thus, like all forms of discrimination, Islamophobia is legitimized and reproduced through the actions of the state, normalized through the rhetoric of our politicians, and reflected back into society for all to consume.

After a long morning of back-to-back meetings, mostly with the staff of elected officials, we were ready for a break. As we made our way toward St. Mark's Episcopal Church—the event headquarters—we felt uplifted. Most of our meetings that morning had been cordial encounters, and most of the representatives whose offices we had visited supported the legislative agenda we were advocating. In 2017, that agenda included three main issues. The first and most important was supporting legislation that protected the constitutional rights of American Muslims, including the Freedom of Religion Act of 2017, which sought to block the Muslim ban, and the No Religious Registry Act of 2017, which sought to preempt the rollout of a "Muslim registry," which Trump had promised on the campaign trail.[11] Second on the agenda was supporting immigrant communities, particularly the undocumented and liminally documented.[12] Thus, we asked our representatives to support the BRIDGE Act, which would shelter Deferred Action for Childhood Arrivals (DACA) recipients from deportation until Congress took up immigration reform.[13] The third item focused on ending racial and religious profiling by law enforcement, an issue that had become a rallying cry for communities of color.

We arrived at St. Mark's Baxter Hall just as the other delegations of Muslim advocates were beginning to trickle in for lunch. We soon found out that our uncontentious experience as the delegates from Massachusetts, meeting with a roster of predominantly Democratic officials, was far from representative. Delegates from more conservative states, such as Arizona, Kentucky, and Texas, had received a far cooler welcome. Some had received no welcome at all. To my delight, Sarwat Husain, the lively president of CAIR's San Antonio chapter, made her way to the table where I had just settled and began telling me about her experience that morning, as others crowded our table to listen:

> Ted Cruz refused to meet with us! We called his office so many times to try to set up an appointment for a meeting. We have been trying for months and have just been ignored. So we decided to just walk into his office and ask to speak with him. I wasn't expecting much from it, but they told me that every Tuesday, he holds a constituency coffee hour on the second floor, and that he was on his way there now! They must have not known who we were. We rushed to the second floor and were waiting for him to arrive when his staffers asked to meet with us privately to hear about our concerns. They took us to another room and were very nice, but they were just trying to keep us there, to prevent us from meeting him, you know? Once we were done, we rushed to the next room, but he [Cruz] was already gone.

She was disappointed, she said, but still glad she had had the opportunity to meet with Cruz's staff: "I told them, 'We are his constituents and he refuses to meet with us. He is running away from us! It's unacceptable.'" Cruz's staff had promised Husain they would bring her concerns to the senator's attention and follow up with her, but, she said, "I will most likely have to call them back myself."

Observers of American politics are unlikely to be surprised by this account of a US senator's refusal to meet with his American Muslim constituents. As a presidential candidate the previous year, Cruz had called for law enforcement to "patrol and secure Muslim neighborhoods"[14] and for the United States to accept Christian refugees fleeing Syria but not Muslim ones, sending them to Muslim-majority countries instead—a position President Barack Obama denounced as "not American."[15] A week following the Muslim ban executive order, Cruz praised President Trump for "trying to act swiftly to prevent terrorists from infiltrating our refugee program" and blamed the public outcry on "hysteria and mistruths being pushed by the liberal media."[16]

One might reasonably expect this political climate to thwart Muslim American advocacy groups' efforts on behalf of their constituents, but the opposite is true. Organizations and institutions representing the interests of Muslims in the United States are surprisingly visible, engaged, and assertive. This book is an attempt to explain how this has come to be the case despite the great odds they face. What motivates Muslim advocacy organizations to participate in the policy process when their ability to exert an influence in the current political climate seems so limited? How do they mobilize support for their policy positions? Why do they continue to mobilize around contentious foreign policy issues, such as the Palestinian-Israeli conflict, when it seems to be against their interests to do so? Whose interests do these organizations really represent?

As a political scientist and observer of Islam and Muslims in America, these questions piqued my interest. As an immigrant woman with roots in the Middle East, who is often assumed to be Muslim and asked to explain a plethora of things associated with Muslims and Islam—particularly, why I don't wear a hijab—the subject speaks to me on a personal level. And, as someone whose closest, most loving and loyal friends are Muslim—my extended family—I feel a duty to share what I came to learn about Muslim American politics through my research, particularly in light of Trump's election.

I began this study in 2011 as a graduate student at the City University of New York's Graduate Center, that wondrous institution that opened its doors to me, even as an undocumented student, setting me on a path beyond my wildest dreams. I began attending events held by Muslim American organizations, meeting and later interviewing Muslim American leaders, and listening keenly to the individuals who attended those events. I became increasingly interested in the organizational strategies that this vilified and poorly understood minority community used to make their demands on the state—their state. I wanted to know how these organizations negotiated the need to engage and collaborate with the government while opposing and criticizing the structures and policies that targeted them and their faith.

The more time I spent researching the subject, the more puzzled I became about what drove the leadership of these organizations to spend limited resources advocating on domestic and foreign policy issues they knew they were unlikely to influence in a meaningful way. I also wanted to understand the link between these national Muslim American groups and the average American Muslim on the street. When I began this work, I often asked my Muslim friends and acquaintances what they thought about CAIR, the country's largest Muslim advocacy organization, only to be met with blank stares. Most had never heard of it or, for that matter, any of the other organizations I write about.

My friends were not alone. A 2011 Gallup poll found that only 23 percent of American Muslims felt CAIR spoke for them. According to the report, "Many Muslims do not feel that there is a national organization that represents them."[17] Although this has changed as more Muslims become familiar with, and supportive of, CAIR's work, the question of representation remains. Some activists are critical of national-level advocacy organizations, arguing that they are elitists and out of touch, dominated by a group of educated, middle-class, first-generation immigrants who have tried to push the "model minority" trope as a recipe for communal advancement. Namira Islam, a lawyer by training and cofounder of the Muslim Anti-Racism Collaborative, an organization that provides racial justice education and training, summarized this critique during our interview:

> The Muslim space is underfunded. People lack a level of understanding of structural issues, and Muslim American organizations tend to reach out to certain organizations for help and expertise. These organizations tend to be white-majority. And I'm always like, that's great, but ultimately, they [white-majority nonprofit organizations] are not having to deal with the Muslim ban or structural Islamophobia. Why aren't we working with more Black, Latinx, or Native organizations? This is the implicit bias that we, as Muslims, and that our organizations, particularly the top-down ones, carry. We should be able to participate and create new coalitions, but there is a hesitance to do that.

Namira's critique contradicted much of what I had been hearing at national events, which placed great emphasis on the need for cross-sectional coalition building, particularly with other communities of color. In fact, I first met Namira at CAIR's National Leadership and Policy Conference in Washington, DC, where she had been invited to speak about strategies for building equitable and accessible community movements. Based on what I knew about these organizations, my sense was that they understood they needed to change, to become more inclusive, to build even wider coalitions that embraced not only the plurality of the Muslim American experience but also communities besides them. For some activists, however, it seemed the change was not fast or deep enough. I asked Namira to elaborate on why she thought "top-down" Muslim organizations, as she put it, were so slow to reach out to other communities of color. "There are a number of reasons," she said, without skipping a beat,

> The first is simply that this is just the way things have been done and practices are not easy to break. Second, it is also the way that things are structured and set up. The networks that national organizations have built are white; the national [Muslim] advocacy scene is very white. Also, most of the founders are white. National Muslim organizations are led by model-minorities, whether south Asian or Arab. They are upper-middle class, educated, so there is a natural tendency to assimilate into whiteness. Lastly, I would say that there is a lot of anti-Blackness, anti-immigration narratives within our own communities that we have internalized.

As a Bengali American grassroots community leader in Detroit, one of the cities with the largest concentration of Muslims, many of whom live either at or below the federal poverty line, Namira saw a different face of Muslim America than the one the national organizations often displayed. "As a Muslim woman of color," she told me, "I understand the feeling of being ignored." Scholars have also contributed to this depiction of Muslims in the United States as a well-educated middle-class minority. Although many Muslims do fit this profile, the narrative of middle-class success erases the experiences of a large portion of American Muslims, particularly those who are working-class, poor, and Black. They, too, are part of the Muslim American mosaic. In a 2017 Pew Research Center survey, 40 percent of Muslim American households reported an income below $30,000 a year.[18] A 2018 study by the Institute for Social Policy and Understanding confirmed these figures and provided insight into how American Muslims experience poverty along racial lines, stating, "Black Muslim households are more likely than any other Muslim racial group to earn incomes less than 30,000 a year."[19]

Namira's critique of the national organizations I write about was not meant to be disparaging. On the contrary, she was thoughtful and constructive:

> Because there are such few organizations, each one is asked to do so much. Given how diverse Muslim Americans are, I think each organization needs to hyper-specialize. In fact, CAIR does the best with their diversity [in the makeup of leadership and constituents]. They do really well at legislative advocacy, so they should focus on that. Other groups need to focus on other issues, particularly on non-governmental, non-legislative change. There is also the fact that so many members of our community have been ignored by national organizations and overall. Native American Muslims at Standing Rock, the Nation of Islam, Latinx, East Asian Muslims in LA . . . and if you think of Latino Muslims in LA, they are *definitely* not being represented by the national organizations.

These sentiments might seem overly negative, even harsh, but I have found much of the leadership and upper echelons of the national-level organizations I write about to be open and self-reflective with regard to criticism and their record of embracing Black, working-class, and inner-city Muslims. Muslim identities in the United States are as diverse, multifaceted, and complex as the country they call home, and although some prominent individuals and organizations have become the public faces of "Muslim America" (a term I borrow from Khaled Beydoun[20]), Namira's critique is a reminder that no one individual or organization can ever really fully represent the Muslim American experience. This, of course, is true of any other organization that claims to speak for a large and diverse group with multiple, and sometimes contradictory, interests, and I do not believe this fact diminishes from their work, efforts, or achievements.

Methods and Rationale

This book exists at the intersection of activism and identity formation. In the pages that follow, I share a facet (and it is that, just a facet) of Muslim American political life. I do not claim to write about every Muslim American organization, nor do I include every national organization. I also deliberately exclude organizations that identify in ethnonational terms, such as the Arab American Anti-Discrimination Committee and the American Iranian Council. My focus is the national-level advocacy organizations that self-identify in both religious (Muslim) and national (American) terms and aim, or at least claim, to speak on behalf of *all* US Muslims, without concern for ethnonational affiliation.[21]

Thus, my study looks at how Muslim American organizations engage in framing and articulating a Muslim American collective identity through their policy advocacy and claims-making strategies. I conceptualize policy activism as a set of interpretive acts that are essential forms of social definition and, thus, are crucial to our understanding of the collective identity formation of this American minority group. My work includes an in-depth analysis of the foreign and domestic policy activism of some of the largest Muslim advocacy organizations in the United States, including such groups as CAIR, the Muslim Public Affairs Council (MPAC), the US Council of Muslim Organizations (USCMO), Muslim Advocates, and the American Muslim Alliance. I also include smaller organizations that have made important contributions to the national advocacy scene, such as the Muslim Justice League and Jetpac.

Why these organizations? A main impetus for writing this book is a desire to explain how minorities in the United States—in this case, Muslims—begin to see and think of themselves as part of a collective, with common policy goals and interests. I am particularly interested in understanding how elites and the organizations they establish contribute to this process. Second, because I see policy advocacy as an arena in which what it means to be an American Muslim is being negotiated and performed, I include organizations whose primary focus is national-level advocacy, which rely on traditional lobbying tactics, and which have a stated mission of influencing the policy process from within. Whereas mass participation is essential to grassroots and community-based organizations, the vast majority of the work of the organizations I examine does not rely on mass participation. In fact, they are not membership based; they feature elite-based, hierarchical structures, rely on paid staff members, and employ a longer-term, gradualist agenda.

The process of Muslim American collective identity formation is the result of a long process of settlement, integration, and negotiation. Although this occurs at both the grassroots (bottom-up) and elite (top-down) levels—and both are essential to our understanding of collective identity formation—my main concern is with the latter. More specifically, I am interested in how organizations are able to employ certain material and nonmaterial resources to act as representatives of the community on whose behalf they claim to speak. Seen through this lens, their advocacy work is not only an attempt to influence policy but also a means through which to signal what American Muslims stand for and are willing to fight for. It is a way to communicate—and, in the process, help engender—Muslim American interests, values, ideals, and norms.

In many ways, this book tells a familiar story about the continuing struggle of American minorities to claim belonging and gain full citizenship rights. The modern civil rights movement, the mass activism that from 1946 to 1968 sought to secure the full political, economic, and social rights of African Americans, pushed the state to recognize them as bearers of rights. The landmark achievements of the era, the Civil Rights Act of 1964 and the Voting Rights Act of 1965, which outlawed racial discrimination and removed obstacles to voting, inspired other minorities to fight for their rights. In the decades that followed, women, Native Americans, people with disabilities, immigrants, and LGBTQ people borrowed the lessons and tactics of the civil rights movement to lead a People's Movement pushing for their inclusion in American society. Their collective accomplishments would come to transform the United States.

The Chicano civil rights movements of 1965–1975 contested the various measures that kept Hispanics from voting and running for office, thrusting the door open for the political participation of Latinx people today. Farm workers (many of whom were Mexican and Asian immigrants), led by Cesar Chavez and Dolores Huerta, joined and led the struggle for labor rights in America. Native Americans launched the Red Power movement for self-determination, asserting and defending Indian and tribal rights, including tribal sovereignty, treaty rights, and the protection of natural resources. The Stonewall Riots of 1969 reignited the gay rights movement to fight for the decriminalization of LGBTQ people's love and self-expression. The disability rights movement successfully propelled legislation that addressed disability as a civil rights issue, including the Rehabilitation Act of 1973, the 1975 Education of All Handicapped Children Act and the landmark 1990 Americans with Disabilities Act.[22]

Marginalized groups today, including victims of sexual harassment and violence, victims of police brutality, undocumented immigrants, and, yes, Muslims, continue to write this most American of stories. But this book is also more than that: it is about the emergence and maintenance of a collective identity. By framing the Muslim American community's main challenges, identifying its foes, and promoting the responses and tactics that are deemed acceptable, advocacy groups are delineating the contours of that community. For these organizations, engagement in the US policymaking process is as much about communicating a Muslim American identity as it is about pursuing collective rights. Ultimately, this is a story about the integration of Muslims in the United States.

I begin in chapter 1 with the links between discrimination, identity formation, and minority advocacy—how Muslim minorities and immigrants from disparate ethnic, national, linguistic, and socioeconomic backgrounds begin to think of themselves, and act, as members of a collective group with a unified set of interests. Even if the Muslim advocacy organizations I examine have not succeeded at meaningfully influencing policy, their real impact lies in their ability to frame and communicate a particular Muslim American collective identity.

Chapter 2 analyzes the historical trajectory of Muslim immigration, settlement, and institution building in the United States, focusing on the structural conditions and collective traumas that have shaped the lives of Muslims in America, particularly in the post-9/11 period. Characterizing this trajectory is broad ethnic, national, denominational, and socioeconomic diversity among Muslims in the United States and the emergence of organizations aiming, or at least claiming, to represent the collective interests of this wide group. This is not a linear history of Muslim integration; the emergence of Muslim American interest groups is the result of a long process of negotiated integration—a process influenced by the American social, political, and legal context as much as by internal group dynamics.

In Chapter 3, I examine counterterrorism policy as one of the major sites, although not the only one, through which US Muslims are framed as an out-group against which American identity can be measured and defined. This reading of the War on Terror presents hate crimes, bias incidents, and discriminatory state policy not as aberrations, or as the unintended but inevitable result of fighting terrorism, but rather as a productive discourse through which certain groups are constituted as outside the boundaries of the national community. As part of this exploration, I look at the rise of Muslim American advocacy organizations and the domestic and foreign policy issues at the core of their lobbying efforts—surveillance and profiling, protecting religious freedom, Islamophobia, countering violent extremism, the Palestinian-Israeli conflict, the Arab Spring, and human rights in the Muslim-majority world. Through each of these issues, I deepen my inquiry into how US Muslim organizations navigate their entry into the policy process while negotiating their community's place in the American mosaic.

Chapter 4 examines the impacts the US government's targeting of American Muslims has had, and continues to have, on the organizations who aim/claim to speak on their behalf. Government policies associated with the War on Terror have wreaked havoc on Muslim communities. But they have also resulted in a new political structure of opportunity for Muslim American advocacy groups. This idea might seem counterintuitive at first. Being targeted as an out-group has solidified perceptions of, and attachments to, a Muslim American collective identity, further legitimizing the claims-making capacity of the organizations aiming/claiming to represent this community. As a result, Muslim American organizations, particularly those at the national level, have gained previously unimaginable degrees of visibility and access to the policy process, the media, and sources of funding. In other words, anti-Muslim discrimination has had the unintended consequence of providing these organizations with opportunities to access the policymaking process, make claims on the state as an American minority group, and communicate a Muslim American collective identity.

The final chapters elaborate on this idea, starting with a detailed analysis in chapters 5 and 6 of some of the domestic and foreign policy issues driving Muslim American interest groups. Together, these chapters examine how these organizations have relied on a rights-based discourse to access the political process and make claims on the state. In particular, I highlight the varied strategies through which Islamophobia has been framed as a civil rights issue and incorporated into the historical trajectory of the movement for minority rights.

Chapter 6 also answers an important question: Why, following 9/11 and facing increased scrutiny, did these organizations continue to lobby on issues related to US foreign policy? This is particularly puzzling because their foreign policy activism seems to contradict their interests and fuel perceptions of Muslims as outsiders concerned not with American interests but with those of other nations. Unlike some scholars, who posit that Muslims in the United States and Europe are driven by a concern for their "imagined homeland," the Muslim *ummah*, I see foreign policy activism primarily as a means through which these organizations communicate their belongingness to America.

The book concludes by examining the main sources of contention over advocacy and the rights of representation in the Muslim American community. Specifically, what gives these organizations the legitimacy to speak on behalf of US Muslims? Relying on existing survey data, I gauge the degree to which Muslim advocacy organizations reflect and represent the interests of their constituents on a variety of policy issues. What I find is that these organizations are constrained by two rationales: the logic of membership (or the need to respond to their constituents' preferences) and the logic of influence (or the need to focus on issues that appeal to the policy establishment). These two logics often converge, but not always. Advocacy on questions of Islamophobia and anti-Muslim discrimination, for example, is highly reflective of the interests and preferences of American Muslims. When it comes to foreign policy, however, national-level advocacy organizations are less representative of the preferences of American Muslims, the vast majority of whom are very interested and engaged in these issues. In the post-9/11 context of increased suspicion, these organizations sought to distance themselves from foreign policy advocacy in an attempt to forestall the accusation of "dual loyalties" that is so common in times of war. These and other issues offer insights into how Muslim advocacy organizations attempt to navigate between the need to respond to their constituents' concerns and the need to gain access to the policy establishment.

The questions that motivated me to write this book are unlikely to disappear anytime soon. In a decentralized system with multiple points of access to the policy process, individuals will organize themselves and seek to advocate for their preferences. And as long as any group of individuals is marginalized and targeted because of their religion, ethnonational background, race, or any other identity marker, they will mobilize around that identity and make claims as a minority group. Simply put, discriminatory state policies will continue to engender the minority and identity politics that have come to define our current political climate.

DISCRIMINATION, ADVOCACY, AND COLLECTIVE IDENTITY

Muslim American advocacy is not new. It's always been there. It's always existed. It's always going to be there. It's part of our Muslim identity, and it won't stop because Muslims are at the center of the justice space right now. . . . But Muslims today cannot identify themselves as being for Muslims and not for anybody else. You can't do that. That's not in the prophetic example, that's not in the teachings, and that's not who we are.

—Jaylani Hussein, author interview, October 20, 2018

Anti-Muslim prejudice has rather deep roots in American history. From its inception, the nation adopted the European Orientalist discourse through which Islam is constructed as a false religion and Muslims from around the world are racialized as Arab, nonwhite, and therefore biologically and morally inferior.[1] Until 1944, Muslims (along with other immigrants who did not meet the criteria of being "free white persons") were barred from becoming American citizens. Arab Christians were also denied citizenship, partly due to their perceived cultural closeness and racial mixing with Muslims.[2] Thus, from early on, Muslims in the United States were racialized as nonwhite and, consequently, undeserving of full inclusion. And though they would eventually win the battle to be considered "white" by the US government, the designation did not shelter them from racial prejudice and institutionalized discrimination.[3]

Muslims today continue to be seen through the prism of race. Indeed, the best predictor of anti-Muslim bias is the existence of deep-seated racist beliefs about the inherent inferiority of African Americans and other marginalized groups.[4] In their pioneering work measuring old-fashioned racist attitudes toward Muslim Americans, Lajevardi and Oskoii find that, among a set of more than one thousand survey respondents, Muslims rank as the most dehumanized group in the United States.[5] These racist attitudes have real social, economic, and political consequences, as we know so well from the experiences of African Americans and other marginalized communities. Not surprisingly, Lajevardi and Oskoii find that racist attitudes toward Muslims are a strong predictor of support for policies that target and exclude them, such as patrolling "Muslim neighborhoods" and curtailing immigration from Muslim-majority countries, and of support for the politicians who espouse such policies, including President Trump.[6] Muslims have been the source of much political debate and vitriolic rhetoric since the 2016 presidential campaign, a period that has also seen a steady rise in hate crimes against this group.[7] For better or worse, citizens tend to take their cues from the political elites they follow and admire.[8]

As data on rising hate crimes against Muslims show, the intensification and mainstreaming of anti-Muslim bias has led to a number of important outcomes for American Muslims and the organizations that represent them. At a most basic level, these facts have cemented Muslims' status as a major out-group in American society, an internal other, whose religious beliefs and practices make them inassimilable, "suspect citizens" deserving of surveillance and, when necessary, punitive action. However, being targets of suspicion, disdain, and aggression has also made Muslim advocacy organizations more visible, helped engender clear policy goals among them, and, consequently, strengthened a sense of shared Muslim American identity.

As we know from the experience of other panethnic groups in America, there is nothing natural or inevitable about the Muslim American identity marker. Groups are made, not given. And while the process of group making is influenced by both cultural and structural factors, the latter have been consistently found to be more significant.[9] Sustained intragroup interaction, common economic interests, external threats, government policies, and membership in a community of faith all positively influence panethnic identity formation and collective action among marginalized groups.[10] In the United States, where the race construct has historically been a major tool for structuring society and maintaining domination, external racialization tends to be the initial catalyst for panethnic group formation.[11] This largely punitive process occurs through acts of discrimination and antigroup violence, but it can also include positive incentives, such as affirmative action and state policies that inadvertently strengthen panethnic affiliations.[12] The emergence of Asian American panethnicity is a case in point. Violence, discrimination, and racial lumping by the larger society all played a role in the making of an Asian American identity, but so did official designation as a legal minority and eventual eligibility for affirmative action and other rights.[13]

When it comes to intragroup relations, the simple act of labeling and lumping people into a certain category has enormous consequences. The social psychologist Henri Tajfel was one of the earliest scholars to argue that prejudice was not the result of certain personality traits or authoritarian tendencies, as commonly assumed, but rather the result of an ordinary process of categorization. He and his student, John Turner, went on to elaborate these findings into the theory of social identity, a framework that has continued to guide scholarship on intragroup relations, prejudice, and discrimination. According to Tajfel and Turner, differentiating between an in-group (the group to which one belongs) and an out-group (external groups) helps individuals make sense of their sociopolitical environment and the other individuals who inhabit that environment. This social comparison is an important aspect of the process of individual and group identity formation, as people attempt to enhance their self-esteem by comparing perceived out-groups less favorably than their own.[14] Accordingly, individuals always have an in-group bias in how they think of their own identities, and are less likely to trust, accept, and relate to those who seem to belong to other groups.[15] In other words, we derive our sense of self from the social categories to which we belong, those from which we are excluded, and the sociocognitive characteristics we assign to each.

The American consciousness includes multiple out-groups, but not all are viewed in the same way, and their positions are not static. A group can certainly move from out-group status to become part of the majority group—Catholics, Irish, and Italians being prime examples. However, there are important distinctions between out-groups that help explain why, in time, some become more accepted by the broader society than others. In general, people are more likely to have a positive view of groups perceived to have tried to assimilate to the majority group, versus those seen to reject the norms and values of the broader society. Scholars have found that the position of Muslims tends to be especially precarious in America, as they are perceived as members of multiple out-groups:[16] *Muslim* is a religious label, but Muslims have also been conceptualized as a monolithic and culturally deviant foreign group.[17] For Muslims in the United States, "religion intersects with skin tone, gender, language, and nation of origin," further influencing how the broader society perceives them.[18] In short, Muslims in America are simultaneously a religious minority, whose practices are believed to deviate from the Judeo-Christian tradition; a relatively recent immigrant population with perceived inassimilable foreign cultural norms; and an ethnic minority, often understood through the prism of race.

Discriminated-against minorities in the United States are more likely to emphasize their dual identities (as both ethnic and religious minorities and citizens), especially when communicating with audiences who may question their belonging and identity claims. As Matt Barreto and Karam Dana argue, "perceptions that members of a group share common structural constraints is the foundation of any form of politicized collective identity."[19] An environment in which actual or perceived threat is heightened also increases voter mobilization as a means of defense.[20] Not surprisingly, then, periods of backlash against American Muslims, such as the 2016 presidential campaign, have resulted in their increased mobilization and political participation,[21] a finding that is in line with the broader literature on minority activism.

In addition to these external threats, collective action and contestation are important drivers of group making.[22] Indeed, panethnic organizations play an important role in framing collective grievances and presenting a unified agenda through their advocacy. However, their work and influence continue to be a source of much debate. Whose interests do these organizations represent, and whose do they ignore? Are the advocacy issues they choose to focus on a reflection of bottom-up pressures or top-down choices? Do they seek a radical transformation of the existing system that would benefit all marginalized groups, or do they seek simply to be accepted at the proverbial policy table? These questions are neither new nor unique to the Muslim American case. However, they are necessary to understand the still understudied role that Muslim American advocacy organizations play in framing and communicating a Muslim American collective identity.

Advocacy Organizations: Splits and Fissures

In her 2006 book on South Asian politics, Monisha Das Gupta argues that national-level panethnic Asian organizations played a formative role in the struggle for Asian American civil rights, but that they did so mainly through a discourse of assimilation, not one of "radical transformation."[23] According to Das Gupta, most of the top-down, national-level organizations focused on demanding citizenship rights, consequently legitimizing the nation-state as the giver of rights and conforming to the trope of the model minority. But there were other panethnic Asian American organizations, operating predominantly at the local and grassroots levels, that rejected the notion that rights were based on citizenship, working instead to make room for all underprivileged and underrepresented groups in their communities, including noncitizens, undocumented people, the poor, working-class people, and LGBTQ people.

The split between minority organizations fighting for increased access and representation and those working to build the radically new society that Das Gupta theorizes is a divide I thought of often while writing this book. Some of the organizations I studied, such as MPAC, are clearly and proudly top-down policy organizations that believe change for the community will only come about through increased access and acceptance. Salam Al-Marayati, MPAC's executive director, exemplifies this view. "Keith Ellison has a great quote," he told me during one of our meetings in his Los Angeles office in late 2017. "If you're not at the table, then you'll be the menu of the table!" We both chuckled.

Al-Marayati was at ease, with his sleeves rolled up and his shirt slightly unbuttoned. The air conditioning in his office had broken down, so we decided to sit by the reception area near the entrance. From that vantage, I could see the large conference room next to us, where a group meeting was taking place. I overheard a woman's voice coming from another room, as she tried to coordinate a meeting with someone on the phone. Given the local news trucks parked outside the building, delivering journalists who were there to interview Al-Marayati, I assumed the person on the phone was hoping to do the same. Interest in Muslim Americans had soared since the 2016 elections and the enactment of the Muslim ban, and individuals like Al-Marayati and the organization he represented were there to fill the gaps.

Despite the commotion around us, Al-Marayati was focused and seemed eager to talk. "The biggest mistake I think people make, is thinking that our [MPAC's] work is civil rights," he began, catching me slightly by surprise. Had he read the piece I had recently written, arguing that Muslim American organizations were working to fight Islamophobia and demand their community's civil rights?[24] I nodded, trying to disguise my self-consciousness. He went on:

> If you want to be a civil rights group, then join the civil rights movement, the ACLU, the National Immigration Law Center, the National Lawyers Guild. Those are all great civil rights groups. But they don't work on policy per se. They work on cases of discrimination and then they hold government accountable. Policy work is more about changing the policy so that there aren't as many of these problems that you see in the community involving discrimination and harassment. . . . And we do that through a stepladder approach. You have to first establish a presence, then gain respect, then gain acceptance, and only then you can become influential. But we are far from there yet. . . . So, I'd rather just leave civil rights work to the ACLU and then spend my energy meeting with the members of Congress, meeting with the White House, meeting with coalition partners and coming up with an action plan to change a policy.

Al-Marayati was clear in his view of how progress happens—gradually—and wanted his organization to have a narrow policy focus. I have found this divide between views on gradualist versus radical transformation to exist not just between Muslim organizations but also within them. Indeed, some of the fiercest critics of national-level Muslim American organizations I met were individuals deeply involved in them. During the meetings and events I attended at CAIR, for example, it was not unusual to hear invited speakers critique the organization's record of advocacy around victims of the war on terror and its inclusion of Black Muslims, converts to Islam, or Muslim inmates in US prisons.

Maha Hilal, a scholar, grassroots activist, and lone advocate for Muslims imprisoned at Guantanamo Bay detention camp, was one such guest. CAIR invited her to speak on a panel on Islamophobia in late 2018. During the discussion, she began talking about Islamophobia *within* the Muslim American community, arguing that many Muslims had internalized the trope of "the enemy terrorist" and that organizations such as CAIR had shown very little concern for Muslims held at Guantanamo or those accused of terrorism and never prosecuted or convicted.

When the panel ended, I made my way to the front of the room, hoping to ask Hilal a few questions. I found her speaking with two audience members who were thanking her for her remarks and inquiring about an exhibit she had organized, showcasing artwork by Guantanamo Bay detainees. As the two young women left, I extended my hand to her, introducing myself. I told her how much I had enjoyed the panel and her presentation. She smiled widely and thanked me, seeming slightly unconvinced: "I don't know why they keep inviting me back and are always surprised by what I have to say! They know my work, they know what I'm going to say!"

Articulating a Muslim American Political Identity

The organizations I examine choose varied approaches and pursue different goals, but all claim, rather unreflectively, to be pursuing the interests of American Muslims. This assertion must be taken with a grain of skepticism, for several reasons. For one, it is unclear whether the majority of Muslims in the United States really think of themselves as members of a collective group. Similarly, there is nothing obvious about what comprises Muslim American interests. Are the interests of poor, working-class Muslims the same as those of educated, upper-middle-class professionals? Does the focus on the post-9/11 backlash speak to a generation of Muslims who feel temporally and experientially removed from it? Poll after poll shows that the majority of Muslims in the United States, like all Americans, are concerned with bread-and-butter issues such as the economy, health care, and, increasingly, climate change, yet these are not the core issues for Muslim advocacy organizations. The narratives we tell ourselves matter, as do those that others tell about us; they become the building blocks of our individual and collective identities. These identities, in turn, influence how we come to understand our interests and work to achieve them.

It is difficult to think of discrimination and Islamophobia as *productive* to the process of collective identity formation and claims making, but that is precisely what other examples of minority activism in the United States suggest. At an institutional level, Muslim advocacy groups require the existence, or active construction, of Muslim Americans as a group that views itself (and that others view) as a collective. Being the target of discrimination has dramatically hastened and strengthened the development of a collective Muslim American identity—an important precursor to political participation. This is because, as a broad body of research on race in the United States shows, targeted identities become "salient," a term that refers to the level of importance an individual places on any of their multiple identities.[25] And the more one identifies with a group, the more likely one is to take part in collective action on behalf of that group.

Hence, the othering of Muslims and Islam also explains why individuals have tended to mobilize around their Muslim identities as opposed to, for example, their ethnonational ones. The focus on individual acts, policies, and discriminatory state practices that performatively constitute US Muslims as an out-group is therefore, quite literally, foundational for Muslim American interest groups, since it is precisely the othering of Muslims that grants these groups the legitimacy to speak on behalf of this constructed, and in many ways imagined, community.[26] As Roger Brubaker explains, "By distinguishing consistently between categories and groups, we can problematize—rather than presume—the relation between them. We can ask about the degree of groupness associated with a particular category in a particular setting, and about the political, social, cultural, and psychological processes through which categories get invested with groupness. We can ask how people—and organizations—*do things* with categories. . . . We can study the politics of categories, both from above and from below. From above, we can focus on the ways in which categories are proposed, propagated, imposed, institutionalized, discursively articulated."[27]

My main interest in this book is examining how perceptions of common threat have strengthened the claims-making capacity of Muslim American advocacy organizations, providing them with an opportunity to access the policymaking process and communicate a set of common policy interests and demands. Specifically, anti-Muslim discrimination has resulted in three distinct opportunities for Muslim advocacy organizations: (1) it has granted them an audience interested in "the Muslim American perspective"; (2) it has helped solidify a collective consciousness among US Muslims; and (3) it has provided a unifying discourse to contest, namely, Islamophobia and the unconstitutional denial of individual and group rights. Muslim advocacy organizations have used these opportunities to position themselves as the official representatives of Muslim America, demand a seat at the policy table, and make claims on behalf of this targeted minority group.

When I describe the work of Muslim organizations, the questions I hear most often revolve around impact: Are they effective? Are they able to influence policy? Does anyone in power actually listen to them? The short answer to these questions is no, or at least, not yet; their ability to meaningfully influence policy has

been largely insignificant. But this does not make them irrelevant. Their advocacy efforts are as much an attempt to influence policy as they are a mechanism
through which they articulate and propagate a Muslim American group identity.
Their focus on the top-down articulation of a collective identity should not suggest, however, that identities are constructed from above. On the contrary, as
Brubaker and others have aptly shown, the process of collective identity formation is too complex to be explained away by a single variable. It involves the top-
down articulation and mobilization of *groupness* by political elites; the bottom-up
and micropolitical processes through which individuals internalize, appropriate,
and subvert certain social categories; and the sociocognitive ways in which individuals come to understand themselves and others around them. But if our goal is
to scrutinize how categories of people (in this case, Muslims in the United States)
are reified and imbued with the characteristics of a group (Muslim Americans),
we must seriously consider the performative roles of ethnopolitical entrepreneurs
and the organizations they establish. It is through their everyday acts that these
organizations and individuals help engender the group on whose behalf they seek
to speak. In other words, "by *invoking* groups they seek to *evoke* them, summon
them, call them into being. Their categories are *for doing*—designed to stir, summon, justify, mobilize, kindle, and energize. By reifying groups, by treating them
as substantial things-in-the-world, ethnopolitical entrepreneurs can, as Bourdieu
notes, 'contribute to producing what they apparently describe or designate.'"[28]

My decision to focus on the top-down role that national Muslim advocacy
organizations play in articulating a Muslim American group identity should not
be taken to suggest that this is the only variable at play, or even the most important one. Nonetheless, understanding their role matters. Through their exposure
to these national organizations, Muslims across the United States learn about issues affecting fellow Muslims and are exposed to news about Muslims in other
parts of the country that they would not otherwise encounter. Muslims are also
invited to think of themselves as active citizens, voters, and participants in American democracy. In this way, the work these organizations do around citizenship
empowerment and voter registration campaigns must be conceptualized as more
than a mere strategy to amplify their constituents' political voice. Rather, it is a
tool for shaping their constituents into citizens with collective interests. These
campaigns invite Muslims to join the American national narrative as a minority
fighting for equality and legitimacy, striving to change the status quo by engaging in the democratic process, and dreaming of making their country a better and
more just place for all Americans.

MPAC's "I Am Change" program reflects many of these themes. According to
Adina Lekovic, the organization's director of policy and programming, the program aims to build the citizenship capital of American Muslims and to encourage

them to become active citizens and embrace their rights, as Americans, to work with decision makers and build a better future. In a promotional video introducing the initiative, Lekovic provides a religious framework to both justify and promote Muslims' political agency: "In the Qur'an, God says that he won't change the conditions of a people unless they change what is within themselves. More than a thousand years later, Gandhi told us to be the change that we wish to see in the world."[29] The message is clear: Muslims must transform themselves from passive victims, upon whom policies are enacted, into citizens who play an active role in shaping the character, policies, and future trajectory of their nation. In a letter introducing MPAC's 2012 Election Community Toolkit, Salam Al-Marayati makes this point succinctly: "Every eligible person should register to vote. A person that is not registered to vote is politically non-existent and has no voice."[30] MPAC and other organizations foster political engagement not for what it can allow Muslims to achieve but for what it enables them to become. It is through their participation in the political process, *as American Muslims*, that this community comes into being.

This understanding of advocacy and claims making as constitutive of Muslim American group identity also allows us to see the performative character of national advocacy events like the Muslim Hill Day I describe in the introduction. Even though CAIR has held Hill Days for years, it was not until 2015 that the event began to take on a more inclusive and national character, bringing together representatives from Muslim organizations from across the country. Under the stewardship of the US Council of Muslim Organizations (USCMO), Muslim organizations were encouraged to send delegates to Washington, DC, to lobby their elected officials to support the "priorities of the American Muslim community."[31] Multiple organizations have sent delegates to these events, including national advocacy and charity groups such as CAIR, the Islamic Circle of North America (ICNA), and the Muslim Legal Fund, as well as local and religious groups such as the North American Imam's Federation, the Islamic Society of Boston Cultural Center, and the Islamic Shura Council of Southern California.

Since 2015, these Hill Days have advocated for policy priorities focused on racial and religious profiling, immigration, equality, and social justice. The USCMO selected, negotiated, and decided these priorities in consultation with other member organizations, but with very little input from average American Muslims. Average individuals might indeed support these policy priorities, as survey data suggest, but we must be clear in recognizing these organizations as the chief protagonists in Muslim American claims making—at least, at the national level. These organizations may see themselves, and be seen, as organizations *of* and *for* American Muslims, but simply equating their interests and identities with those of the group they seek to represent would be a mistake, just as it would be with *any* organization that claims to speak or act in the name of a racial, ethnic, or religious group.

Creating a Virtual Muslim American Public Space

It is astounding that these small, underresourced, and overburdened organizations have been able to set and promulgate a national Muslim American agenda and publicize their community's plight. They have put the Internet to good use in this endeavor, establishing a strong social media presence. Digital media tools have helped foster a platform for sharing and using information and allowed individuals to communicate and interact with distant others who share similar struggles, concerns, and experiences.[32] This is a particularly important function for national Muslim organizations that seek to speak to, and on behalf of, a relatively small community (less than 1 percent of the US population) that is divided along many lines and geographies across the United States. Mucahit Bilici, a sociologist and Muslim American scholar, has described the power of such spaces: "For a religious minority dispersed across the country, collective spaces of interaction and spheres of representation are crucial for the development of codes and standards that define the group."[33] Even if we consider the reliance on social media to be the result of a purely strategic calculus (a cost-effective way to build their institutional brands, disseminate information, distribute material, coordinate online and offline protests, and amplify their voices), it nonetheless has significant consequences in terms of group-making.

Indeed, research suggests that the Internet facilitates new avenues for the development of social identity. Members of virtual groups may develop an identity associated with that group, even if the relationships and interactions exist only virtually.[34] An apt example can be found in the burgeoning of white supremacist groups who have organized and spurred themselves into the national political scene, in large part due to the role of online communities. Their rise underlines how digital forums can help build and sustain communities of like-minded individuals and forge a collective identity among them. Nascent scholarship in this area has begun to delineate a theory of social movement online community, or SMOC, to capture this phenomenon. Unsurprisingly, a key characteristic is that "participants focus on the building of community and identity within the virtual walls of the Internet."[35] Muslim advocacy organizations also rely heavily on the Internet and social media to communicate their policy goals, highlight issues affecting American Muslims (particularly those related to Islamophobia), and mobilize support for their cause. Thanks in large part to their social media presence, these groups have reached a diverse community of Muslims and begun communicating, framing and signifying the issues that should concern this community.

Most of these organizations were born in the age of the Internet, but the humble websites CAIR and MPAC established in the early 1990s are now sophisticated operational command centers and logistical hubs—the main mechanisms for reaching their audiences and disseminating their work. These sites are also important platforms for countering the dominant narrative on and about Muslims and defending their organizations and communities against damaging accusations. One of the most common accusations is that Muslim leaders and institutions have not done enough to condemn terrorism—a belief also held by a plurality of American Muslims.[36] CAIR, for example, dedicates a section of its website to "Dispelling Rumors about CAIR."[37] The organization has also used its website and social media presence to respond to specific cases of terrorism, sending out alerts condemning the acts when they happen and, for a time, keeping a tally of statements it had made in response to terrorist acts since its establishment in 1997.

Other common examples of online activism include action alerts, encouraging individuals to contact their public officials and make specific demands (usually with transcripts spelling out those demands), and letter-writing campaigns. In addition to these traditional forms of online engagement, CAIR, MPAC, the USCMO, and other organizations have dedicated resources to building their social media presence, including hiring interns and deploying communication strategists (often just one person per organization) to fill the role of social media communicators. During one of our conversations following the 2016 elections, CAIR's government affairs director, Robert McCaw, conveyed a combination of exasperation and admiration in describing his organization's use of social media. He apologized for not being able to point me to a particular resource, because the website was "in the perpetual process of being updated." But he also praised his team for what they had been able to accomplish under difficult circumstances: "All the great statements you see put out by CAIR are the direct result of the work of Ibrahim Hooper [CAIR's national communications director and spokesperson]. The man works 18-hour days. He's always on. It's amazing." This comment was meant as a lighthearted reflection on the inner workings of an organization that has been sporadically thrown into the national limelight (as in the post-9/11 period and during the 2016 campaign cycle) and has had to learn to improvise with the limited resources at its disposal. But it is also a reflection of such organizations' savvy of the media world in which they operate and the ways they try to leverage it to their advantage.

A great deal of what these organizations do, and do well, is to provide interpretative frames and narratives for labeling and explaining the Muslim American experience and, in the process, labeling the policy issues they support as "Muslim American" issues. This is perhaps their most important role. As Goffman and others have argued, by imposing a particular frame on an event, we both interpret that which we seek to explain and help constitute it.[38] Applying the lens of ethnic violence to explain conflict, for example, leads us not only to interpret the violence itself to result from ethnic differences and/or animosity but also to assign a level of *groupness* to the actors involved in the violence, even if this sense of groupness is not reflective of how actors involved in the conflict experience it.

Framing and Combating Islamophobia Online

Given the political climate surrounding the 2016 presidential campaign, combating anti-Muslim hate crimes and sentiments became a focal point for these groups' advocacy and outreach efforts—efforts that, in the process, framed their communities as an American minority group fighting for their civil rights. The vast majority of these campaigns have taken place online and relied on the interpretative framework of Islamophobia to make sense of the discriminatory acts Muslims have experienced in recent years. Although this might seem to be a commonsense interpretation of events, it is important to question the taken-for-granted nature of these frames and consider alternative ways these experiences could be perceived and understood. For one, violence against Muslim Americans could be seen through the frame of antiminority or anti-immigrant discrimination. It could also be interpreted as a manifestation of a broader wave against diversity and multiculturalism taking place across the United States and Western Europe. These frameworks are not mutually exclusive, but each leads to very different understandings of the experiences we are trying to explain, as well as the type and level of groupness we assign to the actors involved. Framing discriminatory practices against Muslim citizens as part of the broader backlash against multiculturalism and minorities, for example, constitutes them more readily as a nonwhite minority group, leading to different conceptions of group membership and belonging. Thus, relying on the framework of Islamophobia has important consequences for how individuals come to perceive and understand the lived experiences of US Muslims and for how the category of "American Muslim" comes to be constituted as a group.

Identifying, describing, and contesting anti-Muslim discrimination has been a core mission of Muslim advocacy organizations since their inception. However, in recent years, the Islamophobia framework has become a master framework through which the experiences of US Muslims are perceived and explained—and through which US Muslims are encouraged into action. In 2015, CAIR published a *Challenging Islamophobia Pocket Guide* with the subtitle, "Islamo-phobia can be stopped. It takes people like *you* to take action and make a differ-ence. *Be an agent of change.*" The guide provides a lengthy and detailed definition of the term, its key characteristics, and steps to combat it:

> Islamophobia is fear or hatred of Islam and Muslims. It has existed for centuries, but has become more explicit, more extreme and more dan-gerous in the aftermath of the 9/11 terror attacks.
>
> This phenomenon promotes and perpetuates anti-Muslim stereotyp-ing, discrimination, harassment, and even violence. It negatively im-pacts the participation of American Muslims in public life.
>
> Features of Islamophobia:
>
> Muslim cultures and Islam are seen as monolithic and unchanging.
> Muslim cultures are viewed as wholly different from other cultures.
> Islam is perceived as inherently threatening.
> Muslims are seen as using their faith mainly for political or military advantage.
> Muslim criticisms of Western societies are rejected out of hand.
> Fear of Islam is mixed with racist hostility to immigration.
> Islamophobia is assumed to be natural and unproblematic.[39]

One of CAIR's signature projects in this area was Islamophobia.org, a website it established in early 2015 to "monitor and combat Islamophobia." CAIR used the site to disseminate a wide variety of resources, including lists of Islamophobic organizations and individuals, a record of Islamophobic rhetoric by political can-didates, and a set of antiprejudice tools that individuals were encouraged to use when confronted with anti-Muslim discrimination.[40]

In June 2016, CAIR launched Islamophobin.org, a satirical public awareness campaign to challenge "growing Islamophobia in America." The campaign in-volved the sale of a mock medicine (actually a sugar-free chewing gum), promis-ing to provide "Multi-Symptom Relief for Chronic Islamophobia," and featured a video explaining the affliction ("blind intolerance, irrational fear of Muslims, and U.S. Presidential Election Year scapegoating") and the side effects of taking Islam-ophobin ("loss of Islamophobia and bigotry, development of the ability to think rationally," and the development of "warm feelings toward Muslims, immigrants, or refugees"). Individuals were encouraged to join the campaign by purchasing and handing out packets of Islamophobin, and by mailing them to political candi-dates and asking them to pledge to combat anti-Muslim discrimination.

According to CAIR's executive director, "We hope humor will help create pub-lic awareness about the harm Islamophobia does not only to ordinary American

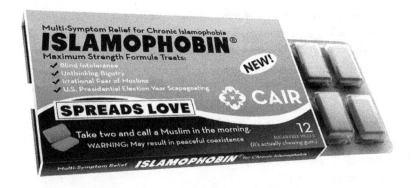

ISLAMOPHOBIN® IS FUNNY. ISLAMOPHOBIA IS NOT.

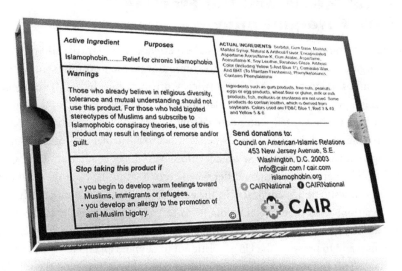

FIGURES 1A AND 1B. Islamophobin packaging, part of CAIR's satirical anti-Islamophobia campaign. Reproduced with the permission of the Council on American-Islamic Relations.

Muslims, but also to the values of equality and religious freedom upon which our nation was founded." The campaign is part of a larger mission to use creative social media campaigns to counter negative representations of Muslims and Islam. Indeed, as post-9/11 scholarship on Muslim Americans has shown, there has been an upsurge of Muslim ethnic comedy by individuals and groups seeking to reclaim their narratives and challenge their perceived "otherness."[41] Ethnic humor is part of the Americanization process, as society is invited to witness, question, and ultimately laugh at the stereotypes that minorities have to endure. As the Islamophobin example demonstrates, Muslim advocacy organizations have appropriated these tactics, using satire as a tool to empower Muslims to claim their belonging to their nation, reclaim their agency, and take control of the narrative of Islamophobia. The goal is for Muslims to be recognized as fellow Americans and fellow humans. The "undoing of otherness" that happens through humor plays an important role in "abolish[ing] the gulf that separates the in-group from the out-group."[42] As Jewish comic Rabi Bob Alper put it, "You can't hate the person you've laughed with."[43]

Social Media and the Framing of US Foreign Policy

Aside from framing group grievances and experiences, social media also provides these organizations with a platform to communicate their positions on US domestic and foreign policy. Muslim advocacy organizations have little influence on foreign policy decisions, but the latter is nevertheless a topic that a majority of Muslims in the United States care deeply about. The Palestinian-Israeli conflict in general and the 2014 Gaza-Israeli conflict in particular are good examples through which to examine these organizations' social media advocacy tactics, including whether and how these differ when compared to their use of social media for domestic policy advocacy. In the early days of the Gaza conflict, Muslim organizations used their social media feeds to counter the prevalent US narrative, which blamed Hamas's rocket attacks on northern Israel for inciting Israel's response, and to pressure the US government to demand an end to Israel's attack on Gaza. This online activism accomplished three things: it turned the conflict in Gaza into a *Muslim American issue*; it presented a unified set of Muslim American demands and plans of action; and it positioned them as the representatives of the community's interests.

Take MPAC's "I Speak Out Because" campaign, which encouraged participants to use Twitter, Facebook, and Instagram to "speak out against injustices that we are witnessing in Palestine, Syria, Iraq, Myanmar, Nigeria, China, and around the world."[44] MPAC launched the campaign on August 7, 2014, as a direct response to the Gaza conflict and the restraining of US public debate about Israel's actions. In the process of making claims about a foreign policy issue, MPAC framed those claims around a discourse of constitutionally protected rights, specifically, the right of Americans to voice their political opinions without fear of repercussion: "Many public figures have spoken out against the ongoing injustices in Gaza, only to face sharp criticism and pressure to retract their statements. Intimidation has led many people to practice self-censorship on topics deemed taboo out of fear of ramifications. When we are intimidated into censoring ourselves, our right to free speech is threatened. . . . 'Now more than ever we must raise our voices collectively to speak out for human rights.'"[45]

Significantly, the war in Gaza was happening at a time when the issue of police brutality in the United States was finally beginning to gain media attention following the killing of Michael Brown, an unarmed African American man, in Ferguson, Missouri, and the mass protests that erupted in response. MPAC's social media campaign visually and thematically linked the Gaza civilians' experience of military violence to the police violence against African Americans and other minorities in Ferguson, and across the United States, thereby framing the conflict in Gaza (and the Palestinian struggle for self-determination) as an issue of basic human rights.

MPAC shared a poignant example on Twitter. Two juxtaposed photographs depict two boys caught in screams of anger and despair, the first captioned "young man in Gaza" and the second, "young man in Ferguson." The tweet reads, "#ISpeakOutBecause their screams for justice aren't being heard. These young men deserve to live. #Gaza #Ferguson."[46] For its part, CAIR's social media strategy on Gaza centered on the illegality of Israel's actions, paying particular attention to violations against American citizens. In early July 2014, the organization took on the case of Tariq Khdeir, an American teen who had been brutally beaten by Israeli police while attending a riot in Jerusalem. The riot broke out a day before the funeral of Khdeir's cousin, who had been murdered by three Israeli extremists.[47] In addition to calling on the US State Department to immediately investigate the beating of Tariq Khdeir and holding a press conference on the topic, CAIR was active in publicizing the teen's plight.[48] The image of Khdeir's bloodied and swollen face was shared on social media multiple times, often juxtaposed with an image of him before the beating, visually emphasizing the brutality of the violence committed against him. In case any lingering doubt remained about the identity of the perpetrators of this violence against an American citizen, the image caption was clear: "Israeli Army brutally beats Florida High School student."

Social media communication around these events also signaled solidarity with grassroots action by US Muslims. Symbolic demonstrations of support for contentious action play an important legitimizing role for advocacy organizations that, as we will see, often meet with criticism from their constituencies for collaborating with the government and pursuing a tactic of policy engagement. Similarly, these organizations commonly shared and retweeted news articles concerning the conflict. These articles tended to focus on Israel's disproportionate military response and human rights violations committed in Gaza, thus helping further shape a narrative of unilateral Israeli brutality, US acquiescence, and Palestinian victimization. Sharing this kind of information serves two important functions: it is a way for these organizations to signal to their audience what narratives are adequate and reliable, and it legitimizes their policy positions by substantiating their claims with information from reputable sources, such as the BBC, Reuters, and the United Nations Human Rights Council. Social media is therefore an important claims-making forum, since it provides these organizations with an opportunity to articulate and share a set of demands discursively constituted as *Muslim American* demands. In doing so, these advocacy groups communicate the ideals and values that, as they see it, define what it means to be an American Muslim, and thus help in crystallizing a Muslim American political identity.

As this chapter has shown, anti-Muslim discrimination is neither new nor unique to the Trump era but rather deeply rooted in an American history of exclusion of, and discrimination toward, minority groups. As other marginalized communities have done in the past, through myriads of acts, big and small, American Muslims strive to resist, counter, and reshape the predominant narrative through which they are constructed as suspicious citizens at best, and enemies within at worst. National Muslim advocacy organizations play an important role in this process. Through their engagement on both domestic and foreign policy issues, they communicate what American Muslims care about and thus help shape a Muslim American collective experience. Islamophobia provides these organizations with an important framework to interpret and translate the individual and structural discrimination experienced by their community. In doing so, American Muslims are positioned as an American minority group clamoring to be seen as fully and wholly American, and pushing America to live up to its own principles and aspirations.

FROM MUSLIMS IN AMERICA TO AMERICAN MUSLIMS

> Many of our parents had built many of our first institutions and we built upon them. But where we had to figure out how to do so, our parents, raised in Muslim circumstances, didn't. They were born into an Islam they carried here, and sometimes thoughtlessly reproduced. We, on the other hand, were determining what to keep and what to let go of.
>
> —Haroon Moghul, *How to be a Muslim: An American Story*

What does it mean to be an American, and what is the process through which an immigrant becomes one? Can immigrant communities ever fully integrate into the receiving society? How much political influence do immigrant groups wield in the policy process? Much of contemporary American political discourse seems to be motivated by these questions—a fact that should come as no surprise. Immigrants are central to the establishment and identity of the United States; those fleeing violence, oppression, poverty, and persecution have helped constitute America as the bastion of freedom, justice, and democracy. Immigration is what defines the American melting pot; without it, the country would be something else entirely. Immigrants' collective identity is also, inevitably, shaped and influenced by the social and political context of the United States. Thus, the dialectical relationship between immigrants and America: each a product and producer of the other.

But being an immigrant is not a permanent condition. Irish, German, and Italian immigrants are but a few of the groups who were once viewed as foreign but today are considered native or "authentic" Americans. Others, previously secure in their belonging, have been made foreign, something that became all too clear during the Red Scare of the 1950s. And while some immigrants have been granted full entry into the American national community, many others remain perpetual outsiders, regardless of citizenship status. This outside status, rather than having anything to do with an immigrant's ability to assimilate and adopt American norms and values, results form a particular process of exclusion, or what the legal and race scholar Bill Ong Hing refers to as "de-Americanization."[1] Immigrants who are de-Americanized experience vigilante violence at the hands of their fellow citizens, and legal violence at the hands of their state, which affirms their otherness through discriminatory laws and practices.[2]

Who belongs? Who is excluded? Who is a real American? And, perhaps more importantly, what is America? Questions of identity construction, evolution, and influence—far from being an academic fad—are central to understanding the political behavior of collective groups and the societies they produce. It seems that this is all the more important when we are examining immigrant groups and their impacts on the political and cultural landscape of the United States.

Collective identity is neither primordial nor naturalized, but contextually and historically grounded. As such, historical narrative is a central building block of collective identity. And just as individuals, groups "are constituted in their identity by taking up narratives that become for them their actual history."[3] It is this aspect of identity, as narrated, that allows multiple and often contradictory experiences to form a coherent collective reality. It would thus be impossible to examine Muslim American policy advocacy, and the collective group it simultaneously represents and engenders, without first examining the historical narrative of Muslim integration in the United States.

This is important because the preferences of Muslim American advocacy organizations and the policy interests they pursue are a result of the broader historical experience of Muslims in America. History, as we are often reminded, "always proceeds from history."[4] The need to take history seriously is acute when examining Muslim American advocacy, since it is as much a product of internal group dynamics as of the broader US social and political context. For these reasons, any analysis of Muslim American claim-making must also explore how the policy terrain in which interest groups function developed and, consequently, how that terrain shapes what these groups can legitimately demand, expect, and pursue.[5] The development of policy advocacy groups aiming, to pursue the interests of the Muslim American community is the result of a long process of integration. Examining the process leading to these organizations' development is thus important for contextualizing, and hence better understanding, their policy engagement and claims-making strategies.

This is by no means a complete chronicle of the Muslim American experience, if such chronicle could be written. Luckily for the reader, historical exploration of political phenomena requires a degree of selection and condensation. It requires us to "simplify reality by designating some elements as salient and omitting many more as not significant."[6] My focus here, and in the next chapter, is on three critical phases that have proven foundational for Muslim American institutional development: (1) the passage of the 1965 Immigration and Nationality Act, which ushered meaningful and long-term Muslim immigration to, and settlement in, the United States; (2) the post-9/11 backlash against Muslims, which generated a new political structure of opportunities for Muslim American organizations; and (3) the 2016 presidential campaign and its aftermath, which saw a rise in anti-Muslim political rhetoric, bias incidents, and discriminatory state policies. These events have changed the trajectory of Muslim life in America. They are thus the keys to understanding the political evolution of US Muslims and the strategies of the groups that emerged to advocate on their behalf.

Out of Many, One

Although the US Census does not collect data on religious affiliation, estimates by the Pew Research Center and other polling organizations indicate that there are 3.35 million Muslims in the United States today, roughly 1 percent of the total population.[7] Some three-quarters of that figure comprise first-generation immigrants and their US-born children. Only 2 percent of the foreign-born arrived in the United States before 1970.[8] Thus, the Immigration and Nationality Act of 1965 marks a foundational moment for Muslim American life—what political scientists refer to as a "critical juncture"—creating the conditions necessary for group development, integration, and political institution building.

Although they make up a majority of Muslims in the United States, immigrant Muslims did not introduce America to Islam. The earliest Muslims to arrive in North America were enslaved African people, many of whom continued to practice their religion in secret.[9] Then, in the late nineteenth and early twentieth centuries, Muslim missionaries introduced diverse denominations of Islam to the United States. The Ahmadiyya movement, for example, gained followers among African Americans, many finding the tenets of the religion, particularly those dealing with racial equality, justice, and brotherhood, to resonate with their lived experiences. African Americans who arrived in the Northeast and Midwest during the Great Migration that occurred between 1916 and 1970 also began looking at Islam as a uniquely African religion and an alternative to white Christianity. The Moorish Science Temple and the Nation of Islam, both established in the interwar period between 1919 and 1939, appropriated and reinterpreted the teachings of Islam through the lens of the struggle for black liberation. They associated Islam initially with Black Nationalist causes and, later on, with the broader struggles of the civil rights movement.[10]

In other words, due to the sociohistorical context of African American conversion to Islam—a context characterized by institutionalized racism and inequality—race became the salient identity around which most Black Muslims mobilized. Today, the Southern Poverty Law Center lists the Nation of Islam as an extremist group because of its theology of Black superiority and the anti-Semitic and antigay rhetoric of its leader, Louis Farrakhan.[11] However, most US-born Black Muslims, who comprise about 13 percent of the total adult Muslim population, practice mainstream forms of Islam. According to the 2017 Pew survey, only 3 percent of them identify with the Nation of Islam; the rest are evenly split between those who identify as Sunni Muslim and those who have no denominational affiliation.[12]

Meaningful Muslim immigration to the United States began after the passage of the Immigration and Nationality Act of 1965 (also known as the Hart-Celler Act), one of the most consequential pieces of immigration legislation in US history.[13] The 1965 act overturned the Immigration Act of 1924, whose purpose was to keep America white. The 1924 act sought to accomplish this by severely limiting the number of immigrants from Asia, Eastern Europe (especially Jews escaping persecution), and the Middle East and by using race and ethnicity to exclude people of "Asian lineage" from entering the United States, effectively stalling immigration from the Muslim world.[14]

By doing away with the quota-based immigration system established in 1924 and upheld by the McCarran-Walter Act of 1952, the 1965 act dramatically changed the demographic and ethnic composition of the United States. Whereas under the old system, admission largely depended on an immigrant's country of birth (70 percent of the immigrant slots available under the quota system were allotted to natives of the United Kingdom, Ireland, and Germany), the 1965 act established family reunification as the bedrock of migration to the United States. Not surprisingly, census data show that immigration began to increase rapidly after its passage. In 1960, the foreign-born comprised slightly less than 5.4 percent of the total US population, a figure that rose to 13.4 percent by 2015.[15] Most of these new immigrants were from non-European countries. Immigrants from South and East Asia, for example, comprised 3.8 percent of the foreign-born population in 1960. By 1980, that number had quadrupled, and by 2017, they made up 27 percent of the total US foreign-born population.[16]

Until recently, there was little convergence between immigrant and African American Muslims, but that has slowly begun to change. In the post-9/11 context, Muslim American organizations have increasingly acknowledged and drawn from the lessons of the civil rights movement in their efforts to access the policy dialogue and gain what they consider to be full and equal citizenship rights. They have also built alliances with other marginalized groups, bringing them closer to the African American community and Black Muslims.

Immigration, Assimilation, and the Development of Group Consciousness

For much of our country's history, assimilation of white Protestant norms was the encouraged course of action. Muslims, like all other immigrants and minorities, were expected to shed their previous identities and adopt "American values."[17] These expectations were codified into law beginning in the late 1800s. The Naturalization Act of 1870, for example, codified racist beliefs regarding the inability of certain cultures to achieve the qualities required to be an American;[18] the impetus for this law was not only that concern but also the concern that their traditions and habits were polluting the political body. These nativist trends culminated in the Americanization movement, which posited that background behavior needed to be instilled before immigrants would be ready to participate in the political life of the nation. Language classes were a key component of this training, but so were classes in hygiene, child-rearing, housekeeping, and public behavior.[19]

With the outbreak of the First World War, many questioned the allegiance of German and other immigrants to the United States. Americanization was imagined as a mechanism through which to secure immigrants' loyalties and hasten their adaptation into the dominant social, cultural, and political practices of citizenship. Today, these programs are viewed as paternalistic, disciplinary, coercive, and racist, but this was not the case at the time when they were conceived. In fact, progressive liberals were their primary proponents, considering the programs as important mechanisms for connecting immigrants to resources, easing their integration into the United States, and molding them into "ideal Americans." Social and civic organizations, churches, schools, factories, and labor unions were all involved in Americanization.[20]

Although we do not tend to think of the labor industry as a site of Americanization, this was indeed the case. Ford Motor Company, whose employees were predominantly immigrants (including many Muslims from the Middle East), is a telling example. Henry Ford himself reflected many of the anxieties that gave rise to the Americanization movement. "We are bringing up a generation of children undernourished and underdeveloped morally as well as physically," he lamented. "We are breeding a generation of workmen weak in body and mind, and for that reason bound to prove inefficient when they come to take their place in industry."[21] Instilling the work habits and discipline that Ford and other industrialists considered both essential to their workforce and lacking in immigrant workers became a major goal for the Ford Motor Company. The ideal American citizen was thus conceptualized and shaped as an ideal, efficient, and compliant worker. The company established a sociological department to advance the process of workers' Americanization and brought in a number of "investigators" to report on their progress.

Commenting on the case of Mustafa, a young Turkish worker, one investigator stated that although he "used to wash his hands and feet five times a day, as part of their religion before praying . . . today [he] has put aside his national red fez and praying, no baggy trousers anymore. He dresses like an American gentleman, attends the Ford English School, and has banked in the past year over $1,000."[22]

As one might expect, Muslim immigrants entering this social and political environment viewed assimilation as the appropriate course of action. Anglo-conformity was promoted as the basis for citizenship and "like the millions of immigrants who passed through Ellis Island, [Muslims] followed the patterns of integration and assimilation that refashioned them into American citizens."[23] As with most other nineteenth-century immigrants to the United States, Muslim immigrants strived to shed—or, at the very least, suppress—those aspects of their identities that marked them as different. There is perhaps no clearer mark of this than the name changes recorded at Ellis Island: "Mohammad became Mo, Rashid became Dick, Mojahid became Mark, and Ali was recognized as Al."[24] Many of these early immigrants also enlisted in the military, serving as American soldiers during World Wars I and II and demonstrating both their loyalty and their belonging to their new country.

The Immigration and Nationality Act of 1965 marked a radical shift in US immigration policy, and post-1965 Muslim immigrants differed markedly from their earlier counterparts. Whereas the first-wave Muslim immigrants strove to assimilate into American society, those who immigrated after 1965—the great majority of Muslim immigrants—were far more likely to want to retain their religious and ethnic affiliations. "[They] often found the accommodation of the earlier immigrants too high a price to pay, especially since America began defining itself as Protestant, Catholic, and Jewish . . . they believed that difference and distinctiveness were a necessary means of affirming a place for Islam."[25]

This trend must also be understood in terms of the broader cultural and political changes that were taking place in the United States. Encouraged by the advances of the civil rights movement of the 1960s, many minorities began organizing to demand their civic, political, and cultural rights. Underprivileged social groups such as women, LGBTQ people, people of color, and indigenous peoples resisted normative expectations to assimilate into a hegemonic American culture and sought to fundamentally redefine notions of integration and belonging. The metaphoric melting pot, in which differences dissolved, gave way to the idea of the American mosaic, where difference coalesced to form a whole.[26]

Thus, the America to which post-1965 Muslim immigrants arrived was fundamentally different from the one their nineteenth-century counterparts had experienced. Not only was complete assimilation no longer expected, but also multiculturalism was increasingly promoted, allowing immigrants to conceive of different forms of belonging. Not surprisingly, it is this post-1965 generation of

Muslim immigrants that began thinking of Islam as an identity signifier. It would be years, however, before the contours of a particular Muslim American collective identity would take shape and become politically manifest, for although post-1965 Muslim immigrants rejected the assimilationist tendencies of earlier immigrants, most still thought of themselves primarily in terms of their ethnonational identities.[27]

In fact, Muslim immigrants arriving to the United States were deeply divided along ethnonational lines. As studies of other immigrant communities in the United States demonstrate, home-country politics can play a major role, mobilizing immigrants around their (trans)national and, to a lesser extent, ethnic identities. Although traditional assimilation theorists treat transnational linkages as anathema to integration, more recent scholarship understands transnationalism and integration as simultaneous processes:[28] "Movement and attachment is not linear or sequential, but capable of rotating back and forth and changing direction over time."[29] Involvement in home-country politics and transnational issues does not have to inhibit engagement in US politics. On the contrary, it can be largely conducive to the political participation and incorporation of first-generation immigrants, as it allows them to conceive of themselves as agents in the process, who are actively involved in negotiating the terms of their integration and can meaningfully contribute to their new homes through the forging of global interactions.[30]

It is unsurprising that Muslim immigrants arriving to the United States in the 1970s and 1980s (and their US-born children today) continued to be concerned with home-country politics, particularly since many of them were leaving behind countries that had only recently gained independence and were still marred by intrastate conflicts. For immigrants from the Middle East and North Africa, the Arab-Israeli conflict and the twin ideologies of nationalism and pan-Arabism were formative components of how they related to the countries they were leaving and the country they were entering. Similarly, the violent legacy of partition of the Indian subcontinent following independence from British rule in 1947, as well as the establishment of Bangladesh in 1971, shaped the early collective identity and mobilization of South Asian immigrants.[31]

The diversity of post-1965 Muslim immigrants to the United States and the initial focus on home-country politics meant they were less likely to identify as members of a Muslim American collective group.[32] But this was a fleeting condition. Encouraged by the example of the African American civil rights movement, many minorities began organizing politically, leading to a burgeoning in the number of minority- and identity-based organizations throughout the 1970s. Home-country politics and the rise of an Islamic response to the sociopolitical failures that many attributed to Arab secularism also aided in the emergence of Islam as a salient identity marker. Muslim American organizations began to be established in this social and political context, helping to mold and articulate a collective Muslim American identity for Muslim immigrants attempting to negotiate their place in their new surroundings. However, it would take the tragic events of September 11, 2001, and the subsequent and persistent targeting of individuals based on their perceived religious identity, for Islam to become a salient collective identity marker and for members of these varied ethnonational backgrounds to begin thinking of themselves as members of a collective group.

Establishing Roots: Negotiating Islam in America

Muslim immigrants encountered the United States long before their migration began. The United States was becoming more meaningfully involved in their home countries, particularly those in the Middle East, and this fact influenced how many of them perceived the United States and their place in it. Some scholars have gone as far as to argue that this wave of Muslim migrants is best viewed as "collateral damage" of US foreign policy in their countries of origin.[33] What is clear is that one reason these immigrants came to the United States was to escape military, economic, and political crises in their home countries—crises that often resulted from US interventions or were exacerbated by them. These immigrants' perceptions of America before their arrival thus inevitably influenced the process of integration. The United States' involvement in Muslim-majority countries continues to influence how Muslims perceive, integrate, and adapt in America, making US domestic and foreign policy a major determinant of Muslim settlement and integration.

Well into the 1980s, however, most Muslim immigrants related to the United States as a transient place to get an education or some work experience before returning home.[34] Soon enough, and to their surprise, these immigrants realized that they were setting down roots, that America was becoming home. There is, of course, nothing essentialist about a home. Rather, it is the very process of inhabitation that makes a place—any place—become one. As Mucahit Bilici beautifully puts it, "What is crucial for the sense of home is the experience of dwelling. . . . The subject appropriates a given space as home only after she projects into that space her subjective being, that is, when she dwells."[35] Looking at the process of dwelling and the everyday practices it entails is one of the keys to understanding how the United States went from being a transient place for Muslims to becoming the home of a thriving American Muslim community. Physical and cultural settlement becomes an attempt to mitigate the loss, rupture, and disequilibrium of immigration by (re)claiming the attachments to one's surroundings, even if a new self must be born in the process. It is this process of settlement that allows Muslims to think of themselves as citizens; citizens with rights to enter the political process and make claims toward the achievement of their individual and collective rights.

How did these immigrants experience, interpret, and appropriate their new homeland? We know from the study of other immigrant groups that symbols, myths, and rituals play a crucial role in the settlement process.[36] We must, therefore, examine the common narrative provided by Islam—its texts, rituals, practices, and myths—as discursive building blocks through which Muslim Americans build and interpret their collective experience and reality.

Constructing Home, Conceptualizing Belonging

Migration has played an important role in the historical narrative of Islam. Whether to escape persecution, to proselytize, or to conquer other lands, Muslims and Islam have been in constant movement.[37] This narrative, found in Islamic jurisprudence, gave immigrants a way to interpret their social surroundings and make sense of their experience. Islamic jurisprudence is thus an important part of the discourse of Muslim American integration and a major way through which Muslims explain and rationalize their immigration, settlement, and belonging in America.[38] One of the most important aspects of this narrative comes from the theorization of a binary opposition between *dar al Islam* (abode of Islam/Muslim-controlled lands) and *dar al harb* (abode of war, chaos/the rest of the world). The perception is that Muslims living within *dar al Islam* inhabit a familiar place and belong to a bounded and recognizable community. Classical Muslim jurists concerned with protecting the community, or *ummah*, saw no reasons for Muslims to move permanently to *dar al harb*, unless their departure was due to necessity. This, then, becomes the lens through which early Muslim immigrants both experienced and legitimized their migration to the United States: migration resulted from economic or academic necessity and was, therefore, temporary. Many Muslim immigrants also considered living in America as potentially dangerous, an exposure to possible moral decay. Of course, not all Muslim immigrants were, or are, concerned with a religious-philosophical interpretation of their experience, nor do they all seek a religious justification for their presence in the United States, but these questions play an important role in the historical narrative of the community, and thus in the development of a collective identity.

Until the 1970s, most Muslim immigrants wanted only to avoid the negative effects of living in America, to remain "pure" for their return to *dar al Islam*.[39]

Some thinkers of the time went as far as to promote isolationism—living in separate Muslim enclaves—as a way of preventing the corruption that could come from living in the United States. Voicing this sentiment most starkly was Syed Abu Al Hassan Ali Nadwi, an influential Muslim speaker from India, who argued that "should there be the least danger to faith, go back to your native land, or to any other place where there is the security of faith; go, and take your family, go even if you have to go on foot."[40] This isolationist tendency changed over time, mainly as a result of an internal process of reinterpretation of the relationship between *dar al Islam* and *dar el harb*. Rather than an either-or dichotomy, Muslims began reintroducing juridical concepts such as *dar al dawah* (abode of mission) and *dar al ahd* (abode of contract), which made it possible to begin seeing and thinking of America as a place of settlement.[41] The concept of *dawah* is particularly significant, as it has played an important role in mobilizing the community around domestic and foreign policy issues, including disaster relief at home and abroad, and raising awareness about human rights crises affecting the *ummah* in Palestine-Israel, Kashmir, and Myanmar—a subject we will return to later in the book.

Paradoxically, another factor aiding the process of settlement in the United States was the fact that many Muslim-majority countries were governed by secular dictatorships that largely constrained religion to the private sphere; living in a Muslim-majority country did not guarantee (and often prevented) freedom of religion. A common theme in my interviews with Muslim Americans was that the United States, as a democratic, open, and pluralistic society, was the only place where Muslims could practice "true" Islam, free from compulsion or corruption. Since 9/11, many Muslim scholars and leaders have criticized the entire notion of abodes, arguing that rigid dichotomies do not make sense in a globalized world. Instead, they argue, the world is a single *dar*, a single abode. These internal modes of conceptualizing belonging are significant, in that they provide the seeds for the institutionalization of Muslim American life and the development of a minority group identity, factors that are crucial for mobilizing political participation in the US context. And although these concerns may seem to be specific to the Muslim American community, they are part of a familiar, broader story. Questions of religious rituals and practice (more than beliefs per se) often acquire new significance for immigrants struggling to adapt to new and unfamiliar surroundings. As Charles Hirschman argues,

> Religious belief and practice can serve as ballast for immigrants as they struggle to adapt to their new homeland. . . . Immigrants must confront the existential question of "Who am I?" In a new social context, immigrants could often find meaning and identity by reaffirming traditional beliefs, including the structures of religious faith that may have been

taken for granted before. The certainty of religious precepts can provide an anchor as immigrants must adapt and change many other aspects of their lives and habit.[42]

Reenacting the familiar becomes a central way of making sense of what appears foreign.

Establishing Belonging: Making Islam Visible in US Public Spaces

Settlement and integration are thus best understood as a process of gradual familiarization and claiming of one's surroundings, both physically and metaphorically. For Muslim immigrants, this was of immediate concern, since fulfilling their religious duties and facing Mecca during prayer required a deep familiarization with their physical surroundings. As other minority groups before and after them have done, Muslim immigrants began establishing places of worship in their adopted homelands. And, as has often been the case, these religious institutions became major drivers of immigrant integration and political participation.

Contrary to the commonly held "clash of civilizations" assumption that the values and attitudes of religious Muslims are incompatible with democratic norms, mosque attendance has been found to strengthen social networks, foster political participation, and make individuals more interested in civic life—a finding in line with the broader literature on the role of the Black church in mobilizing African American voters.[43] This is because religious institutions expose individuals to a broader community of fellow participants and religious leaders and to the informal social gatherings that take place outside of the religious services. Mosque involvement is also positively associated with nonelectoral forms of political participation, such as attending a rally or community meeting, donating to a cause, or contacting an elected official. In short, US Muslims who attend mosque and follow the precepts of the Qur'an are more likely to think of Islamic and democratic values as compatible and participate in the civic and political life of their nation.[44]

Imam Hussein Karoub established the first American mosque in 1921,[45] but US mosques, like Muslims themselves, are primarily a post-1965 phenomenon. Fewer than 13 percent of American mosques were founded before 1970, but by 2011, there were 2,106 across all fifty states, with more than half of these built after 2000.[46] How these physical spaces have evolved and changed is, in many ways, representative of the journey of Muslim American integration. In the beginning, American mosques were often humble spaces, such as homes, commercial buildings, or businesses, that had been converted into community gathering places. Most had a room for prayer (the only real requirement of a mosque) and a hall for weddings and parties, akin to a church.[47] It was also not uncommon for Muslims to congregate in the mosque on Sunday, the Christian day of rest and worship. In other words, mosques were largely invisible; from the outside, there was almost no sign that a building was a mosque.

This began to change dramatically in the late 1980s. America was becoming home, and the architectural structures of mosques were reflecting that reality.[48] Mosques built in the 1990s were architecturally assertive structures that epitomized American Islam. Their designs combined elements of traditional Islamic architecture and American architecture and sought harmony with the surrounding landscape. The Islamic Cultural Center of New York is one example of this approach. Built with traditional Islamic motifs and geometric forms, it is nevertheless a strikingly modern structure, fitting, complementing, and adding to its New York City surroundings. Other examples include the Islamic Center of Virginia, whose cobblestones blend with the existing architectural environment, and the Islamic Center Village of Abiquiu, New Mexico, which complements the local adobe buildings and Spanish architecture of the region.[49]

Like Muslims themselves, the evolution of the American mosque is an ongoing process. Reflecting the growth and diversity of Islam in America, the nation's only Spanish-speaking mosque, Centro Islamico, opened its doors in Houston in January 2016. Centro Islamico serves Latinx converts, one of the fastest growing congregations of Muslims in the United States. It celebrates Cinco de Mayo festivities and is decorated with motifs that echo the arches of the Mesquita de Cordoba, a mosque in southern Spain that dates to the tenth century. Similarly, the Women's Mosque of America opened its doors in Los Angeles in 2015. As its name suggests, the mosque is a space only for women. Female *khateebahs* deliver the Friday *Jumma'a* prayer service, something traditionally done only by men, and run every aspect of the institution. According to its founders, the mosque seeks to reclaim a long tradition of women's religious scholarship in Islam, provide a safe space for all women, and promote women's leadership skills.[50]

What began as a hesitant attempt to make space for Islam in America, and to make Muslim religious life possible, has become a much more confident manifestation of Muslim American settlement, belonging, and integration. Mosques today are not just religious institutions. They are incubators of civic and political life, places where Muslims encounter others like—and not so like—them, gain exposure to relevant social and political issues, and are spurred into action. They are also places where the meaning of *American Islam* and what it means to be Muslim is being negotiated and shaped, often in unanticipated ways. In short, mosques are products and reflections of the broader society, outcomes and mirrors of the demographic and sociocultural changes that are shaping this country. As such, they have also become major sites of contestation. For some, they represent a physical encroachment by immigrants who, rather than assimilate, are imposing their own, foreign cultural norms. For others, the debate is about religious liberty and the denial of a community's basic constitutional rights. Though this debate predates the "Ground Zero Mosque" debate of 2010, the latter is one of its clearest manifestations; a case study through which we can examine the broader ideological battlefield over the place of Islam in the United States—a topic to which we will return in the next chapter.

Building the Foundations of Home: Civic and Political Institutions

Mosques are not the only institutions Muslims have been interested in establishing. Soon after their arrival, the young professionals and graduate students who migrated to the United States in the 1960s and 1970s began establishing civic organizations, institutions that would eventually become the foundation of Muslim civic and political life in America. For those recently arrived immigrants, however, as for most first-generation immigrants, the need to survive and achieve economic security was paramount. Politics was secondary. Reflecting this reality, early Muslim organizations in the United States were primarily concerned with meeting the community's immediate needs for spiritual development, education, and charity. Explicitly political and advocacy-focused organizations came a few decades later, as these new Americans began to build the resources necessary for political engagement and recognize the importance of promoting and securing their rights.

The earliest civic organizations were established in the middle of the twentieth century: the short-lived Federation of Islamic Association, established in 1953, and the Muslim Students Association (MSA), established in 1963, which later became MSA National, a nonprofit umbrella organization dedicated to supporting independent, student-run Muslim organizations across college campuses and "empowering the students of today to be citizens of tomorrow's community."[51] In 1982, a group of MSA student leaders went on to establish the Islamic Society of North America (ISNA), with the stated goal of providing some cohesion to the various mosques and outreach organizations that had been developed up until that point. In the 1990s, ISNA extended its work to include education and outreach to other faith communities and interfaith organizations. Today, it is the largest North American Muslim umbrella organization and remains primarily concerned with issues of religion, education, outreach, and humanitarian relief.[52]

ISNA also publishes a bimonthly journal, *Islamic Horizons*, and organizes an annual convention that brings together more than thirty thousand people.

Similarly, the Islamic Circle of North America (ICNA) was established in 1968 to educate American Muslims and others about Islam. *Dawah*, the process of conveying the message of Islam and inviting people to understand the worship of God through the Qur'an, was, and remains, one of ICNA's top priorities. In 1999, the organization launched an ambitious (and, to some critics, controversial) project: Why Islam. The project gained attention after a number of eye-catching billboards started appearing across US highways, inviting people to visit the website and call the Why Islam hotline. Critics see these ads and the work of Why Islam in general as proselytizing, at best, and the work of global, hardline *Salafis*, at worst. Those behind the project argue that they are seeking only to "provide accurate information about Islam . . . [and] dispel popular misconceptions about Islam and Muslims."[53]

What these debates often miss is the highly political nature of the project. A billboard installed in Tampa, Florida, in the summer of 2017, for example, read, "Making America Great with Love, Compassion & Mercy" in a style evoking Trump's campaign signs and slogan. Another billboard included three images: a nun, the Virgin Mary, and a woman in a hijab, alongside the words, "They wore it for the same reason." The intent, of course, is to call out the double standards of those who discriminate against veiled Muslim women. A billboard in Dallas, Texas, simply read: "Islam = racial equality," a clear message in the current context of racial injustice in America.

FIGURE 2.   Billboard in Tampa, Florida, 2017. Reproduced with the permission of whyislam.org (877-WHY-ISLAM).

Aside from their more ostensible functions, civic organizations such as the MSA, ICNA, and ISNA provide the basis for Muslim American presence, visibility, and social connectedness. Through their community programs, outreach events, and basic service provision, Muslims in America physically encounter and engage with one another and the society around them. These institutions were, in many ways, the first spaces where diverse groups of Muslims encountered each other beyond the local level (which they had historically done at their mosques), allowing them to begin to think of themselves as members of a larger, imagined community[54] of Muslim Americans. As Robert Putnam and other social scientists have demonstrated, civic organizations such as these play a central role in the process of cultural and political integration. Among other things, they help promote the basic norms of civic engagement and foster members' "social capital," which includes qualities like collaboration and social trust—essential precursors for political participation.[55]

As these emergent organizations were nurturing the development of social connectedness among Muslims across the United States, debates about the religious permissibility of permanently residing outside Muslim-majority countries were continuing, a fact that greatly thwarted the community's political participation. It was not until 1986 that ISNA (then the largest Muslim organization) took a position favoring citizenship and participation in mainstream US politics, thereby ushering in the establishment of explicitly political organizations.[56] Whereas earlier organizations had focused primarily on religion, education, community outreach, and *dawah*, the organizations established in the late 1980s and early 1990s shifted their efforts to the policy process. Their guiding principle was simple and familiar: Muslim American integration and empowerment would only occur through political engagement and advocacy. For them, the question was not *whether* to pursue assimilation or isolation but *how* to achieve the collective interests of US Muslims and meaningfully contribute to the American homeland. They viewed engagement, or, as they like to put it, "having a seat at the policy table," as the best way to promote their community's interests and secure their full citizenship rights.

These organizations did not emerge in a vacuum. As is the case for the other minority and immigrant groups that began emerging in the 1970s, the example, sacrifices, and advances of the civil rights movement created the conditions necessary for their mobilization. This shift encouraged minorities to think of the possibilities of mass action, provided them with a collective symbolic vocabulary from which to draw, and enabled them to conceptualize their claims in terms of rights they were entitled to as Americans. These organizations and their leaders have sought to naturalize Islam and Muslims in America, to articulate and represent the demand of this marginalized and often-targeted community and, as one

FIGURES 3A AND 3B. "Recognize Muslim Roots," House Resolution 869 advocacy flyer. Reproduced with the permission of the Islamic Circle of North America Council for Social Justice (icnacsj.org).

of the leaders I interviewed put it, "to take the torch from those who have struggled and made gains before us, push it forward, and pass it on to the next group of Americans who will be targeted."[57] ICNA's "Recognize Muslims Roots Campaign" depicted in figures 3a and 3b is a compelling example of this mission.

Indeed, "were it not for the African American triumph over racial prejudice, immigrants of color would not have found an open door in America."[58] For the next few decades, American Muslims would try to thrust open that door, pushing it a little further each time.

The Impacts of September 11 on Muslim American Institutional Life

The 1990s saw a real explosion in the number of new Muslim advocacy organizations. Most were short-lived and could not survive the pressures following the 9/11 attacks and the passage into law of the USA PATRIOT (Uniting and Strengthening America by Providing Appropriate Tools Required to Intercept and Obstruct Terrorism) Act of 2001. CAIR, established in 1994, is now one of the largest and most influential US Muslim advocacy organizations. It was also one of the few to meaningfully survive after 9/11. Many others, including the American Muslim Committee and the American Muslim Alliance, became practically defunct, as government officials distanced themselves from them.[59] Others, such as the Holy Land Foundation (HLF), at the time the largest Muslim charity organization in the United States, were shut down by the government and saw their leaders prosecuted. Five members of the HLF's senior leadership were arrested, accused of providing material support to Hamas, and sentenced to fifteen to sixty-five years in prison.[60] The HLF and other Muslim organizations, including CAIR, maintain that the funds went to support humanitarian causes in the West Bank and Gaza. The HLF was not a political advocacy organization, but its demise sent chills down the spines of American Muslims, particularly those in leadership positions. Under the Patriot Act, making financial contributions to what the government deemed questionable nonprofits became a punishable act, even if the individual contributor was not aware of how the organization handled its donations. People stopped contributing to Muslim causes and organizations for fear that the US government would go after the charities. Many grew mistrustful of the government and questioned the prudence of political action at a time when their communities were under enormous pressure. However, for CAIR and the other advocacy organizations that survived (and those that would come into being in the years following 9/11), silence and disengagement were not options. These groups turned the pressures of 9/11 and the Patriot Act into an opportunity to promote and defend the civic, political, and social rights of Muslims in the United States; to spur them to political action; and to access the policymaking process as the representatives of this community. September 11 became a catalyst for American Muslims, simultaneously engendering and solidifying a distinct Muslim American group identity while opening the space necessary for meaningful integration and naturalization of Muslims in the United States.

Intellectual debates about Islam's relationship to pluralism and democracy did not begin with the attacks of 9/11, but the attacks made them all the more important in the context of new questions and demands from American pundits regarding Islam's (in)compatibility with democracy. From the early treatment of minorities to encounters with colonialism, dealing with non-Muslims has been a major pragmatic and intellectual concern for Muslims and Islam.[61] Historically, the issue had been how to deal with non-Muslims in Muslim lands, but immigration to the United States (and other non-Muslim majority countries) turned this question on its head. Muslim American intellectuals advocated for a pluralistic Islam, grounded in the Qur'anic teachings of coexistence and equality of humankind.[62] The inherent compatibility of Islam and democracy became an important component of this pluralism discourse—a discourse both constituted by and constitutive of Muslim American integration and cultural settlement.

An Evolving Narrative of Muslim Identity in America

The organizations I examine are fundamentally products and producers of this discourse. Their establishment resulted as much from the intellectual developments within the Muslim American community that made their vision of an American Islam possible as from the social and political context of American democracy. Their goals and work center on a vision of Islam that is not only compatible with, but also part of, a pluralistic American democracy. As MPAC's president, Salam Al-Marayati, put it:

> We have to be part of a pluralistic model wherever we live. Even if we are part of the 99 percent Muslims, well, there are some Muslims who are not practicing, some Muslims who have different lifestyles—some are nationalists, some are atheists, some are communists, some are socialists, and so on—so the goal is to construct a pluralistic model of government. To me, that is what the Prophet did when he was in Medina, because he brought the Jewish tribes and the Christian tribes and they

formed a covenant called the Medina Charter, which was based on security, common citizenship, and equality.[63]

By highlighting the practices (citizenship, deliberation, security, and equality) that today signify American democracy as representative of "true" Islam, Muslim American leaders are advocating on behalf of their constituents, but they are also communicating a particular group identity, based on the core values of individual rights, equality, and social justice. This discourse becomes an important basis from which the organizations I examine seek access to the policy dialogue as an American minority group making rights-related claims.

The historical narrative of Muslim settlement in the United States is complex, nonlinear, and still evolving. It includes the assimilationist tendencies of nineteenth-century Muslim immigrants as much as the isolationism, and later integrationism, of those who came to the United States after 1965. It is best understood as a process of negotiation through which Muslim immigrants attempt to appropriate their surroundings while reinterpreting them to fit their needs. At its core, it is a narrative about how collective identities are formed, how they evolve, and how they change. Today, a Muslim American collective identity is emerging and, although it is still developing—as all identities always are—it is also increasingly clear, confident, and comfortable in its surroundings. The Immigration and Nationality Act of 1965 was the first critical juncture in this historical narrative of Muslim life in America, catapulting long-term Muslim immigration to and settlement in the United States. The events of September 11, 2001, were the second, and perhaps more important, watershed moment, both because of the pressures it imposed on Muslims and for the opportunities it engendered, particularly for Muslim American institutions.

FROM THE PATRIOT ACT TO THE "MUSLIM BAN"

9/11 is the B.C. and A.D. of the Muslim American community.

—Dr. Maher Hathout, author interview, June 2, 2013

Institutional Islamophobia makes individual Islamophobia easier, it makes it easier for the public to agree on policies that discriminate against a particular group.

—Dalia Mogahed, author interview, December 5, 2018

I still cringe when I recall the days and weeks immediately following the 9/11 attacks. The fear, grief, and anxiety I felt engulfed everything and everyone around me. Living in Bay Ridge, Brooklyn, at the time of the attacks, a neighborhood with a large concentration of Arabs and Muslims, forever shaped me. One of our neighbors lost their son, who worked at Cantor Fitzgerald, on the 105th floor of One World Trade Center. He was twenty-eight years old. I did not know them, but I cried for days after I found out. I just couldn't believe it. A few years later our street would be renamed to commemorate him.

As the reality of the tragedy was starting to sink in, my best friend's mother, concerned about the safety of her daughter, asked me to return to our high school first and see whether it was safe for "the Muslim kids" to go back. It was, though you could feel the anger and accusatory stares of many of our peers. The same week of the attacks, I went to my afternoon shift at the bakery where I worked after school. My coworker, Kimberly, was there, her blonde hair tied in a beautiful long ribbon of red, white, and blue. When I went to hug her and ask if she and her loved ones were OK (as most New Yorkers around me were doing in those dreadful days), I was met with a cold, angry stare. "Arabs did this," she told me. I felt my face burning with shame, though I wasn't sure why.

Rumors soon started to circulate that the FBI was rounding up people. I will never forget the helplessness in the eyes of one of the hairdressers in the salon I frequented whose husband had been afraid not to heed the FBI's request for an interview, too trusting that he would be cleared as a nonthreat and simply allowed to go home to his family. He had lived in the United States for more than a decade, had never broken any laws other than overstaying his visitor's visa from Egypt, and had paid his taxes. He had two young American-born children. He was detained for months and deported to Egypt. People seemed to disappear over-night, picked up by the federal authorities in the days after the attacks, taken into custody, and—when nothing other than an expired immigration status was found—deported.

On Trauma, Victimhood, and Belonging

For Muslim Americans, as for all Americans, the collective traumas caused by the 9/11 attacks are still felt, lived, experienced. The physical and metaphorical vio-lation of the homeland disrupted the sense of home that comes, in part, from feel-ing safe and in harmony with one's surroundings. Collective mourning became a way to interpret the events, grasp the loss, and attempt to overcome as a nation. For Muslim citizens, however, the trauma was amplified. Not only were they vic-tims of an attack on their nation, they were also blamed and victimized as some-how culpable, their purported culpability stemming from nothing other than sharing the religion of the perpetrators. Their identities as American Muslims—their very being—marked them as dubious. This experience has been unabat-edly replicated every time a terrorist attack involving a Muslim perpetrator takes place in the United States, or anywhere else in the world. Muslims are continu-ously asked to condemn these acts—and, thus, demonstrate their loyalty to their nation—but their condemnations seldom reach a wider audience.

In addition to being (temporarily?) excluded from the imagined American community, American Muslims have also been alienated from their institutions of government, as they became the domestic targets of their government's War on Terror. Such hardship can stimulate, build resilience, and be developmentally helpful, however. According to CAIR's former national legislative director, Co-rey Saylor, his organization had tried for years to convince the community that their political participation was a necessity. The backlash from the 9/11 attacks was a wake-up call, he told me: "It really made people aware that we couldn't just hang out in our mosques and be comfortable and enjoy the privileges and free-doms that come from living in America. Just because freedom is on paper it doesn't mean it exists in reality. You really have to struggle for it."[1] Muslims in the United States became increasingly politically mobilized. They realized that to claim their place in America, they would have to fight for the civic and political rights their Constitution granted them. However, Muslim American organizations were utterly unprepared to meet the demands imposed on them in the aftermath of 9/11—a fact that actually proved conducive to their institutional development and the broader integration process. Lacking organizational resources and know-how forced them to build alliances with other minority and advocacy organizations, something that they had started to do before the attacks but that necessity dramatically hastened. Moreover, members of the government and the media were eager to gain the "Muslim American perspective" and thus granted organizational elites a previously unimaginable degree of attention and access, legitimizing them as the official representatives of the Muslim American community in the process. These elites became the public spokespeople of a community under siege. In the coming years, they would use this newfound influence to push for their policy demands and further the social and political integration of American Muslims.

But 9/11 is no longer the only foundational moment for the Muslim American community. Indeed, there is an entire generation of younger Muslims who relate to 9/11 as history, not the lived, painfully visceral experience it continues to be for many of us old enough to remember the gruesome details of that day, the wars fought in supposed retaliation, and the policies enacted under the auspices of national security. The post-9/11 backlash galvanized an entire generation of activists, but for younger Muslims, it was the 2016 campaigns and the election of Donald Trump that made them recognize just how much work remained for them to do.[2] As Khaled Beydoun put it, "for younger Muslims, Trump's election was their 9/11."[3]

During each of these catalytic events, Muslims have responded by making claims as citizens, demanding their constitutional rights, and mobilizing to defend and promote what they perceive to be core American values. The targeting and marginalization of Muslims that government policy has perpetuated since the 9/11 attacks, and which manifests overtly in our current political discourse, has strengthened the organizations that claim to represent them. I do not mean to suggest that these organizations are immune to backlash or that they have not suffered as a result of the government's policies. They most certainly have. Documents leaked in July 2014 show that CAIR's executive director, Nihad Awad, was under strict government surveillance from 2002 to 2008, even as his organization worked closely with the FBI and other government agencies on counterterrorism and efforts to prevent radicalization.[4]

Events like these, and the many other violations against Muslims and those perceived to be Muslims—collectively known as the "post-9/11 backlash"—are well documented.[5] Less deeply examined are the opportunities that the post-9/11 crisis and Trump's election engendered for Muslim American organizations. The very policies that have constituted US Muslims as an out-group have also created the structural conditions necessary for the participation of Muslim American interest groups and, to a great extent, determined their strategies and claims-making capacity.

The War on Terror and the Criminalization of Islam

A mere seven days after his inauguration in 2017, President Trump translated his campaign promise of a "total and complete shutdown of Muslims entering the United States" into Executive Order 13769, which temporarily barred entry to the United States to immigrants from seven Muslim-majority countries.[6] In the hours and days following the announcement, organic mass protests took place in airports across the country, civil rights organizations mobilized against what they saw as a religious (and thus unconstitutional) ban, and legal challenges against the administration's decision began to mount. What seemed absent in the ensuing discussions about the executive branch's authority over immigration[7] was any placement of Trump's "Muslim ban" in a broader policy context. Contextualizing the ban would mean considering the legislation, special registrations, extrajudicial deportations, and detentions that the US government had already actively employed as domestic tools in the War on Terror—tools through which Muslims are framed as potential threats to "our" national security. Well before the 2016 presidential election, the War on Terror had lived inside the American national homeland, with Muslim Americans as its main domestic target.[8] Trump's immigration ban must be understood in its place along a broader legal and policy spectrum that has targeted and criminalized Muslims both inside and outside the United States.

There are clear examples of how official US policy, implicitly and explicitly, codifies anti-Muslim discrimination. Most of this analysis centers on the post-9/11 era, the period when Muslims as a *category* of individuals became the focus of policymakers and law enforcement officials in charge of waging the War on Terror, but it is worth remembering that the policy response to 9/11 did not emerge in a vacuum. It was possible thanks to a long-standing paradigm in which Muslims and Arabs have been historically constructed as targets of exclusion. As the historian Ibrahim Al-Marashi notes, "Trump's fiat is therefore embedded in a deeper American history of conceiving Middle Eastern populations as security threats."[9]

The first time Arabs and Muslims were targeted for special exclusion in the United States was after the Munich Olympics attacks of 1972, when Palestinian militants affiliated with Black September (a military offshoot of Fatah) took hostage and then killed eleven Israeli Olympic team members and a German police officer. Hours after the attack, President Nixon issued a memorandum establishing a Cabinet Committee to Combat Terrorism.[10] What began as a visa-screening program focusing on people from the Middle East traveling to the United States expanded into a campaign of domestic surveillance and intimidation of Arab individuals and organizations, code-named Operation Boulder.[11] In 1972, Abdeen Jabaran, one of the targets of FBI surveillance, enlisted the help of the ACLU to sue the FBI and other security agencies. Jabaran was a prominent Arab American civil rights attorney and cofounder of one of the largest Arab American organizations, the American-Arab Anti-Discrimination Committee. The National Security Agency was forced to admit, for the first time, that it had been spying on American citizens.[12]

Following the events of September 11, 2001, the ACLU again found itself at the forefront of the national security–civil liberties debate. Almost immediately after the attacks, Congress began drafting legislation that became the USA PATRIOT Act, one of the most expansive and ambiguous pieces of legislation dealing with the War on Terror, and thus among the most important legal and discursive sites in the construction of Muslims as an out-group.[13] As ACLU president Susan Herman put it in a 2011 speech, "The idea that in October 2001, Congress knew exactly what was required to intercept and obstruct terrorism seems, in retrospect, like fear-induced swagger."[14] The Patriot Act, an abstruse document of more than 340 pages, is a collection of hundreds of amendments to previously existing laws. Its main purpose and rationale was to facilitate evidence-gathering procedures and expedite the prosecution of suspected terrorists. To accomplish this, it granted the government increased powers to monitor and surveille individuals and organizations perceived to pose a potential threat to national security. In the process, the act resulted in a vast expansion of the government's surveillance capabilities and posed a grave threat to the civil liberties of all Americans. Herman sums it up as follows: "A panicky American public wanted to believe the government could keep them safe and was willing to barter constitutional rights for safety."[15]

In fact, Americans were conflicted about how much to sacrifice their civil liberties in the fight against terrorism. A Gallup survey conducted in January 2002, just four months after the attacks, found Americans evenly divided on this question, with 47 percent saying that the government should take steps to combat terrorism, even if civil liberties are violated, and 49 percent saying that the government should take steps to combat terrorism, but not if those steps would violate basic civil rights.[16] Subsequent polls showed that a majority of Americans were *not* willing to compromise their civil rights in the War on Terror, and by August 2003, two-thirds of them said that the government should continue to take steps to combat terrorism but not violate their civil rights in the process.

Tellingly, during this same period, most Americans did not believe the Bush administration was restricting their civil rights, with a majority saying the government was "about right" or "has not gone far enough" in restricting people's civil liberties to fight terrorism. In other words, Americans were largely opposed to restrictions of their civil liberties but did not believe those restrictions were occurring or that they were subject to them.[17]

Contradictions abounded, as they often do. While most Americans were against having their *individual* civil rights restricted, a majority were accepting of a requirement that "all citizens carry a national ID card at all times" and favored profiling travelers who appeared to be Arab or Muslim for extra screening.[18] Not surprisingly, the Patriot Act did not affect all Americans equally. In the first legal challenge against it, the ACLU argued that the FBI was "targeting ethnic, religious, and political minority communities disproportionately."[19] Interestingly, the act begins with a disclaimer that aims to both preempt and circumvent this critique: "Arab Americans, Muslim Americans, and Americans from South Asia play a vital role in our Nation and are entitled to nothing less than the full rights of every American."[20] Thus, while condemning discrimination against the identified group, it also defines the targets of the post-9/11 societal backlash.[21]

The act also implicitly presents the targeting of US Muslims based, in part, on the presence and visibility of outward markers of Islam, claiming, "Muslim Americans have become so fearful of harassment that many Muslim women are changing the way they dress to avoid becoming targets."[22] Muslims are constituted as not only visibly different from other Americans but also capable of avoiding (or at least attempting to avoid) becoming targets by changing that which makes them visibly different: in this case, a woman's hijab, or headscarf.

What becomes immediately clear upon reading this preamble is that the Patriot Act seeks to assign, and thus shift, responsibility for the backlash against Muslim citizens to the level of the individual. The backlash is thus presented as the result of the actions of a misguided few, an aberration, rather than the result of state policies that not only encourage but also are directly implicated in discriminatory practices against those perceived to be Muslim or of Arab and South Asian descent. As section 102(4) suggests, "When American citizens commit acts of violence against those who are, or are perceived to be, of Arab or Muslim descent, they should be punished to the full extent of the law."[23] In this construction, "the law" is to serve as the protector of the targeted group against the criminal actions of a few. There is no mention of what should be done when the law itself is providing the rationale to target these groups and the state—represented by its political elites and the varied institutions of government, including the FBI, the CIA, and the police—is perpetrating the violence.

In expanding the government's powers, the Patriot Act has led to the erosion of the constitutional and civil rights of all Americans, but American Muslims have been disproportionally targeted. Section 215, in particular, dramatically expands the government's surveillance capabilities and powers, which were previously curtailed by the Foreign Intelligence Surveillance Act (FISA) of 1978. Furthermore, the Patriot Act grants federal authorities (specifically the CIA and the FBI) the right to define and interpret what constitutes suspicious behavior and to identify, prosecute, and punish those suspected. According to the ACLU, "Under Section 215, the FBI could demand a list of every person who has checked out a particular book on Islamic fundamentalism. It could demand a list of people who had visited a particular website. It could demand a client list from a charity that offers social services to immigrants."[24]

The act also made it possible for the FBI to subject thousands of individuals to "voluntary" phone-ins and interviews and, with the INS, to round up and detain hundreds of immigrants for visa violations. Some individuals were detained for months without ever facing charges. Most of these "suspect" citizens were men of Arab and South Asian descent.[25] According to data released by the Department of Justice, the majority were citizens of Pakistan, Egypt, Turkey, Jordan, and Yemen—all close US allies.[26]

In 2002, six of these detainees brought a class action lawsuit against top government officials, including former attorney general John Ashcroft and former FBI director Robert Mueller. The suit claimed that the detainees had been subjected to humiliating beatings, searches, and other abuses. On June 19, 2017, the US Supreme Court ruled in favor of the government. However, in the majority opinion, Justice Anthony Kennedy emphasized that the court was only considering whether the plaintiffs could sue the government for financial compensation, not "whether the petitioners' alleged conduct was proper, nor whether it gave decent respect to respondents' dignity and well being, nor whether it was in keeping with the idea of the rule of law that must inspire us even in times of crisis."[27]

There is also clear evidence that the FBI engaged in profiling based on ethnicity, religion, and national origin. An internal FBI document, *Domestic Investigations and Operations Guide*, which aimed at implementing the 2008 *Attorney General's Guidelines for Domestic FBI Operations*, explicitly authorized the FBI to "identify locations of concentrated ethnic communities . . . if these locations will reasonably aid in the analysis of potential threats and vulnerabilities."[28] Documents the ACLU received through the Freedom of Information Act clearly show how the FBI used this to target predominantly Muslim communities for surveillance. An FBI Detroit field memorandum, for example, states that Michigan is an area of particular concern for radicalization and recruitment due to its large Arab and Muslim population, thus depicting an entire group of people as potential terrorists on the basis of nothing other than their religious or ethnic affiliations.[29] The FBI also targeted American Muslim institutions for surveillance, going as far as mapping the geographic locations, composition, and other characteristics of mosques and other institutions.[30]

Section 805 of the Patriot Act expanded existing terrorism financing laws, allowing US officials to designate individuals and organizations as terrorists, freeze their assets, and punish any material support to them, regardless of intent. In practical terms, this meant that if an individual donated to a charity engaged in disaster relief in the Middle East, and if that charity was later accused of providing material support to a terrorist organization, the individual who made the donation could face criminal prosecution, as happened with the five members of the Holy Land Foundation (HLF) discussed in the previous chapter. According to the ACLU, these laws "disproportionately affected American Muslim charities."[31] FBI agents raided mosques and charitable Muslim organizations and interviewed donors in ways that amounted to the harassment of an entire community. This has had a chilling effect on Muslim American communal and organizational life, significantly restricting Muslims' ability to fulfill one of the five pillars of their religion (*zakat*, or charitable giving) and leading to an overall drop in donations to mosques and other Muslim institutions.[32]

Of the nine US-based Muslim charities that were forced to shut down, only one (the HLF) was convicted of any wrongdoing, and the case against that organization has been deemed seriously flawed.[33] According to the ACLU and other civil rights lawyers that have taken on the plight of the five HLF leaders, the government never produced evidence to support the claim of material support to a terrorist organization (Hamas). In fact, during the 2007 criminal trial, "prosecutors admitted all the money went to charitable aid."[34] Even more damaging for Muslim American institutional life, in a much-criticized move, the Department of Justice filed a list of 246 individuals and organizations as "unindicted co-conspirators" in the HLF case. Among those named were some of the largest mainstream Muslim American organizations, including CAIR and ISNA. These so-called coconspirators were never charged with a crime, and the prosecutors later acknowledged that the labeling was a "legal tactic, intended to allow the government to introduce hearsay evidence against the HLF later in trial."[35]

Nonetheless, the label amounted to a smear campaign against Muslim American institutions and was, not surprisingly, extremely damaging to their reputations. It also provided ammunition to anti-Muslim individuals and groups, who would use the label to discredit the work and leadership of CAIR and other organizations. Civil rights and religious organizations, including the National Council of Churches and the Union for Reform Judaism, criticized the public labeling as a violation of Muslim Americans' constitutional rights. The Union for Reform Judaism issued a powerful statement opposing the government's designation of ISNA. The statement read, in part:

This charge includes no accusation of wrongdoing by ISNA, yet it none-theless has a clear connotation of guilt which could greatly hurt the organization in its work to advance the cause of justice in our country. Particularly concerning are reports that the government has informed ISNA's lawyers that the naming was only a legal tactic and that ISNA is not a target or subject of any criminal investigation. Because ISNA is one of the nation's largest Muslim umbrella organizations, the charge is also damaging, and has a chilling effect on, the entire American Muslim community.[36]

In 2010, the Fifth Circuit Court of Appeals found that the Department of Justice had violated the Fifth Amendment rights of the North American Islamic Trust, another of the organizations named in the HLF case.[37] However, the court refused to expunge these organizations' names from the record, as they had sought.

Looking Beyond the Patriot Act

Although the Patriot Act is among the most exhaustive and far-reaching pieces of legislation dealing with the War on Terror, it is not the only policy that has facilitated the targeting of US Muslims, nor is Trump's immigration ban of 2017 without precedent. Shortly after 9/11, Attorney General John Ashcroft announced the establishment of the National Security Entry and Exit Registry System (NSEERS), which, among other things, called for a special registry for nonim-migrant residents of the United States.[38] The registry initially targeted people with origins in the Muslim world and singled out Muslims, especially males, with origins in "high-risk" countries. When the first registration deadline ap-proached in December 2002, hundreds of immigrants rushed to comply with the rule and were deported, not because they were deemed to pose a threat but on the grounds of having overstayed their visas.[39]

The *Federal Register* also granted the attorney general and law enforcement agents the power to define who was a high-risk nonimmigrant resident. NSEERS section 264 states, "Nonimmigrant aliens who meet pre-existing criteria . . . de-termined by the Attorney General or the Secretary of State to indicate that such aliens' presence in the United States warrants monitoring in the national secu-rity, as defined in section 219 of the Act, or law enforcement interests of the United States."[40] Notably, Trump's Executive Order 13769 rested on a similar rationale—mainly, as the president argued, that the seven countries subjected to the ban "have already been identified as presenting heightened concerns about terrorism and travel to the United States."

The primary justification for NSEERS was that terrorists could be identified and removed before they became a tangible threat. Altogether, the registry resulted in the deportation of more than thirteen thousand individuals, without a single terrorist suspect being found in the process.[41] But although it failed in identifying terrorists, it succeeded in creating and defining a broad category of people believed to be potentially threatening to national security. The fact that no evidence was found does not negate its purpose and achievement as part of a broader set of policies that served to delineate the vague, but nevertheless all too real, contours of the out-group.

Extrajudicial detentions also took place, both within the framework of NSEERS, which detained people for visa violations, and that of the FBI's "voluntary" interviews and raids that targeted Muslim, Arab, and South Asian suspects.[42] These detentions were, and continue to be, shrouded in secrecy, since the Patriot Act made it legal to hold individuals indefinitely and without formal charges, so long as the attorney general has "reasonable grounds" to believe the individuals are involved in terrorism. We can expect these detentions to continue into the foreseeable future. For one, they have bipartisan support. In 2011, President Obama signed the National Defense Authorization Act, allowing for indefinite military detention (including that of US citizens) without trial under the law.[43]

Detentions play a central role in the construction of an out-group. Physically holding individuals marks them as a threat in need of isolation—a danger that, left unchecked, could threaten the social fabric. Physical separation becomes a way to draw, and guard, clear boundaries that differentiate an in-group (those in need of protection) from the out-group (the source of threat requiring protection). As Maha Hilal rhetorically asks us, "Would a U.S. offshore prison that completely and utterly disregards established human rights protections exist if it housed a different religious group?"[44]

The government used methods other than detention to target Muslims and construct the threat against which it claimed to provide protection. Some were short-lived, such as the Terrorism Information and Prevention System (TIPS), which President George W. Bush proposed in the summer of 2002 but never signed into law. The program sought to enlist "citizen observers" to report any activity they thought was suspicious. Mail carriers, utility workers, truck drivers, and other government employees whose jobs gave them access to people's homes were to become citizen patrols—policing the nation against the perceived enemy lurking within its borders. In the words of ACLU legislative council Rachel King, TIPS would have turned these government employees "into government-sanctioned peeping toms."[45]

With strong opposition from civil rights groups, Congress overhauled TIPS on November 25, 2002.[46] Nevertheless, the proposed program helped sow mistrust of Muslim citizens and further depict them as an out-group in need of surveillance. Representing certain individuals as requiring increased surveillance (in this case, not only by the state but by fellow citizens) helps constitute them as potentially guilty, disloyal, and capable of crimes against the homeland. Thus, *potentiality* is perhaps the most important building block in the construction of Muslim Americans as an out-group: as long as the potential threat exists, they need not commit a crime in order to be considered outside the boundaries of the American nation.

It is also worth highlighting that despite Congress's rejection of an official TIPS program, surveillance of the Muslim community did occur, and continues to take place in myriad ways. In 2014, documents leaked by former NSA employee Edward Snowden showed that the National Security Agency and the FBI had been covertly monitoring the telephone and e-mail communications of American Muslims.[47] The FBI recruited and employed informants from within the Muslim American community to gather intelligence on "jihadi sympathizers" and home-grown would-be terrorists, often with no evidence of wrongdoing. Many individuals who refused to serve as informants claim that the government retaliated against them for their decision. Attorneys from the City University of New York's CLEAR Project have represented dozens of victims of alleged government retaliation. According to Amma Akbar, one of the supervising attorneys, "the FBI approaches the vast majority of our clients as potential informants to partake in mass surveillance of Muslim communities, unconnected to any real criminal investigation . . . by using coercion, pressure tactics and intimidation."[48]

Surveillance of Muslims also took place at the state and local levels. Starting in 2002, the New York Police Department (NYPD) Intelligence Division engaged in active surveillance of mosques, Muslim religious and community leaders, college student associations, individuals, and businesses within a one-hundred-mile radius of New York City.[49] A 2007 report from the division rationalizes this constitutional breach by arguing that although Muslims in the United States are better integrated than those in Europe, they are not immune to becoming radicalized: "The powerful gravitational pull of individuals' religious roots and identity sometimes supersedes the assimilating nature of American society."[50] Accepting the overwhelming evidence that US Muslims are well integrated and that radicalization is not a significant problem in this community, the report suggests that only a handful of radicalized individuals are enough for an attack to take place—and, more problematically, that it is only a matter of time until younger Muslims become radicalized:

> The absence of significant terrorist attacks or even advanced terrorist plots in the United States since 9/11 is good news that cannot entirely be explained by increased intelligence and heightened security. It sug-

gests America's Muslim population may be less susceptible than Europe's Muslim population, if not entirely immune to jihadist ideology; indeed, countervailing voices may exist within the American Muslim community. . . . The vast majority of American Muslims reject al Qaeda's violent extremism, although younger Muslims are more accepting of violence in the defense of Islam. Conversely, it may merely indicate that the American Muslim population has not yet been exposed to the degree or variety of radicalization that its European counterparts have been exposed to, and it requires not majorities, but only handfuls to carry out terrorist attacks.[51]

Thus, surveillance becomes a strategic response to the potentiality of radicalization. Indeed, the NYPD targeted places they considered "radicalization incubators," including most of the everyday spaces where Muslims congregate:

> Generally these locations, which together comprise the radical subculture of a community, are rife with extremist rhetoric. Though the locations can be mosques, more likely incubators include cafes, cab driver hangouts, flophouses, prisons, student associations, non-governmental organizations, hookah (water pipe) bars, butcher shops and book stores. While it is difficult to predict who will radicalize, these nodes are likely places where like-minded individuals will congregate as they move through the radicalization process.
>
> . . .
>
> Muslim communities are often more vulnerable to the radicals' agenda—an agenda that uses Islam as the center stage for spreading and justifying extremist views. Radicalization is indiscriminate and those attracted to it include New York City citizens from all walks of life, ranging from university students, engineers, business owners, teachers, lawyers, cab drivers to construction workers.

In other words, what all these New Yorkers have in common is their religion,[52] and religiosity is seen, in and of itself, as evidence of potential radicalism. As recently as 2011, the FBI provided its officers in Quantico, Virginia, with optional training briefings that highlighted Muslim piety as a key indicator of potential aggression. Though the bureau later discontinued and distanced itself from these sessions,[53] they formed (and continue to form) part of a broader discursive field of government-sanctioned policies through which US Muslims have been discretely but readily marked as suspicious outsiders. Counterterrorism policy in the United States is thus one of the major sites in which US Muslims are framed as an out-group, an internal other against which American identity can be measured and defined.[54] This reading of the War on Terror sees discriminatory state policies not as aberrations or as the unintended but inevitable result of fighting terrorism, but rather as a productive discourse through which certain groups (in this case, Muslims) are constructed as latent threats to be monitored, controlled, and, when called upon, neutralized.

Framing the Debate about Radicalization

In March 2011, Peter King (R-NY), chairman of the House Committee on Homeland Security, began convening hearings on "The Extent of Radicalization in the American Muslim Community and the Community's Response." Throughout 2011, he held five hearings on subjects ranging from "the threat of Muslim American extremism" to "Al-Shabab recruitment within the Muslim American Somali community" and "Muslim American radicalization in U.S. prisons." Clearly, the underlying impetus for these hearings was the assumption that Muslim radicalization differed from other forms of radicalization, and thus merited specific attention. In his opening remarks, King explicitly stated that "there is no equivalency of threat between al-Qaeda and neo-Nazis, environmental extremists, and other isolated madmen. Only al-Qaeda and its Islamist affiliates in this country are part of an international threat to our nation."[55]

Congressional Democrats overwhelmingly opposed the hearings and sharply criticized King for focusing only on American Muslims. In an emotional plea, Keith Ellison (D-MN), the first Muslim to be elected to Congress in 2006, argued that singling out Muslims was "the very heart of stereotype and scapegoating." He told the story of Salman Hamdani, a twenty-three-year-old first responder who lost his life on 9/11. "His life should not be identified as just a member of an ethnic group or just a member of a religion, but as an American who gave everything for his fellow Americans."[56] Other Congressional Democrats, including, among others, Sheila Jackson Lee (D-TX), Bennie Thompson (D-MS), and Laura Richardson (D-CA), who called the hearing "an abuse of power," joined him in his outrage.[57]

King claimed that although some of the critiques were "measured," others bordered on hysteria. He asserted the hearings were necessary because "al-Qaeda is actively targeting the American Muslim community for recruitment." Although he was quick to note that the majority of US Muslims were patriotic citizens who contributed to their nation, he cited a 2007 Pew survey of US Muslims that found that 15 percent of Muslim American men under the age of thirty believed suicide bombings could "often or sometimes be justified in the defense of Islam."[58] King and those in favor of the hearings argued that this was the segment that al-Qaeda was targeting for radicalization and that the problem of homegrown radicalism could not be ignored, particularly in light of high-profile incidents that preceded the hearings, including the 2009 mass shooting at Fort Hood, Texas, and an attempted 2010 bombing in Times Square.

Critics viewed the decision to focus solely on Muslim radicalization as misguided. Bennie Thompson, a member of the Committee on Homeland Security who testified during the hearings, cautioned that "a narrow focus that excludes known threats lacks clarity and may be myopic."[59] A *New York Times* editorial elaborates this point further: "It might be perfectly legitimate for the Homeland Security Committee to investigate violent radicalism in America among a wide variety of groups, but that does not seem to be Mr. King's real interests. Instead, he is focusing on one group that appears to have obsessed him since the Sept. 11, 2001 attacks, resulting in slanders and misstatements that might have earned him a rebuke from his colleagues had they been against any other group."[60]

Among King's most controversial claims during the hearings was that Muslim Americans refused to cooperate with the FBI. Many within the law enforcement community argued that this was not only false but also counterproductive, as it undermined their efforts to reach out to and build trust with the community. Lee Baca, who was sheriff of Los Angeles County at the time, said that there was simply no evidence to support King's claims and that the burden of proof should rest on the congressman, not the Muslim American community at large. Furthermore, given the FBI's record of unconstitutional surveillance of Muslims, it is not difficult to understand why Muslims would hesitate to cooperate with the bureau and other government agencies. Whereas King believed loyal and lawful citizens should have no qualms about cooperating with law enforcement, his assumption belied the realities of American Muslims and other minority communities who have been targets of the FBI and other government agencies tasked to protect them.

Two of King's most reiterated demands during the hearings were that US Muslims should do more to combat radicalization and that "moderate leadership" needed to emerge from within the Muslim American community. His comments suggested that Muslims are not doing enough to prevent and respond to radicalization (although what, exactly, they are supposed to be doing remains unclear), thus erasing the efforts, realities, and experiences of national and grassroots Muslim American leaders and organizations. His remarks also represented a broader trend, which saw any outward expression of Muslim religious and political identity as incompatible with moderation. Before the hearings, King claimed that there were too many mosques in the United States and that radical fundamentalists controlled 80 to 85 percent of them.[61]

In his opening remarks, he singled out CAIR as a "discredited group," citing its designation as an unindicted coconspirator in the HLF terrorist financing case (not only a hollow accusation but also a clear attempt to undermine and discredit the organization). In written testimony submitted in response to the hearings, CAIR conceded that "King did prove what was already known: that a small number of individuals within the American Muslim community are susceptible to violent extremism," but it rejected his accusations as "demonstrably false" and questioned his motivations, particularly in light of his long pattern of factually inaccurate and anti-Muslim statements.

King's comments, and the narrow focus of the hearings, served to further associate Muslim political or religious identity expression, in any form, with extremism and radicalism. In the narrative of the hearings, the community lacked moderate leadership, individual Muslims did not do enough to support law enforcement, and their houses of worship were little more than breeding grounds for radicalism. Not surprisingly, the ACLU and other civil rights organizations condemned the hearings as "unfair, unwise, and unconstitutional."[62]

Islamophobia in the American Public Square

United States government policies and rhetoric that have criminalized Muslims since 9/11 have been coupled with a rise in organized grassroots efforts dedicated to opposing public manifestations of Islam. In recent years, these anti-Muslim movements have increasingly promoted and relied on a characterization of Islam as a political ideology, not a religion. Critics see this as a clear strategy to attempt to circumvent First Amendment protections granting individuals the right to freely establish and exercise their religion. According to John Robbins, executive director of CAIR's Massachusetts chapter, "this tactic allows them to masquerade their religiously motivated hatred as a national security concern and portray any form of Muslim religious expression as extremism."[63] Identifying Islam as a political ideology, as former national security advisor Michael Flynn and others in the Trump administration have done, transforms Muslims from a religious minority group, entitled to specific constitutional protections, into a potential threat grounded in extremist ideology.

Coming onto the national stage in 2010, these movements focused predominantly on two issues: opposing the building of new mosques and introducing "anti-sharia" legislation in US courts. The public became aware of these groups following a national controversy surrounding the Park51 project, a mosque and interfaith community center due to be built two blocks away from Ground Zero in New York.[64] In the summer of 2010, a network of anti-Muslim activists and organizations led a national campaign against the project, which they dubbed the "Ground Zero Mosque." One of the main voices behind the campaign was Pamela Geller, a conservative blogger and anti-Muslim activist who claimed that Park51 was part of "an Islamic pattern to build triumphant mosques on the cherished sites of conquered lands."[65] The campaign succeeded in foiling the project and "is credited as being the spark that instigated organized grassroots anti-Muslim efforts in the United States."[66] Over the next few years, mosques would become a centerpiece of these campaigns.

Individuals who oppose the building of mosques in their communities usually claim their objections are based on practical zoning considerations, such as traffic, parking, noise level, and property values. Similar arguments are often made against proposed churches and other houses of worship, so these complaints on their own do not suggest particular anti-Muslim bias.[67] Since 2010, however, antimosque protests have explicitly called for the banning of Islam and Muslims from America, with some protesters openly carrying arms.[68] It is not difficult to see how this has helped create an environment that, as the ACLU puts it, "conflicts with our Founders' vision of religious liberty and tolerance."[69] Further reinforcing this environment is the rise in violent crimes and vandalism against existing mosques, with documented cases of arson, shootings, the defacing of Qur'ans, letters and voicemails threatening violence, and the leaving or throwing of pork products at mosques.

According to research conducted at the Othering and Belonging Institute at UC Berkeley, the racial anxieties that surfaced following the election of the first Black US president in 2008, and which catapulted Tea Party candidates to victory in the 2010 midterm elections, help explain the anti-Muslim movements' ability to win some legislative victories. A large share of their efforts has been spent on pushing state legislatures to adopt "anti-sharia bills," limiting a court's ability to consider foreign laws in general and sharia law in particular. They have found ready allies in Tea Party representatives, with 194 such bills introduced in state legislatures across the country from 2010 to 2016. Eighteen of these passed and were enacted into law.[70] Since the Constitution already states that foreign laws cannot supersede US law, critics contend that the bills are nothing other than a response to a manufactured threat and an attempt to legalize discrimination against Muslims. There is evidence to support their views. David Yerushalmi, founder of the grassroots anti-Muslim movement leading the anti-sharia efforts (and whom the Southern Poverty Law Center classifies as an extremist), admits that the purpose of the bills is "heuristic—to get people asking this question, 'What is Shariah?'"[71]

The Road to Trump's "Muslim Ban"

Many people assume anti-Muslim prejudice is the result of terrorism in general and of the 9/11 attacks in particular, but the reality is more complex. In fact, American public opinion of US Muslims improved in the two months following the attacks. Similarly, while hate crimes against Muslims saw an almost fifteen-fold increase in the same period, from 33 crimes in 2000 to 546 crimes in 2001, these numbers quickly began to wane, decreasing to 155 incidents in 2002.[72] Many credit President George W. Bush for this trend since, in the aftermath of 9/11, he aimed to distance Muslims and Islam from the terrorists who were responsible for the carnage. During a visit to the Islamic Center of Washington, DC, on September 17, six days after the attacks, he declared, "The face of terror is not the true face of Islam. . . . Islam is peace"—a statement that proved crucial in setting the national tone. He would reiterate the message in an address to a joint session of Congress on September 20, even as his policies, both at home and abroad, implicated and related to Muslims as potential threats.[73]

As the ebb and flow of hate crime statistics against Muslims show, rhetoric from our national leaders matters, particularly in times of crisis. It is not surprising that following the deadliest attack on US soil—an attack carried out by terrorists claiming to be acting in the name of Islam—hate crimes against US Muslims rose to unprecedented levels. However, the spike was short-lived; the following year, anti-Muslim hate crimes precipitously declined, partly because of "a concerted effort on the part of President George W. Bush using the Presidency as a bully pulpit to unite America."[74] These rates would remain rather stable (between 105 and 160 hate crimes per year) until 2014, but in 2015, the FBI recorded the second-sharpest rise in hate crimes against Muslims since the bureau began collecting data in the mid-1990s.[75] It is important to note that the FBI derives its hate crime statistics from annual official reports from law enforcement and that hate crimes are vastly underreported to police for a variety of reasons, including victims' fear of retaliation, mistrust of the police, and cultural and linguistic barriers, to name a few.[76]

Explaining the rise in hate crimes in 2015 seems more difficult, lacking a major event like the attacks of 2001. Although it is impossible to isolate a specific explanation for the rise in anti-Muslim bias and hate crimes during this period, considering a number of intertwined factors helps in drawing some conclusions. News of the Syrian conflict and the escalating refugee crisis, the seemingly overnight rise of ISIS, and the violent extremist attacks against Western targets orchestrated or claimed by ISIS all contributed to the rising prejudice against Muslims at home and abroad.

Political rhetoric is also an important piece of the puzzle. Just as George W. Bush is credited for having almost single-handedly changed the national narrative about Muslims and Islam in the immediate aftermath of 9/11, political rhetoric throughout the 2016 election cycle, beginning with the primary elections of 2015, is credited with helping normalize anti-Muslim (as well as anti-Semitic and anti-immigrant) sentiments. Scholars have found that political rhetoric can prime citizens' predispositions and influence their positions, particularly on issues for which they hold less crystallized attitudes.[77] Politicians, public officials, and political candidates play a particularly important role in cuing their constituencies and helping shape public opinion.[78] This agenda-setting ability to determine what issues are considered important and how individuals should think of and interpret these issues is particularly relevant during highly contested election cycles. This is because, as John Zaller puts it, "frames of reference and elite leadership cues . . . enable citizens to form conceptions of and, more importantly, opinions about events that are beyond their full personal understanding."[79] In other words, the complexity of the political world requires individuals to take cues from political elites they trust in order to make sense of a flood of information, allowing them to form an opinion.

There are two important factors to recognize when thinking about prejudice in general and anti-Muslim sentiments in particular. The first is that racial appeals can be explicit or implicit. Whereas past studies found that people disliked explicitly racist appeals and were therefore more likely to respond to political rhetoric that relied on implicit messages, covert biases, and "color blind" language,[80] more recent studies find that both explicit and implicit racial appeals are quite successful.[81] And the more white Americans perceive themselves as a threatened group, the more likely they are to be receptive to explicitly racial appeals.[82] The second factor is that prejudice does not have to be conscious. In fact, most prejudice is held at the subconscious level, which explains why an individual can make an openly discriminatory statement while vehemently denying racism or intolerance.[83] Research has also demonstrated that political elites have relied on racially divisive appeals as a strategy to attract voters, even when the appeals contradict privately held opinions and inclinations.[84]

Anti-Muslim political rhetoric picked up speed following the Paris attacks of November 15, 2015, and in the wake of the shooting in San Bernardino, California, less than a month later, on December 2. In an interview with Fox News, then presidential candidate Donald Trump stated that he would consider shutting down mosques as part of his counterterrorism strategy. "Islam hates us," he said in another interview a few days later. It would not be long before those sentiments found expression in the form of bias incidents and hate crimes. According to Brian Levin from the Center for the Study of Hate and Extremism at California State University, San Bernardino, political rhetoric has an independent effect on the propensity of hate crimes. In the aftermath of a terrorist attack, Levin finds, "a tolerant statement about Muslims by a political leader was accompanied by a sharp decline in hate crimes, while a less tolerant announcement was accompanied by a precipitous increase in both the severity and number of anti-Muslim hate crimes."[85]

The normalization of anti-Muslim discourse that took place throughout the 2016 election cycle also helped secure a degree of public support for Trump's proposal to ban Muslim immigrants from entering the United States, something he began calling for as early as 2015, long before his executive order of January 27, 2017. A 2016 public opinion poll by the Texas Politics Project at the University of Texas at Austin found that the majority of Americans either strongly supported (31 percent) or somewhat supported (22 percent) banning Muslims from entering the United States.[86] A few weeks before Executive Order 13769, nearly half of Americans (48 percent) still supported the ban. Having painted Islam and Muslims as sources of violence, the next natural step was to prevent individuals from Muslim-majority countries from entering the United States. Interestingly, once Trump signed the order and his proposal became a policy reality, public opinion turned swiftly against it. It is still unclear what caused such a rapid shift in public opinion (this is rare, as most public preferences are highly resistant to change, particularly in the short term[87]), but scholars have argued that the mass protests following Trump's announcement and the flood of information portraying the ban as being at odds with American principles changed the environment in which individuals made their decisions.[88] In short, political rhetoric matters a great deal. Particularly when individuals lack sufficient information, they will rely on the cues of political elites they trust, and with whom they share values, to form their policy preferences. However, these elites also function within a larger information environment, where mass protests, organizations, the media, and other influences can present counter-cues that, although rare, can generate meaningful changes in public opinion.

Discriminatory state policies, such as the Patriot Act, the normalization of anti-Muslim political rhetoric, and the more recent rise of grassroots movements dedicated to opposing expressions of Muslim identity in the American public square have been scourges for the Muslim American community. People's lives have been upended, and families destroyed. This chapter has attempted to chronicle some of the major ways in which structural, state-sanctioned Islamophobia shapes and influences the lives of Muslim America. The detrimental and oppressive impacts are clear. But, as I argue throughout this book, it is also through the collective pain of their struggle that a Muslim American identity has become more salient. Indeed, the very policies through which US Muslims are targeted and constituted as an out-group have been foundational for Muslim American interest groups, since it is precisely this othering that grants these groups the legitimacy to speak on behalf of this targeted minority community. Since 9/11, each time Muslims have been vilified and targeted, their organizations have had a choice: to lie low or to demand better for their community. They have consistently chosen the latter. Cloaking themselves in the protective mantle of the Constitution, finding solace in the experience of other minority movements, and stubbornly believing that the American dream applies to them too, they have marched forward. But is their conviction justified? What explains their ability to endure? What do they hope to achieve, and how much are individual leaders willing to sacrifice?

THE RISE OF THE MUSLIM AMERICAN LOBBY

Legislation is a tool for social change. The social and cultural changes come only after the legislation changes, not the other way around.

—Robert McCaw, author interview, May 3, 2017

Hassan Shibly arrived early at Tampa International Airport. He wanted to make sure nothing prevented him from boarding this particular flight to Washington, DC. He was on his way to the nation's capital to meet with Valerie Jarett, a senior advisor to President Obama, to discuss rising discrimination against the Muslim community. He had devoted his life to this subject. As a civil rights lawyer, activist, and imam, Hassan was acutely attuned to his community's plights and needs. He had represented dozens of plaintiffs in discrimination cases, lectured on university campuses across the country, and served as a consultant to NGOs and government agencies. He was also on the US government's Watchlist.

By his own estimate, Hassan had been stopped roughly twenty times by airport security or at border crossings in the past decade, sometimes with his wife and young children. On the day he was traveling to DC, he was unable to check in for his flight on American Airlines, and he knew what this meant; the agent would have to call the Department of Homeland Security to clear him. The process would take around an hour, keeping him from reaching his gate on time, but he had few choices. If he wanted to make it to the meeting, he would have to pay the extra money to buy a new ticket, this time on Southwest, an airline that had stopped flagging him for extra security, due to the absurdity of the Watchlist system. And that is what he did, just making it to his meeting at the White House in time. "It's ironic that I am deemed safe enough to visit the White House to talk about Islamophobia, but I'm not trusted to board a plane," he said, summarizing the travesty he and hundreds of other Americans on the Watchlist have had to endure.

In August 2018, Hassan and his colleagues at CAIR filed a lawsuit against the federal government on behalf of twenty individuals targeted by the Watchlist system and the Transportation Security Administration's Quiet Skies program.[1] Hassan was a plaintiff in the case. During his deposition, he recounted the trauma of his ordeal, which began in 2004, the first time he was stopped at a point of entry, detained for hours, questioned, and treated "like a common criminal." There would be many more such instances—too many to recall, "all meshing into one," as he would remind the government lawyer questioning him over and over again. Some things, however, are not easily forgotten. For Hassan, being put in shackles in front of his grandmother at the US-Canada border, being asked whether he "recruited people to Islam," and being told that "on the border you had no rights" are seared in his memory.

He also recalls the moment when he had had enough. It happened during one of the routine stops he endured at the US-Canada border on his way back to his hometown in Buffalo, New York. He was pulled over for secondary questioning, as he had been countless times before, but this encounter was different. He was part of a group returning from a Muslim religious gathering in Canada. "The officer calls me and says, 'So, do you all go to the same mosque?' And I say, 'Excuse me? Is none of your business whose mosque we go to. That's our constitutional[ly] protected right. Let me speak to your supervisor.' So, right away I think he understood, now you're dealing with a different, empowered citizen, a citizen who knows their rights and isn't afraid to stand up for them."

Hassan Shibly was not the only fed-up American Muslim who was ready to fight back.

Discrimination and Targeting as Unintended Opportunities

Rather than passively resigning themselves to being targets of hatred and bigotry, American Muslims are increasingly visible, engaged, and assertive in demanding their rights. Through their advocacy efforts, they have sought to challenge discriminatory state and social practices, to empower their communities, and to proudly assert their belongingness to their nation. The othering they have experienced since 9/11, and which intensifies during every election cycle, has also strengthened the perception of a cohesive Muslim American group identity, both within the Muslim community and among the broader American public. This has legitimized US Muslim organizations as the official representatives of a targeted minority, made their voices part of the broader social justice movement, and provided them with a degree of access to the policymaking process that was difficult to conceive when the organizations were first established.

In short, the targeting of Muslims has had the unintended effect of amplifying their voices, and that of their leaders. The US institutional context, with its history of minority groups' struggle for civil rights, has established the background conditions that allow these groups to present and advance their demands. The US policymaking process, with its varied points of access, became the chariot through which Muslim advocacy groups would propel their community's demands. The Constitution and the Bill of Rights form the legal and moral basis through which they communicate and frame their claims. Indeed, Muslim advocacy organizations have adopted the lessons of the civil rights movement to articulate what I call a *pursuit of justice framework*, a frame that speaks not only to their group experience but also to the broader struggle of minority rights and the building of a more inclusive union, where all citizens see themselves reflected in the American national narrative. Indeed, centering their advocacy efforts on the pursuit of justice serves to legitimize their demands, position them as a US minority group making rights claims, and open (some) access to policymakers.

And, counterintuitive though it may seem, anti-Muslim policies and bias have resulted in a number of unintended positive consequences for Muslim advocacy organizations and their leaders. Discrimination solidified perception of, and attachments to, a Muslim American collective, further legitimizing the claims-making capacity of Muslim advocacy organizations as the representatives of this targeted community.[2] The targeting of American Muslims also has increased their visibility and those of their organized groups. Following 9/11, journalists and publications seeking the "Muslim American perspective" began reaching out to advocacy organizations and their leaders, providing them with a forum and a previously unimaginable degree of visibility. A similar process took place during the 2016 presidential campaigns and the early months of the Trump presidency: the more Muslim-focused diatribes and policy proposals candidates made, the more space and attention Muslim advocacy groups received to respond to those attacks.

Many of the Muslim leaders and activists I interviewed told me that being targeted had spurred the community to action and motivated them on a personal level. One argued that there had been "a flurry of activity at the organizational level" after Trump's election. Another claimed that in the immediate post-election period, foundations reached out to Muslim organizations, offering much-needed financial support. Referencing a $100,000 donation made by the Bush Foundation, a staff member at one of these organizations told me they "could never sustain this level of activity without that support." Others told me directly that experiencing discrimination firsthand is what drove them to advocacy work. As Hassan Shibly eloquently put it, "Being the victim made me the lawyer. It motivated me to learn the law. My personal experience has given me the passion to fight not just for Muslims but for all Americans."[3]

For better or for worse, moments of crisis have brought Muslim organizations into the limelight. In recent years, many of the local and national leaders featured in this book have appeared in major national news outlets, including CNN, Fox News, MSNBC, the *New York Times*, the *Washington Post*, NPR, and PBS. But even if mainstream media invited them in, it was digital media that propelled them into the public sphere, giving them an important platform to communicate their visions and reach an audience. Aside from their organizations' websites and blogs, many of these leaders contribute to popular blogs, write op-ed pieces, and use their personal social media accounts to amplify their voices. Public officials are also courting them. During the 2016 presidential campaign, Linda Sarsour, one of the country's most prominent Muslim grassroots activists and future cochair of the 2016 Women's March on Washington, served as a national surrogate for Senator Bernie Sanders, campaigning for him and speaking at his rallies.

More often than not, however, politicians tend to include "the Muslim voice" only when it comes to issues related to security and counterterrorism. Regardless, Muslim advocacy organizations agree that discriminatory practices have provided strategic opportunities, increasing the need for organized groups to represent, speak for, and come to the aid of the targeted community.[4] By framing different forms of anti-Muslim bias as manifestations of Islamophobia, these groups have helped articulate a cohesive narrative around which to mobilize. This has opened up important political space, expanding their ability to speak on issues affecting Muslims and other marginalized groups. It is important to note, however, that in spite of their recent growth, CAIR and other national Muslim organizations have relatively miniscule budgets. According to tax documents filed with the IRS, CAIR's 2014 budget was around $2 million. By 2017, their budget had more than tripled, to $6,632,436, a direct reflection of the rise in donations and grant money they received in the wake of Trump's election. MPAC's budget also experienced a boost. Whereas their 2015 budget was around $1.5 million, by 2017 it had reached $2,355,000. But in spite of this sharp increase in funding, their budgets remain small, particularly considering the breadth of the work they are doing. As a point of comparison, the American Israel Public Affairs Committee (AIPAC) had a budget of nearly $96,093,190 in 2017. "Look at the budget of AIPAC, JStreet, and all the other Jewish advocacy organizations. Look at the budget of Christian advocacy groups. Then look at the budget of Muslim organizations," Al-Marayati prodded me. "Their budgets are in the hundreds of millions, and our budget—together, all of us together—is less than $10 million. It's nothing. People think that we [MPAC] are a $5 million organization. We're only a $1.5 million organization."[5]

Lacking necessary institutional and financial resources compelled these organizations to form partnerships with other minority and civil rights groups. These connections have helped position them within the spectrum of American civil rights organizations, granting them crucial material and nonmaterial resources, such as organizational knowledge, solidarity, authority, and, most importantly, legitimacy.[6] Coalition-building efforts began before 9/11, but the attacks were the critical juncture that hastened, intensified, and solidified previously nascent partnerships that gave Muslim advocacy organizations the immediate assistance they needed to aid their communities. Being part of these partnerships also positioned their efforts at social justice work and embedded their missions within the broader civil rights struggle for minority rights in the United States.

The American Institutional Context as a Structure of Opportunity

Until Mancur Olson's classic 1965 study on interest-based groups, *The Logic of Collective Action*, lobbying was seen as a bargaining process between collective groups and government actors, in which legislators (always seeking to reduce uncertainty) exchange access to decision-making processes for information and know-how.[7] Olson, and the many scholars who built on his work, greatly expanded on this transactional model of lobbying by examining the origins and maintenance of interest groups, as well as how incentives (material and nonmaterial), networks, and social capital influence the bargaining process. For example, we now know that selective incentives, leadership, and the ability to secure sources of revenue are keys to the initiation and maintenance of interest groups.[8] And although material resources such as money, labor, and time are important, nonmaterial benefits such as leadership, moral engagement, and solidarity are also vital for motivating collective action.[9] Scholars have also focused on how social networks and alliances influence the choices and strategies of interest groups, as well as their ability to influence policy outcomes.[10]

Importantly, the institutional context in which organizations operate is central to defining how likely they are to gain access to the decision-making process, what strategies they can conceive of, and how likely they are to achieve their goals. Thus, the separation of powers, built into the US Constitution to prevent any one branch of government from becoming too powerful, also grants interest groups multiple points of access to policymakers and provides a fertile institutional ground for lobbying government and elected officials. Further, constitutional federalism, with its diffusion of decision-making power along the local, municipal, state, and federal levels, provides a system of multilevel governance, with various centers of power (and potential access).

The existence of a strong independent judiciary further enhances the power of interest groups, many of which view legal advocacy as an important part of their work. Acutely aware that the courts, not the legislature, have settled some of the most important political issues of our time, Muslim American organizations have used the opportunity to access the judiciary as a means to challenge the government's policies in the War on Terror. CAIR, in particular, has undertaken strong legal advocacy at the national and local levels, filing multiple lawsuits against the US government, as well as amicus briefs with the Supreme Court.[11] According to Corey Saylor, legal advocacy comprises the core of CAIR's efforts, for which the organization employs nearly twenty-five full-time attorneys and legal experts.[12]

In 2002, aware of the immense need for legal advocacy and legal representation, a group of American Muslim lawyers established the Muslim Legal Fund of America, a nonprofit organization primarily dedicated to defending Muslims wrongly accused of crimes by the government. Its stated mission is to "provide funding for cases impacting the civil rights and liberties of Muslims in America . . . [and] turn donations into legal services for select cases with potential civil liberties impact."[13] Representation of individual clients, community outreach, and education are important aspects of the organization's work. In light of the government's surveillance and targeting of Muslim organizations—which, it is important to note, did not begin with, but intensified with, the War on Terror—the Muslim Legal Fund provides valuable information to Muslim mosques, charities, and nonprofit leaders about ways to protect and safeguard their institutions and legal status. As executive director Khalil Meek puts it, the organization "provides the information our community leaders need to help them in navigating the complicated and ever changing legal-landscape in America."[14]

The Muslim Justice League is another legal advocacy organization founded to protect the legal rights of US Muslims targeted in the War on Terror. Established in 2014 as a direct response to the US government's "countering violent extremism" programs,[15] the Muslim Justice League engages in legal advocacy, community education, and cross-movement solidarity. Its work centers on protecting the rights of Muslims approached for questioning by the FBI and the Joint Terrorist Task Force (JTTF). The organization's website cautions, "Please Note: Anyone—including those with nothing to hide—can suffer serious consequences from speaking with an agent without counsel. If you are approached by the FBI or JTTF, please politely tell the agent you do not wish to answer questions without your lawyer and that your lawyer will call them back. Take their phone number, and call MJL's Hotline for Free FBI Representation: 857-256-1310."

None of this work would be possible without the earlier advances made by minority and immigrant groups in pushing for increased civic and political rights. In particular, the legal and moral precedence established by the civil rights movement granted Muslim American organizations an existing legal framework under which to demand their rights—legislative advocacy. Taking the government to court over warrantless surveillance and detentions would have been simply inconceivable before the civil rights movement.[16] Today, the law and the principle of equality under the law has given Muslim American and other minority organizations the legitimacy and political access necessary to make their demands.

Moreover, the long history of institutionalized ethnic and immigrant mobilization in the United States provides an important guiding example. Muslim organizations have used this history to their advantage, learning from and appropriating the techniques of other minority groups. Most of the leaders I interviewed repeatedly referenced the model of the "Jewish lobby" and Jewish immigrant organizations, some of which they work closely with. Many respondents acknowledged that much of their success in litigating against anti-sharia legislation was partly due to support from the Jewish community. As one individual told me, "The Jewish community recognizes that these laws would not only affect us, but . . . many of their practices as well."[17]

Challenges do beget opportunities, but this should in no way undermine just how difficult those challenges have been. Roula Allouch, a trial attorney and chair of CAIR's national board, poignantly reminded me of this during our conversation. "It's overwhelming," she said, almost as soon as I asked her what was keeping her busy these days. "I don't want to paint a rosy picture. We're struggling to keep up. This administration is unlike anything I've ever seen. It's exhausting and overwhelming."[18] As I tried to gather my thoughts moved by her honesty and the weariness in her voice, searching for words of encouragement, she continued: "I try to find hope and optimism even in these times, but it has been a constant struggle. I don't want to undermine how very difficult this time has been. With that said, I think one of the most positive things that we are seeing is a stronger connection of people of different backgrounds. People are standing shoulder to shoulder. That gives me hope. And to see the leadership that has come out of our community has also been encouraging."

Many Muslim leaders echo Allouch's sentiments. Times are challenging, but the only choice they see is to confront them head-on. Resources are scant, but pennies are stretched and volunteers keep signing up, in ever-expanding numbers. Coalition building is hard work, but people recognize their common struggles and unite in a vision of the future that sees all Americans living freely and with dignity. After the horrific mass shooting of June 12, 2016, at the Pulse nightclub in Orlando, Florida, which left forty-nine people dead, Nihad Awad wrote a piece for *Time*, extending his support to the victims and the entire LGBTQ community: "The liberation of the American Muslim community is inextricably linked with the liberation of all minority groups—Black, Latino, Gay, Jewish, Trans and every other community that has faced discrimination and oppression in this country. We cannot fight injustice against some groups, and not against others . . . homophobia, transphobia, misogyny and Islamophobia are all interconnected systems of oppression, and we cannot dismantle one without dismantling the other."[19]

That Awad would make this statement openly and unequivocally is noteworthy. Until recently, mainstream Muslim organizations largely ignored the LGBTQ community, leaving many gay Muslims feeling doubly ostracized by the wider national culture and their own communities.[20] Change is slow, and one statement cannot erase the pain and marginalization of LGBTQ Muslims or alter the belief system of Muslims in the United States who believe homosexuality should be discouraged (48 percent, according to Pew's 2017 survey). But, leadership matters a great deal, as does the public rhetoric of leaders.

Muslim Leaders and the Formation of National Organizations

What drives Muslim leaders to bear the costs of advocacy? Why do they continue to press their demands, despite a dismal ability to effect change? How do they respond to challenges from within their communities and work to build institutions that aim to be representative, inclusive, and pragmatic?

For years, scholars believed interest groups were the spontaneous responses of people facing deprivation and increased frustration. Olson challenged this understanding, arguing that participating in political action requires people to invest time, energy, and resources. However, since people could still reap the benefits of collective action without the cost of participation, he contended that they would participate only with material incentives or under coercion. Although Olson's theory provides critical insight regarding interest group formation and participation, later scholars found that very few interest groups provided the material benefits he thought necessary to attract supporters.[21] These scholars emphasized the role of nonmaterial incentives, such as solidarity, moral engagement, and leadership, in the establishment of interest groups, arguing that inspirational leaders were sometimes single-handedly responsible for spearheading these collective efforts.[22] For better or for worse, group leaders were found to "play an important role in determining the fortunes of individual organizations," often becoming "the prime movers behind interest group formation."[23] According to these scholars, group leaders can be incentivized by personal gain and career advancement, but they are more likely persuaded to bear the cost of participation by moral or purposive incentives.[24]

My interviews corroborate these theoretical insights. When I asked what motivated them to establish (and maintain) their organizations, the leaders I spoke with gave different versions of a similar response. They all claimed to be driven by the teachings of Islam and its emphasis on struggle, justice, and freedom. They interpreted their faith and religious beliefs as a direct call to struggle on behalf of society's most vulnerable and marginalized communities—Muslim and non-Muslim alike. They credited their Muslim faith for giving them the strength and solace they needed to bear the costs of their engagement. And bear the costs they have. According to Al-Marayati, his office has been vandalized several times and he has received threatening phone calls, been unfairly accused of having a radical Islamic agenda, and been criticized by members of the Muslim American community itself for working with the government on initiatives to prevent and counter radicalization among US Muslims. For his part, Awad has had death threats made against him,[25] has been criticized by the far right as a Hamas operative, and was a target of NSA surveillance for years.[26] Shibly put it boldly: "People like ourselves who are very visible, representing the Muslim community, we get picked on, we get targeted. I can't tell you how many American-Muslim leaders—it's just the thing, it's just normal, if you're an American-Muslim leader, you're visible, you're publicly speaking, you're going to be targeted."[27] But most say that rather than discouraging them, the hardship they have faced is what inspires and invigorates their work.

In many ways, the narrative through which Al-Marayati explained MPAC's establishment exemplifies the moral and purposive incentives driving many of these Muslim organizational leaders. He related how, when he decided to establish an organization to advocate on behalf of the Muslim American community in 1988, his goal seemed unattainable, almost laughable. He recounted for me how his work during MPAC's early days reminded him of a story he read to his young children, *The Little Engine That Could*, telling me, "[The engine] went up a huge mountain and it simply said, 'I think I can, I think I can,' and that's how MPAC has survived. It just believes that it can."[28] The story is especially fitting when one learns, as I did from Al-Marayati, that he began the organization with a single staff member (himself) and a budget of $30,000 (the result of his individual fundraising efforts). Today, MPAC has twelve full-time employees and a budget of roughly $2.3 million, which, although relatively small, has allowed the organization to make its presence felt at a national level and speak on a wide variety of domestic and foreign policy issues.

Similarly, CAIR's founders, Nihad Awad and Ibrahim Hooper, credited the negative effects of the "stereotyping and defamation" of Islam on their US-born children and the overall civic paralysis it was causing in the Muslim American community as the main impetus for the establishment of their organization. I asked Awad about this during a brief chat we held in a crowded hallway during a Muslim Advocacy Day event. He told me that he was driven by a desire to address the devastating effect that the stereotyping of Muslims was having on Muslim communities and, in particular, the youth. CAIR was established in 1994. Less than a year later, the Oklahoma City bombing would mark a turning point in the organization's young life. Before Timothy McVeigh was identified as the perpetrator, Muslims were widely suspected of having carried out the attack. As Awad recalls, "When that happened, we [CAIR] had less than a thousand dollars in our account. I got a ticket and borrowed a cell phone. A reporter got me inside the area closed for investigation. Ibrahim sent a news release that we'll have a press conference on the spot. That press conference was historic. Later we met with the governor of Oklahoma and gave a check from the local Muslim community in Oklahoma to help the victims."[29]

The significance of these leaders cannot be overemphasized. They used moments of crisis, and the subsequent opportunities they engendered, to lobby on behalf of Muslims' constitutional rights and to further their legal, political, and cultural integration in the United States. As all political leaders must, these leaders must have specific skills to be effective: the ability to build interpersonal ties, communicate effectively, and serve as inspirational examples are among the most necessary. More specifically, the ability to build coalitions and alliances with other interfaith organizations is essential for these leaders to normalize Islam as an American religion. In recent years, Muslim advocacy organizations have worked closely with leaders of the Jewish community, holding interfaith meetings and workshops and often appearing together when making public statements about civil and religious liberties. These cross-sectional alliances intensified in the aftermath of the 2016 elections (although their longevity remains to be seen).

In June 2017, for example, the Anti-Defamation League, a major Jewish advocacy organization, joined CAIR, MPAC, and one hundred other organizations in demanding that mayors in US cities where anti-Muslim rallies were scheduled to take place disavow the marches. Anti-Defamation League CEO Jonathan Greenblatt argued that such marches "perpetuate harmful stereotypes against Muslims. The ideas furthered by these anti-Muslim groups only serve to weaken our communities."[30] The statement goes on to cite the rise in hate crimes against Jews and Muslims in the United States as a reason for grave concern, highlighting anti-Semitism and Islamophobia as manifestations of the same right-wing extremism.

Mapping Muslim Advocacy Strategies

Lobbying is likely the tactic most commonly associated with advocacy groups in the United States. Often understood as an attempt to pressure and influence elected officials, lobbying also provides information policymakers need to formulate policies and vote on a wide variety of issues on which they may not have deep knowledge. The influence that "Washington lobbyists" exert on actual policy formulation is often overemphasized, but there is little doubt that having access to policymakers, and being able to directly present them with specific views on a policy issue, can be a powerful tool of persuasion.[31]

Learning from the example of other immigrant and ethnic interest groups, Muslim advocacy groups have made lobbying a major component of their advocacy. MPAC, for example, sees lobbying as an important tool "to inform and shape public opinion and policy by serving as a trusted resource to decision makers in government and policy institutions."[32] They view policymakers as often well-intentioned but generally misinformed on issues related to Muslims and Islam. Consequently, they consider educating them and providing them with reliable information to be an important aspect of their work. Realizing the need to be physically close to national centers of power and build the interpersonal relationships lobbyists need to succeed, many of these organizations have their headquarters in Washington, DC, or have established offices there. CAIR-National was founded in DC and is today located only blocks away from the Capitol building. MPAC was spurred to open its DC offices in 2006 because, as it argued, in the post-9/11 era, issues affecting Muslims were being "written about, debated and decided without direct Muslim American voices sitting at the table."[33] Gaining an audience in Washington that was more willing to hear their views was one of the relevant opportunities brought about by the post-9/11 backlash. According to Haris Tarin, MPAC's former DC office director (now a senior policy advisor to the Department of Homeland Security), the minimum goal was to be part of the policy discussion, not only because it directly affected the Muslim community but also because Muslims had something important to contribute.[34]

Muslim organizations are also active in state and local politics. CAIR has established thirty-four chapters in cities across twenty-three states and has seen an upsurge in requests for new chapters since the 2016 elections. National chapter director Lori Saroya told me, "We could have easily had 15 new chapters established this year [2017] alone, but had to limit the pace of chapter development considering the resources and support we have to provide to each new chapter. We are expanding and want to continue to grow, but we have to do it right." Local chapters work closely with CAIR-National and its board of directors but mainly focus on grassroots issues, such as employment and housing discrimination, law enforcement overreach, and hate crimes against individuals and places of worship.

As other ethnic lobby groups have done before them, these organizations frame their policy agenda and demands, both foreign and domestic, around US national interests. For example, support for a two-state solution to the Palestinian-Israeli conflict—one of the most important foreign policy issues for Muslim organizations—is defended on the basis of US interests in the region. Similarly, protecting the civil rights of Muslims at home is promoted as a defense of the legal protection and rights to which all Americans are entitled. In other words, they view and promote their advocacy work on behalf of US Muslims as part of a broader mission to defend American constitutional values and principles. The Muslim Legal Fund's executive director, Khalil Meek, states this sentiment succinctly: "The injustice against Muslims today will be the injustice against every American tomorrow. We're all in this together."[35]

And increasingly, Muslim organizations have sought to challenge injustices in the courts. In 2011, CAIR issued its first amicus curiae brief to the US Supreme Court, the first ever to be issued by a Muslim organization, on *United States v. Jones*, a case related to warrantless GPS surveillance by law enforcement. Since then, Muslim organizations have written and joined other organizations in scores of amicus briefs, including briefs against Trump's immigration ban.

Building Social Capital

While a large portion of institutional efforts is spent in trying to reach elected officials and gain access to the policymaking process, none of the organizations I examined relies solely on insider lobbying to accomplish their goals. For most, community outreach and grassroots contact between their constituencies and elected officials are equally important. Thus, empowering American Muslims, educating them about their rights and responsibilities, and helping them build the skills to fully participate in the democratic process comprise a large and important aspect of these organizations' work.

Examples abound. MPAC, for instance, runs a civic engagement and leadership program, "I Am Change," that provides community training workshops aiming to teach individuals "how to promote civic engagement from an Islamic perspective."[36] CAIR and the USCMO, for their part, have worked ceaselessly to register and encourage Muslims to vote in local and national elections. They hold voter registration and get-out-the-vote drives, and they teach people how to organize drives in their communities and at local mosques. They have made available a wide variety of election-related resources, including sample scripts for get-out-the-vote campaigns, Election Day reminder calls, national voter guides with information on key issues, and a tool kit on questions to ask candidates in town hall meetings. Before the 2016 presidential elections, CAIR launched MuslimsGOTV.com, featuring a variety of CAIR-produced material, such as videos encouraging Muslim voters to register and vote, information on absentee and early voting, a map of polling stations across the country, and a summary of candidates' views on Islam and Muslims. These efforts are significant; according to Pew survey data, only 57 percent of US Muslims are registered to vote and only 44 percent of them voted in the 2016 elections.[37] Minorities are generally less likely to vote than whites, but other minority groups still have higher turnout rates than Muslims. Almost 60 percent of Black Americans voted in 2016, for example. The numbers are more anemic for Asian Americans and Hispanics (but still better than for Muslims). They voted at 49 percent and 47 percent, respectively.[38] Aware of this reality, CAIR established MuslimsGOTV.com as a resource to encourage Muslim American civic engagement and electoral participation. "We have to register every single Muslim to vote in 2016," declared Nihad Awad. "Turn your organizations, Islamic centers and mosques into registration centers for voters and polling stations during the elections. The Muslim vote can be the swing vote in major states. What kind of America we are going to have depends on you."[39]

Notwithstanding these efforts, Muslim advocacy organizations have become increasingly aware that mobilizing the community to vote is not enough. Encouraging and training individuals to run for elected office has become not only desirable, but also necessary to secure the community's long-term inclusion. Toward these ends, in 2007, MPAC launched its Young Leaders Summits, aimed at increasing the presence of Muslim Americans in public life. As part of this program, the organization selects college and graduate students to participate in summer policy summits, where they have the chance to meet and engage with government officials and policymakers. According to the organization, participants have met with President Obama's senior adviser and chief of staff, the undersecretaries for the Departments of State and Homeland Security, and prominent members of Congress.[40]

Other nascent organizations have emerged, such as Jetpac (justice, education, and technology), specifically calling on Muslims to train and run for local office. Founded by Nadeem Mazen, a Cambridge, Massachusetts, city councilor and that state's first Muslim elected official, the organization defines itself as a political advocacy center dedicated to helping Muslims and other minorities "focus on their ground game," applying the same recipes for success that led Mazen to his 2013 election victory (and his 2015 reelection).[41] Youth leadership training is an

FIGURE 4.   MPAC's Young Leaders Government Summit meeting with Rep. Ben Carson. Reproduced with the permission of the Muslim Public Affairs Council.

important component of Jetpac's work. In 2017, it partnered with Al-Noor Academy, an Islamic secondary school in Massachusetts, to launch an advanced placement course in US government and politics. According to the organization, the curriculum "combines grassroots activism strategies with Islamic principles while teaching the fundamentals of American democracy."[42]

As these initiatives indicate, Muslim leaders have come to realize that being invited to the policy table is not enough. Increasingly, they have begun to think of their work as incubating future American leaders, encouraging their constituents not only to vote in elections but also to become the candidates on the ballots. In 2016, Ilhan Omar (D-MN) and Rashida Tlaib (D-MI) became the first two Muslim women to be elected to the US House of Representatives. From 2016 to 2019, 323 Muslims ran for statewide and national elections—a record number.[43] Many of these candidates said they were motivated to run because of Trump's anti-Muslim bigotry and policies.[44] As Roula Allouch, chair of CAIR's national board of directors, told me, "This upsurge in the number of people running and winning elections has filled us with enormous pride . . . and of course, the elections of Rashida Tlaib and Ilhan Omar. It's a historic moment for our community. Many of us will remember where we were and what we were doing when they were elected and when they were sworn into office."[45]

Outreach, Cross-Sectional Alliances, and Coalition Building

As simple as it might sound, one of Muslim advocacy groups' most significant efforts is making lawmakers aware of the impacts that existing or proposed legislation could have on their communities. Often, making that message clear rests on the ability to explain how other American communities are also affected, since many of the policies that target Muslims have grave consequences for others, particularly members of minority groups. Again, "anti-sharia" legislation offers a salient example. Despite its specific targeting of the religious freedom of Muslims, major Muslim organizations have convincingly argued that the proposed restrictions would have a grave impact on the religious liberties of other minorities, most directly American Jews. Mainstream American Jewish advocacy groups have generally agreed, arguing that Muslims apply sharia in much the same way that Orthodox Jews in America apply halacha on issues related to family and property law, while always deferring to civil courts.[46] Similarly, following the announcement of President Trump's first executive order restricting immigration from seven Muslim-majority countries, MPAC joined a broad interfaith coalition (which included the National Council of Churches and a number of synagogues, rabbis, and reverends from across the country) in their amici curiae brief to the US Supreme Court, opposing the ban as "anathema to [the] core tenet that all members of our coalition share."[47]

Interfaith advocacy and collaboration are important ways through which Muslim organizations work to normalize Islam as an Abrahamic religion (and, hence, part of America's value traditions). Reflecting on the rising Islamophobia in the United States, al-Marayati contended that "Islam is as Western as it is Eastern. They are trying to divide Islam from the other Abrahamic traditions. Our job [as American Muslims] is to reunify the Abrahamic religions."[48]

Over the years, MPAC has joined interfaith leaders and organizations in rallies, public statements, and court cases on a wide range of issues, including immigration, terrorism, gun violence, and religious and racial discrimination. In 2012, MPAC joined the Zionist Organization of America and the American Jewish Federation to oppose an invitation extended to Pamela Geller, a well-known anti-Muslim advocate, by the Jewish Federation of Greater Los Angeles. Their joined statement cautioned, "Imagine how hurt Jewish community members would be, and rightly so, if they discovered American Muslims hosting an anti-Semitic speaker."[49] The Jewish Federation rescinded Geller's invitation.

Alliance-building efforts extend beyond interfaith groups to include reaching out to and building coalitions with other minority and marginalized groups, including Latinx (one of the fastest-growing groups of Muslims in the United States), undocumented immigrants, African Americans (roughly a third of the American Muslim population), the Black Lives Matter movement, and the LGBTQ community. These are not mutually exclusive categories of individuals, of course, and Muslims belong to all of these groups, but there is a growing recognition among Muslim organizations that they have not always leveraged these partnerships to the extent they should. Muslim leaders also acknowledge that it might be politically expedient to demonstrate how the issues that affect their communities also affect many other Americans. Awad's statement following the Pulse nightclub shooting reflects this growing awareness, as does CAIR's increasing focus on its principles, goals, missions, and image. Issuing joint news conferences and press releases alongside other minority leaders on topics related to racial and religious profiling, surveillance, terrorism, and immigration has become a staple of Muslim advocacy work. This is an important way of demonstrating support for other targeted groups and positioning the Muslim community in the context of the civil rights struggle for minority rights.

Is Anyone Listening?

In looking at the field of Muslim advocacy, one thing is clear. Muslim organizations are emphatically communicating their visions, demands, and positions, but with whom, exactly, are they communicating? Whom are they attempting to reach? Who is listening to them? Is their primary audience American Muslims, on whose behalf they claim to speak; US policymakers, whose positions they seek to influence; or the broader American public, whose support they need to achieve their long term-goal of integrating and achieving full citizenship rights for American Muslims?

Indeed, in all they do, Muslim organizations always have these multiple audiences in mind. How could we explain the fact that MPAC, for example, initially supported a limited US invasion of Iraq to depose Saddam Hussein, even though 75 percent of US Muslims opposed this position? Perplexing at first, the organization's position becomes less surprising if we understand that in that instance, MPAC was trying to get the attention not of Muslim American citizens but of the US security establishment. Supporting a limited intervention to depose Hussein (which, although highly unpopular with Muslim Americans and the broader American public, was generally supported by the foreign policy and security establishment) must be seen as a way through which MPAC sought to gain legitimacy and therefore access to the halls of power—and, as critics point out, to potential sources of government funding.

What is important to keep in mind is that while speaking on behalf of a minority that is often perceived as disenfranchised, especially institutionally,

Muslim advocacy groups are also aspiring insiders trying to appeal to elite members of the US policy establishment. As interest groups, increased inclusion in the policy process is an important goal.[50] Many leaders are candid about this point, arguing that the interests of the community will be met not through protest but by claiming access to decision makers and making the demands of the community heard.[51] These organizations are thus clear about their tactics, and about the fact that they perceive meaningful change to result from the top down—from changing policies. And while they consider bottom-up activism a necessary tactic to exert pressure on elected officials, their day-to-day work focuses on trying to reach and influence decision makers and those with access to them. In fact, some of these organizations and their leaders have been harshly criticized as elitists and out of touch with the average Muslim person on the street.[52] The outreach coordinator of one of CAIR's regional chapters described it more positively to me: "This is *la crème de la crème* of the Muslim community."

Advocacy and the Construction of Muslim American Political Identity

On the surface, it is easy to understand why these organizations would want to be included in policy debates that deal with the Muslim American community and therefore profoundly influence it. Looking a little closer, however, one finds a far more nuanced relationship. The historical narrative of Muslim Americans leaves little doubt as to the tremendous degree of ethnic, cultural, and theological diversity this group embodies. What is less clear is whether, despite their differences, they identify and see themselves, at least broadly speaking, as a cohesive group that identifies with the "Muslim American" label—and, if this is the case, how this came to be.

Moments of crisis, such as the post-9/11 backlash and the rise in hate crimes during the 2016 election cycle, have tended to strengthen affiliation with a Muslim American collective identity.[53] This finding is in line with social identity theory, which argues that perceptions of shared threat, discrimination, and intergroup conflict can intensify people's attachment to the targeted group.[54] And, as discussed in chapter 1, discriminated-against minorities are more likely to emphasize their dual identities (as both ethnic and religious minorities and citizens), especially when communicating with audiences who may question their belonging to the group and their identity claims.[55] Building on these insights, some scholars have begun emphasizing the communicative and performative aspect of identity, arguing that social identities are articulated with a particular audience in mind and thus gain their meaning, in part, from specific interactions. Moreover, "others' perceptions and expectations impose constraints, which in turn can shape the situational contents and meanings of social identities."[56]

What becomes increasingly clear is that Muslim advocacy organizations are not only concerned with protecting the interests of the Muslim American community. Instead, through the issues they select to engage in, the positions they take, and the tactics they use to pursue their demands, they are performing a particular Muslim American identity—one that is rooted in the principles of social justice, embraces liberal democratic values, is compatible with secularism, and opposes all forms of extremism. Of course, this is one of many possible Muslim American identities; the US policy establishment, our current political climate, and the alliances these groups are building inevitably shape and influence the particular group identity that they communicate and construct.

The "policy acts" these organizations engage in are both reflections and producers of Muslim American interests. While the great majority of Muslim advocacy organizations have focused their efforts on the domestic arena, transnational activism is an inescapable aspect of their work, even if they would rather escape it. This is partly explained by the fact that a majority of US Muslims (58 percent) are first-generation immigrants, a figure that rises to 75 percent when we include their American-born children. The majority of US Muslims are not from the Middle East, but that Muslim-majority region has immense geostrategic importance to the United States, as well as emotional significance to Muslims around the world, including those in the United States.

These facts provide Muslim advocacy organizations with an opportunity to position themselves as relevant to the policy establishment on a wide variety of issues related to the region. Transnational considerations are also relevant to many of the domestic issues in which these organizations engage. In a rapidly globalized world, many of the concerns we may consider to be domestic are, in fact, transnational. Surveillance, counterterrorism and the War on Terror, Islamophobia, immigration reform, and extrajudicial exile cannot be seen in purely domestic terms. These issues cross the national–foreign policy boundary, bringing Muslim citizens into contact with their coreligionists from around the world. The reach of US policy is wide indeed.

The rise and evolution of Muslim American advocacy organizations are the result of both group-specific dynamics (Muslims being victims of discrimination and the leaders who established these organizations) and broader social and political dynamics (the history of minority mobilization in the United States and a decentralized political system that presents individuals with ample opportunities for lobbying, or, in the language of social movement theory, "openings").

Muslim advocacy groups have used these opportunities to make a wide range of claims on behalf of their communities and relied on various tactics to advance those claims—including contestation, collaboration, empowerment, and coalition building. The next two chapters look at these strategies more deeply and present a detailed analysis of the domestic and foreign policy issues comprising the core of these organizations' advocacy efforts.

DOMESTIC ADVOCACY

Between Contestation and Collaboration

We are the foot soldiers of the Constitution.

—Shereef Akeel

Shaima Swileh fought for something no mother should have to fight for: the right to be with her dying child. Under President Trump's travel ban, Shaima, a Yemeni national, was barred entry to the United States unless she obtained a visa waiver. She applied for the waiver, only to hear nothing back. The family reached out to the American embassy in Cairo, where Shaima lived, twenty-eight times. Their desperate pleas were met with automated responses. Meanwhile, Shaima's husband, Ali, and their two-year-old child, Abdullah (both US citizens), were in California, where they had gone to seek better care for Abdullah's genetic degenerative brain condition. It was a devastating situation that was made needlessly cruel by the family's separation.

In mid-December 2018, with Abdullah's condition rapidly deteriorating, the Sacramento Valley chapter of CAIR filed an emergency lawsuit and led a massive media campaign to reunite the family. Three members of Congress from California became aware of the family's plight and petitioned the US Department of State to expedite Shaima's waiver decision.[1] A day after the letter was sent, Shaima was granted the visa waiver to come to the United States. CAIR's campaign had succeeded, but there was nothing to celebrate. Little Abdullah died on December 28, nine days after his mother's arrival. The family's tragedy came to starkly symbolize the human impact of the Muslim ban. As Saad Sweilem, the CAIR-SV civil rights attorney who represented the family, put it in a statement mourning Abdullah's passing: "This family has inspired our nation to confront the realities of Donald Trump's Muslim Ban. In his short life Abdullah has been a guiding light for all of us in the fight against xenophobia and family separation."[2]

As novel as it may seem to some, the Muslim American experience is not unique. Throughout our nation's history, many other minority groups have been marginalized, scapegoated, and dehumanized. And just as Muslims are doing today, previously marginalized groups of Americans have found ways to contest, resist, and challenge the institutions and social practices through which they were systematically excluded from membership in the national community. The civil rights movement would prove to be a watershed moment in the history of collective claims making in the United States, setting the standard for what targeted groups could attain by reclaiming the very institutions that had been used to legitimize their oppression. The Constitution and Bill of Rights are among the most powerful weapons in the struggle for full citizenship rights. Thus, a central strategy of the political movements for equality of the 1960s—including the civil rights movement, the women's movement, and the labor movement, to name but a few—was to rely on constitutional principles to advance individual and collective rights and to make claims as citizens deserving of those rights. Figure 5, which shows a group of Muslim delegates in front of the Capitol building during the 2018 Muslim Hill Day, is illustrative of this strategy.

"Rights-talk," as scholars came to describe this process, has become a definite marker of collective action in the post–civil rights era. Few such value norms have acquired the degree of recognition and acceptance that the value of rights seems

FIGURE 5.   USCMO/CAIR Muslim Advocacy Day on Capitol Hill, 2018. Reproduced with the permission of the Council on American-Islamic Relations.

to hold, leading to a broad degree of acceptance of right-based claims.[3] These demands can be framed around rights to do something (the right to marry, for example) or protections from something (in particular, the overreach of state power).[4] As Ruud Koopmans and colleagues explain, this process "consists of the purposive and public articulation of political demands, calls to action, proposals, criticisms, or physical attacks, which, actually or potentially, affect the interests or integrity of the claimant and/or other collective actors."[5] Thus, groups that are able to frame policy issues, particularly contentious ones, around rights can gain an important degree of legitimacy for their cause and, consequently, meaningful levels of access to the political dialogue.

American Muslims have joined a range of other groups, including the LGBTQ community, Black Lives Matter, the pro-choice and pro-life movements, and immigrants (including the undocumented among them), in applying a discourse of rights to put forth their claims. And, as with many groups before them, they have received severe backlash. Making claims is difficult and generally not readily accepted by those of whom the demands are being made. Indeed, a 2017 poll by the University of Pennsylvania's Annenberg Public Policy Center found that a full 22 percent of Americans did not believe (or know whether) Muslims in the United States had First Amendment rights.[6] Remarkable numbers of Americans also refuse to accept that Islam is a religion and are thus willing to strip their fellow Muslim citizens of their constitutionally granted legal rights to religious liberty. As the legal scholar Asma T. Uddin writes, their complaint can be summarized starkly: "Islam is not a religion, but rather a geopolitical system bent on instituting jihadist and sharia law in America."[7]

Uddin has meticulously documented the concrete legal impacts that the political strategy of stripping Muslims of their claims to religious protections has had on the lives of American Muslims, including her own. "Religious liberty," she writes, "is what the drafters of international law would call a dignity-based right. That means it is inherent to human beings and cannot be negotiated away, nor is it something that one has to earn or contract for. Under American law, it stands as the 'first freedom'—it's covered in the first part of the first sentence of the first amendment, privileged even above freedom of speech, press, and assembly."[8]

Although it is, by far, the most common way Muslim advocates have framed their claims, the effectiveness and desirability of framing group grievances in terms of legal entitlements is not universally accepted. Critics contend that relying on a discourse of rights turns individuals into passive petitioners, dependent on the state. Others argue that rights-talk fosters social division by magnifying disagreements, particularly if the rights being demanded are seen, rightly or wrongly, to come at someone else's expense. Unquestionably, however, the practice of claims making is a practice of reaffirming an individual's fundamental human rights and values, making minority groups visible, promoting and communicating collective political identities, and, ultimately, as proponents would argue, making the state more responsive to and inclusive of all its citizens.

Whatever an individual's position on these tactics, minority groups in the United States continue to rely on them as an important strategy for collective action. Not surprisingly, the debate over whether this is the most effective way to promote a community's interests is one that Muslim organizations have grappled with and is reflected in the issues in which they choose to engage. Is the fight for constitutional rights the best way to achieve the community's demands? Should Muslim organizations be pragmatic and work to improve existing policies that affect the lives of Muslims and other marginalized communities, or seek a deeper and more meaningful transformation of society? What is gained, and lost, when we ask the state to grant us rights? And, how far do Muslims have to go to be considered good citizens, deserving of those rights? These were some of the questions occupying many of the Muslim leaders I spoke with. The responses and positions they offered are diverse, nuanced, and often difficult. How Muslim American organizations demand their community's rights ranges the spectrum—from cooperating and pressuring the government to contesting specific policies and fighting for radical transformation.

No subject better captures the complexity of these organizations' claims-making strategies than that of counterterrorism policy in general and the Obama-era program of countering violent extremism (CVE) in particular.

Counterterrorism and the Debate over Countering Violent Extremism

In August 2011, the Obama White House released a national strategy aimed at preventing radicalization in the United States, which came to be known as countering violent extremism. CVE was promoted as a local intervention that sought to empower communities to "disrupt the radicalization process before an individual engaged in criminal activity."[9] It did this by providing grants to community organizations and police departments working to reach people believed to be at risk. From its inception, however, many Muslims voiced apprehension about the program, viewing it as yet another attempt at government surveillance of their communities. National Muslim organizations were deeply troubled about the CVE initiative but equally concerned about how to respond to it. They had cooperated with the government for decades, striving to be seen as allies and partners in the war against al-Qaeda and terrorism. While severely critical of specific policies, many prioritized accessing and collaborating with the government, arguing that meaningful change required engagement. In the post-9/11 era, they worked tirelessly to entrench Muslims as loyal American citizens, whose love of country was wrongly and unfairly questioned.

The framing of CVE as a community partnership that sought to relate to US Muslims as allies in the war on terror presented these organizations with a real conundrum: although they considered the program a deeply flawed initiative that both perpetuated and repackaged the surveillance of Muslim communities, any opposition to it had to be tactful so as not to jeopardize the partnerships they had spent years cultivating, including the growing acceptance of Muslims as partners in the war on terror. Even the most vocally anti-CVE organizations reflected this tension. Following the government's rollout of the initiative, CAIR released a restrained statement, declaring that although it strongly supports law enforcement efforts to protect US national security, it questioned the rationale and effectiveness of the CVE paradigm, adding that the program was "not an effective use of public resources."[10]

This tone would change in 2015. When Congress passed the Countering Violent Extremism Act, moving CVE to the Department of Homeland Security, the Muslim American response was anything but subdued. Muslim and other civil liberties groups argued that ideology was not a clear predictor of terrorism and rightly pointed out the dangers of policing thought rather than action. CAIR contextualized its response, writing that its disapproval emerged "from a backdrop of a decade long history of the federal government and law-enforcement elements, absent evidence of criminal activity, targeting mosques and community organizations for intelligence gathering."[11] MPAC, for its part, argued that the decision to move CVE under the DHS "formalizes and institutionalizes a program that is vague and lacks transparency."[12]

Nevertheless, MPAC applied for and was initially given a CVE grant of nearly $400,000 (which the Trump administration later rescinded), which it vowed to use to buttress its Safe Spaces Initiative on extremism, a program it defined as "an alternative to both heavy-handed law enforcement tactics and government-led countering violent extremism." The decision caused a stir in the Muslim American community. Critics accused MPAC and organizations such as the lesser-known Detroit-based Leaders Advancing and Helping Communities (formerly the Lebanese American Heritage Club) of being "native informants," whose support allowed the government to disguise and deflect the structural Islamophobia underpinning the program.[13] As Salam Al-Marayati explained:

> Muslim organizations . . . and people on the left were also criticizing us
> for that grant. But [the Safe Spaces Initiative] was intended to empower
> communities to handle the problem, not law enforcement. And it made

it a strong demarcation between community and law enforcement. Here's what the community is going to deal with: social issues, counseling issues, religious issues, theological issues. . . . [Currently] you either call the FBI, which is what happens in some of these cases—like in Northern California there was this case where this guy called the FBI and now his son is going to be gone for 30 years. So that's one way of doing it . . . or they do nothing, and then it gets worse. But here is the middle way of doing something about it but not treating the person as a criminal right off the bat.[14]

In addition to condemning these organizations as sellouts, critics claimed that their cooperation invited the FBI into the community and thus "securitized" daily interactions. Other attacks were more personal. Some have claimed MPAC was a "revolving door" for people to enter careers in government as "experts" on the Muslim community, pointing to the fact that Haris Tarin, MPAC's former Washington, DC, director and CVE supporter, went on to work for the Department of Homeland Security on issues related to CVE.[15] When I asked him to reflect on the criticism, Al-Marayati was unrepentant, convinced that his work was needed:

Being anti-CVE is a *cause celebre* right now. . . . To be anti-CVE is to be cool. But there has been this misunderstanding and distortion of facts really. Of what we are able to do by engaging that these other groups are not readily acknowledging. They don't want to acknowledge that we've made a difference on some of these issues. . . . Or the other thing is that they don't want to acknowledge that there's a problem with extremism . . . and we're not going to deny that a problem with extremism exists. We see it, there's been San Bernardino, Orlando, here was Boston. It's our responsibility to engage. You can complain, you can litigate, but at the end of the day you've got to come up with solutions.

Criticism of the CVE program from within and outside the Muslim American community is rooted in a broader critique of government surveillance and the way the surveillance power of the state is used to target particular groups of people. CAIR has voiced concern over the vagueness of what could be deemed a potential red flag of radicalization under the program's parameters, arguing that "government programs to counter violent extremism, which incorporate steps for 'intervention' can too easily slip into policing ideology" and thus lead to potential First Amendment violations—something civil liberties groups, including the ACLU, have also argued.

Echoing these concerns, in February 2015, the USCMO issued a press release stating its apprehension over CVE and its skepticism toward the program and those mandated to implement it: "Law enforcement outreach and CVE programs may be accompanied by intelligence gathering activities or other abusive law enforcement practices."[16] Documents obtained via Freedom of Information Act requests by the Brennan Center for Justice suggest these concerns were well-founded.[17] In an internal memo, FBI officials acknowledge that engagement with radical ideology is not a predictor of terrorist acts but argue that the CVE program can nevertheless help enhance the bureau's intelligence-gathering abilities.[18]

Concerns over overzealous government counterterrorism initiatives have spurred a variety of grassroots responses, opening the door to newcomers in the realm of Muslim American advocacy. In 2014, four Muslim women (three attorneys and an anthropologist) founded the Muslim Justice League in Boston as a direct response to the US government's decision to make that city one of its CVE pilot locales. The organization argued that CVE was a disguised attempt at "soft-surveillance," with the government providing financial incentives for mosques, schools, and community-based organizations to report on potential "vulnerabilities" or signs of extremism.[19] Accordingly, it contended that these counterterrorism initiatives have caused serious harm to American Muslims, divided communities, and instilled fear and mistrust of law enforcement, all of which is ultimately counterproductive.

I met Stephanie Marzouk, one of the Muslim Justice League's cofounders, on a warm summer afternoon in 2019. By then, she had stepped away from her day-to-day involvement with the organization, although she still served on its board. I asked her to take me back to those early days following the Boston Marathon bombing of 2016 and the FBI's response, since it was what had earned Boston its spot as a pilot city in the CVE program and catapulted her organization into being. Marzouki explained:

> After something like the marathon bombing, the FBI is doing a real investigation, and they knock on people's doors and say: "Hey can we talk to you," and people say, "Sure, come on in." And of course we're not trying to prevent people from sharing information if they have any to share, but just letting them know that they have a right to an attorney in those moments. . . . We're very conscious of the risks of participating in CVE, the risks of engaging with the federal government, especially the US Attorney's Office, on these issues. But the community was very torn. . . . I think a lot of community leaders were looking for legitimacy. I think that many Muslim leaders and organizations wanted to show that they did have connections with the government, that they are good people, doing good things. It was a way for them to say: "Look we're working together, we want to help you, we're Americans too . . . and I

think some people always knew that wasn't a great idea." Some organizations were thinking: "Well, we can take the money, being cleared-eyed about what it is and what we're doing with it, or someone else will take it, who's maybe not going to be so clear-eyed." There is a lot of tension. And a lot of times, especially for organizational leaders, there isn't really a good choice. You're answering to a lot of people. You're answering to other people you work with. You're answering to the government at some level and there is real concern out there. These are not easy problems to solve.

As Marzouk recounts, the Muslim Justice League decided to focus its advocacy efforts on empowerment—educating the community about its rights and providing free legal representation to people contacted by law enforcement for questioning. Their main advice? Do not invite FBI agents into your home or answer any questions without an attorney. To clear any confusion, they provided a script of how to respond in these cases: "Be confident and polite and repeat yourself as many times as necessary: 'I don't wish to answer questions without an attorney. Please leave your number. My attorney will call you.'"[20]

These tactics should not be read as proof of disengagement on issues related to counterterrorism. Even the most stringent critics of the government's domestic war on terror recognize that radicalization is an issue among a minute number of American Muslims. They argue, however, that the federal government's response should not be to target an entire faith community. "This is not normal," Marzouk would tell people. "The US Attorney is not meeting with the Jewish community, the US Attorney is not meeting with the Sikh community. . . . They are really not here to help you in the way you think they are. They play a very important role in law enforcement, and that helps all of us, but what is your goal in trying to interact with them? And are you really going to accomplish [that] through these means?"

Muslim leaders do not deny the existence of radicalization and extremism. What they argue is that the government's surveillance of an entire community is not only unconstitutional but also highly ineffective. It is, simply, not the best way to respond to these threats. Instead of spending limited resources on counterproductive programs, they argue, the government should empower communities—people who already have a long history of cooperating with law enforcement—to freely express their dissent (which works to reduce the appeal of injustice narratives that terrorist organizations use to recruit)[21] and then acknowledge and reform its unconstitutional surveillance of US Muslim communities. Perhaps more controversially, Muslim advocacy organizations unanimously agree that any serious government-led initiative to counter radicalization must address how US foreign policy decisions are implicated in the radicalization process—a topic we will turn to in the next chapter.

What is clear is that CVE did not emerge in a vacuum. Rather, it is part of a broader spectrum of government initiatives that have sought to gain the trust and cooperation of Muslim communities.[22] This outreach has provided Muslim American interest groups with an opportunity to reach policymakers, share their perspectives, and voice their criticism of what they largely perceive as a failed US counterterrorism strategy. By adding their voices to the counterterrorism discussion, no matter how faint, these organizations are communicating what they posit as "the Muslim American perspective" and, inevitably, are shaping, delineating, and defining the collective identity of the group they claim to represent.

As is the case for all collective identities, their counterterrorism advocacy illustrates that difference and differentiation are keys to the construction of a Muslim American group identity. Indeed, as identity scholars put it, "all identity is constituted in relation to difference."[23] In this case, the impetus is to differentiate American Muslims from what I refer to as "the foreign Muslim radical," the popular image that the West, and in particular the United States, has of Muslims and Islam.[24] It is worth noting that this is also the image of Muslims that President Trump and other GOP candidates propagated throughout the 2016 election campaign, espousing the term "radical Islamic terrorism" as a rallying cry that many saw as a coded racial appeal to attract the white nationalist vote. Dispelling this image of Muslims and Islam, and disassociating American Muslims from it, became a central goal of Muslim American advocacy. In fact, what Muslim American leaders seem to be saying is that "we" are not what you have wrongly made us out to be by taking the worst among us as a depiction of our entire community. And they are not only correcting that image but also, through the process, engendering, defining, and redefining what it means to be an American Muslim in the age of counterterrorism.

Contesting US Counterterrorism Policy: A Muslim American Response

At the height of the War on Terror in 2003, MPAC published its first policy report on counterterrorism, a document that provides a number of important insights on the nexus of US counterterrorism policy and the articulation of a Muslim American identity.[25] The report exemplifies a key advocacy tactic, linking counterterrorism strategies, radicalization, and the erosion of domestic civil liberties as manifestations of the same ailment—misguided US policy. Accordingly, MPAC presents the document as a tool to educate policymakers and aid in the development of an "appropriate" counterterrorism response. Central themes are the need to disassociate Islam and Muslims from radicalism and the need to problematize the ease with which people, groups, and nations are labeled as terrorists. Rather than treating American Muslims as potentially dangerous suspects, MPAC suggests they should be seen as key allies in the fight against terrorism. Thus, there is a clear effort to demarcate the parameters of Muslim American identity by, first and foremost, disassociating Islam and Muslims from foreignness, fanaticism, and violence. As basic as this may seem, it is a point worth highlighting, since it is what these organizations were established to do, and long after their establishment it continues to sit at the heart of their mission.

MPCA's counterterrorism report begins with a preamble, clarifying critical aspects of Islam and Islamic jurisprudence. Why would a report on counterterrorism strategy begin in this way? The answer, according to MPAC, is that crude representations of Islam have led to the alienation of the Muslim American community, a fact that "harms both the American Muslim community and the intelligence gathering capacity of the United States."[26] In other words, harm inflicted on the Muslim American community is harm done directly to the nation—by hurting its intelligence-gathering efforts and, thus, its security. Linking harm done *to* Muslims (versus the overriding public narrative of harm done *by* Muslims) with harm done to the homeland repositions American Muslims as an integral and inseparable part of the United States. The first step in this process is to highlight the synergy between Islamic jurisprudence and American values.

The following year, 2004, another report made a similar claim: *Counterproductive Counterterrorism: How Anti-Islamic Rhetoric Is Impeding America's Homeland Security* is dedicated to exposing the dangers of racist and Islamophobic organizations and, in the process, presenting them as a threat to US national security.[27] Steve Emerson's Investigative Project receives special attention as one of the worst examples of Islamophobia in America. MPAC is clear that Emerson "has the right to do and say whatever he pleases," presenting itself as a fierce protector of the First Amendment even as it is the target of hateful and erroneous speech. However, just as Emerson's freedom is protected, the report calls on Americans "who know more and do more for the cause of fighting terror" to speak out and contest his misguided views: "In the fight against terror, it is crucial that we use the insight of all segments of our pluralism. The work of Emerson and his colleagues is blunting the opportunities for American Muslims to participate in our democracy. [His] lack of insight and aptitude has led to faulty analysis and sensationalized claims that misguide the public's search for truth and squander the resources of our government in defending America. We as Americans should not allow those who are interested in the profitable industry surrounding terrorism to steer us down the path of dividing America in the war on terror." With such statements, MPAC reframes Anti-Muslim rhetoric as not just a civil rights issue but also a threat to national security, since it leads the government to squander limited resources to respond to manufactured threats. In other words, anti-Muslim activists are a threat to both the Muslim American community and to the American nation. Figures such as Emerson are thus constituted as the real traitors for seeking to divide "us" while profiting from "our" collective national security. Through this kind of discourse, Muslim advocacy organizations assert themselves as members of the American in-group: it is Emerson and Islamophobes like him who fall outside its boundaries.

Echoing a common criticism from Muslim and other civil liberties organizations, these publications condemn US counterterrorism policy for the ways in which it implicitly—and explicitly—associates terrorism with Islam and Muslims and identifies "terrorism with the identity of the perpetrator, rather than the nature of the act itself."[28] MPAC recommends that law enforcement focus its counterterrorism efforts not on thought but on criminal behavior. The core of the argument is that extremist beliefs do not equate to violent behavior; it is not extremists who should be cause for concern but people's behavior and actions. In making these claims, MPAC emphasizes that freedom of thought and expression, no matter how radical, are protected under the Constitution, adding that "ideological approaches" to law enforcement constitute "a profoundly un-American activity that does not enhance security."[29]

Positioning themselves as defenders of core American principles—freedom, justice, liberty, and equality—is a central building block in the articulation of Muslim American identity. It also links Muslim advocacy groups to other American minorities who have advanced the cause of civil rights. In the words of CAIR's Corey Saylor, "Right now, we are under the lens and what I say to people is, this is our opportunity. All these other groups before us have defended liberty in this country. We have the African American community to thank for the Civil Rights Act of 1964, which we use all the time to defend our community. Today the lens is on us; we have to hold the line and try to defend those civil liberty protections."[30]

MPAC's reports are written primarily as appeals to policymakers and other government officials, but the organization is acutely aware that their audience also includes the constituents they aim to represent, as well as the broader American public. Thus, in a section of *A Review of U.S. Counterterrorism Policy* titled "Recommendations for the American Muslim Community and Organizations," it argues that "while some individual Muslims, motivated by political agendas rather than religious guidance, have sought (and may still seek) to inflict harm on American citizens and interests, the American Muslim community . . . is an integral component of American civic and political life, and can have a positive impact on American civil society."[31] Claiming that the main impetus driving some Muslims to seek to harm the United States is political, the report clearly attempts to disassociate the broader religion (and thus the majority of Muslims) from the "politically motivated" acts of a few. Further, distinguishing between the teachings of Islam, on the one hand, and politically motivated acts, on the other, can be seen as an echoing of the American separation of church and state—and thus as a way to further naturalize Islam, and Muslims, in the United States.

The report's specific recommendations to the Muslim American community provide a fascinating glimpse of elite representation of Muslim American identity. The recommendations present Muslim organizations as reasonable, moderate, and mainstream policy actors seeking to guide their communities in ways that are acceptable and conducive to the aims of the broader policy establishment. They are thus best understood as representations of American Islam. Take, for example, the following guidelines:

- National Muslim organizations should develop educational materials and other initiatives designed to educate law enforcement officials.
- The nation's leading Muslim organizations should work in concert with other civil liberties groups to protect America's constitutional freedoms.
- Muslim religious institutions should take steps to mitigate extremism and angry rhetoric by establishing educational and training programs that emphasize the importance of tolerance, citizenship, and social/civic responsibility as Islamic values; and educate mosque officials about their responsibilities regarding irresponsible speech and/or activity on their premises.[32]

As can be gleaned from this advice, some of the key qualities Muslim American grassroots leaders and organizations should possess and promote are tolerance, civic values, responsibility, and cooperation. It is worth bearing in mind that this discourse differentiates Muslim American identity not only from the image of the foreign Muslim radical but also from illiberal and conservative interpretations of Islam, such as Wahhabism, which the same report describes as "an exceptionally austere and puritanical interpretation of Islam that rigidifies the faith." Through these policy recommendations, Muslim organizations are countering what they view as fringe conservative interpretations of the religion, while constituting a liberal, democratic, and tolerant American Islam.

Dr. Maher Hathout, a senior advisor at MPAC, expressed these sentiments forcefully, describing fundamentalist interpretations of Islam as having no place in the United States. Speaking of American Muslims who follow conservative (as Hathout put it, "puritanical") interpretations of Islam, he advised, "If you are fascinated by the ways things are done in Saudi Arabia, be my guest, go there! But don't try to implant Saudi Arabia here, because this is a foreign body that will be rejected."[33] The other, in this case, is represented as an illiberal and dogmatic Islam, a foreign other that will be rejected by American Muslims upholding the real essence of Islam.

Challenging the Construction of the Suspect Citizen

Government policies do not exist in a vacuum. The subject of unwarranted surveillance, profiling, and policing that CVE underscores came to the national limelight after the passage of the Patriot Act and again in 2013, following the leaking of classified documents by former CIA employee Edward Snowden. The documents revealed what many American Muslims already knew: their government was spying on them. Unwarranted surveillance became a key domestic issue for Muslim advocacy organizations in the post-9/11 period, but Muslims (and many other Americans) had been the targets of government surveillance long before that fateful day. In the 1960s, as Edward E. Curtis reminds us, African American Muslims (the Nation of Islam in particular) were key targets of FBI surveillance.[34] At that time, the Counter Intelligence Program, better known as COINTELPRO, was used to target "the radical left." Key targets included individuals perceived to have Communist sympathies, African American Muslims, and charismatic figures such as Malcolm X and Muhammad Ali.[35]

The first time national Muslim organizations engaged in a concerted effort to advocate against the threat of government surveillance was 1995, when CAIR (founded the year before) and MPAC joined the now-defunct American Muslim Council and a number of civil rights organizations in lobbying against the Omnibus Counterterrorism Act of 1995, introduced by then-Senator Joe Biden on behalf of the Clinton administration and which many consider a predecessor to the Patriot Act.[36] CAIR argued that the Counterterrorism Act violated fundamental constitutional rights and unfairly stereotyped Muslims, "singling them out for investigation, surveillance, and prosecution without adequate evidence."[37] The bill died in the Senate, but CAIR and other Muslim organizations would return to this issue often, particularly in the post-9/11 period.

In 2006, long before the Snowden exposé, CAIR joined the ACLU, Greenpeace, the National Association of Criminal Defense Lawyers, and other organizations in filing a lawsuit against the National Security Agency (NSA) over its Terrorist Surveillance Program, a secret program the NSA had started in 2002 to intercept the international telephone and internet communications of individuals within the United States. The plaintiffs argued that by engaging in warrantless spying, the NSA had violated the privacy rights granted to all under the Constitution. A federal district court judge ruled that "the wiretapping program violated the Fourth Amendment by operating without warrants," and the case was ultimately dismissed on appeal.[38] It would become the first of many legal challenges that CAIR would bring to the courts over the issue of warrantless surveillance, part of the organization's long battle against what it sees as the unconstitutional targeting of US Muslims.

In conjunction with the legal challenges to contest the government's surveil-lance power, Muslim organizations also worked to voice their concerns within the intelligence community and other government agencies. When reports of un-lawful surveillance began to appear in the national press in the mid-2000s, MPAC was relentless in requesting meetings with the Department of Justice, in-cluding the FBI, and the Department of Homeland Security. In 2005, when Mus-lim leaders were angered by reports that the FBI had engaged in radioactivity monitoring of US mosques and other Muslims organizations after 9/11, MPAC asked to meet with the bureau, which it did in January 2016. How MPAC chose to frame its concerns and demands is telling. MPAC's president told the FBI, "It is crucial that the American Muslim community be informed of and included in discussions about homeland security. . . . The more information we have, the bet-ter our ability to help our government protect our nation, while ensuring that the civil rights of all Americans are protected."[39] By highlighting their eagerness to join the government in defending the homeland against potential threats, MPAC was contesting the construction of American Muslims as subjects in need of sur-veillance, establishing itself instead as an important partner in the fight against terrorism. At the same time, MPAC was reasserting that homeland security should not come at the expense of individuals' civil rights, positioning both issues as mu-tually dependent.

Travel Bans, Old and New

It is easy to understand why CAIR and other Muslim organizations would con-sider the balance between counterterrorism and civil liberties to be of critical con-cern. Many of the gravest violations against the rights of Muslim citizens have been committed under the guise of security and the war on terror. None of these violations ring truer than the No Fly List and the practice of placing citizens on it *while* traveling abroad, a practice CAIR has deemed tantamount to the "extra-judicial exile of American citizens."[40] In contesting the practice, CAIR argued that the government was denying citizens some of their most basic constitutional rights, as protected by Fourteenth Amendment citizenship guarantees. In Janu-ary 2011, the organization sued the Department of Justice and the FBI on behalf of Gulet Mohamed, an eighteen-year-old American who was placed on the list while traveling to Kuwait and claimed he had been tortured and coerced to an-swer questions without legal representation while in detention. CAIR's lawsuit states, "The United States [was] depriving Mr. Mohamed of perhaps the most ba-sic prerogative of American citizenship: the right to be in the United States."[41] Following the lawsuit, the federal government agreed to arrange for Mohamed's return to the United States while the case was pending. In 2014, the court ruled that the DHS redress program in place for those who had been placed on the list was "constitutionally inadequate."[42] In September 2019, the same federal judge, Anthony J. Trenga of the Fourth Circuit Court, ruled that the government's database of "known or suspected terrorists" violated the rights of Americans on the list.[43]

MPAC was also active in contesting the No Fly List, but rather than going to court or drawing media attention to the issue, Al-Marayati told me he had worked closely and quietly with the Bush administration to get people off the list: "We actually engaged on homeland security to get the rights afforded to our community that they deserve, like every other American."[44] Al-Marayati had personal experience with the No Fly List. In December 2004, he recounted, in a poignant open letter, his detention and interrogation after returning to the United States from a family vacation to Mexico: "We returned home to Los Angeles, only to face some disconcerting homeland insecurity."[45] He was interrogated about the purpose of his travels, his charitable donations, and whether those charities sent money overseas. Throughout the ordeal, he states, his main concern was that his children would witness something that would cause them to resent their homeland. He recounts a question his twelve-year-old son asked while they were in detention: "What about the Pledge of Allegiance, where it says liberty and justice is for all. Don't they have to believe in it, too?"

Countless Muslim citizens have complained about undue harassment and religious questioning by agents of Customs and Border Protection (CBP)—an agency that has, for years, engaged in religious profiling and violated the constitutional rights of Muslim citizens by unlawfully questioning them about their personal religious beliefs and practices.[46] In early 2017, CAIR filed a complaint with the CBP, the Department of Homeland Security, and the Department of Justice "over reports of systematic questioning of American-Muslim citizens by CBP about their religious and political views," including such questions as "Are you a devout Muslim?" "What mosque do you attend?" "Do you pray five times a day?" and "Why do you have a Quran in your luggage?"[47]

For many people, traveling elicits a mix of feelings—fear, anxiety, the thrill of the unknown. For Muslim citizens, these feelings are heightened, as traveling and borders become a test and measure of their belongingness to their nation. As the sociologist Mucahit Bilici has noted, "Airports are the internal borders of the nation. As entry and exit points to the nation, airports provide a unique perspective on questions of sovereignty and identity."[48] No recent event has lent as much credence to this insight as President Trump's January 27, 2017, executive order banning immigration from seven Muslim-majority countries, known to critics as the "Muslim ban."[49]

The executive order and two subsequent iterations were the focus of much public and legal dispute. The president and his supporters argued that it was a necessary and long-overdue step to address national security concerns and begin the process of protecting US national borders. Critics contested that it was an unconstitutional violation of religious freedom and pointed to Trump's campaign promises of "a total and complete shutdown of Muslims entering the United States"—a message that remained on the Trump website long after his inauguration. An amicus curiae brief filed by the Southern Poverty Law Center and other civil rights organizations argued forcefully that the order was "born as a political maneuver designed to spark and capitalize on religious and racial animus [and] entrenched into law at the first opportunity after the current administration took office."[50] Although the majority of the world's Muslims were not barred from entry, Trump's original executive order barred *only* people from Muslim-majority countries, an act many saw as a demarcation with chilling consequences for Muslims living in the United States. The other two iterations of the order, including version 3.0, allowed to go into full effect on June 26, 2018, by the Supreme Court of the United States, did little to conceal the fact that Muslims were the main target group.[51]

From the day President Trump announced the ban, Muslim American organizations began to contest it. CAIR, MPAC, the Muslim Justice League, and others filed multiple lawsuits and amicus briefs (and joined other coalitions' legal challenges) on behalf of Muslim citizens and foreign nationals residing in the United States. In a press release announcing the filing of the first of these lawsuits in January 2017, Nihad Awad said that policies such as the Muslim ban were not only discriminatory, they were outright dangerous: "Trump is threatening who we are as Americans."[52] According to CAIR's national attorney Gadeir Abbas, the executive order amounts to religious gerrymandering, dividing people into favored and disfavored groups based on their faith. He feared the ban would not only affect those foreign nationals denied entry to the United States but also extend to Muslim citizens and permanent residents, who would be unable to reunite with family members, renew immigration documents, or be seen as equal citizens under the law. Abbas's fears were well-founded; the human impacts of the ban have been heartbreaking, as Shaima Swileh's case makes clear. Families have been separated, individuals have been prevented from seeking life-altering medical care, and students have had their futures upended.

In addition to engaging in litigation and public pressure campaigns, organizations also mobilized around the Muslim ban by engaging with elected officials and making their discontent—as voters—known. For anyone keeping tabs, MPAC made available an impressive document listing the public stance of all sitting senators, house representatives, attorneys general, and governors re-

Let's repeal the ban!

Two years ago, you showed up at airports, took to the streets, and offered legal aid. Will you show your support once more?

Take action and urge Congress to support the **NO BAN Act**. It will terminate the Muslim Ban, better protect individuals from being denied entry on the basis of their faith, and limit the ability of future Presidents to impose similar bans.

mpac.org/nobanact

FIGURE 6.   "Let's repeal the ban!" action alert. Reproduced with the permission of the Muslim Public Affairs Council.

garding the executive orders, along with their specific comments on the issue, the year in which they would be up for reelection, and their contact information.[53] The message was clear: American Muslims would not accept being turned into second-class citizens. They would use their constitutionally granted rights to contest the ban through the courts, make their demands clear to their elected officials, and demonstrate their influence at the voting booth. The Supreme Court decision to allow the last version of the ban to remain in effect indefinitely was a heavy blow for Muslim and other organizations that had fought against it. In a press conference held on June 26, 2018, the day of the ruling, Nihad Awad said that the decision gave the Trump administration "a free hand to inject discrimination against a particular faith back into our immigration system, which was rejected more than fifty years ago."[54]

During its early days in office, the administration toyed with other policy ideas through which to target Muslims. Fears of a "Muslim registry" began soon after reports started circulating that Trump was open to the idea.[55] Nonetheless, he was not the first to plant this idea; it emerged in the aftermath of the 9/11 attacks, with the Bush administration's NSEERS special registry, discussed in chapter 2. CAIR responded through its "Register Me First" campaign, establishing a website where non-Muslims could do just that. The site stated simply, "If they want to register American Muslims, they will have to #RegisterMeFirst," before prompting individuals to sign their names.[56]

At the many public events I attended in 2017 and early 2018, Muslim community leaders regularly voiced fears of a Muslim registry, reiterating the need to create a "protective wall around the most vulnerable amongst us." One leader encouraged the audience to each donate one dollar to a Muslim American organization of their choice to "get on the Muslim registry," the argument being that the government would use records of charitable giving to Muslim organizations to compile such a list.

Unmasking the Islamophobia Network

Why do often well-intended public officials agree to policies and legislation that disproportionately affect Muslims? What explains the rise of anti-Muslim sentiment? Who is really behind the efforts to demonize Islam, Muslims, and, by extension, the 3.35 million Muslim citizens who call America home? Answering these questions, and making those answers widely known, is an important domestic mission of Muslim advocacy groups. They have concluded that behind many of the most overtly anti-Muslim policies and proposals being promoted is a group of small, ideological, well-financed, and deeply committed group of individuals, a group they have dubbed "the Islamophobia network." Their mission, according to CAIR, is to "promote prejudice against or hatred of Islam and Muslims" and ensure that anti-Muslim bias is codified into US law.[57] A recent report published by the Othering and Belonging Institute at UC Berkeley confirms these claims. It finds that Islamophobia in the United States has become an increasingly strategic national movement with a well-defined policy and legislative agenda, particularly since the 2010 "Ground Zero Mosque" controversy. According to Basima Sisemore, one of the report's authors, anti-Muslim groups have sought "to legalize the othering of Muslims, as well as to perpetuate a fear of Sharia, Islam and, ultimately, Muslims."[58]

Exposing how they work to accomplish these goals, as well as the links between donors, elected officials, and anti-Muslim activists, has become an important mission of Muslim advocacy organizations in the United States. They do this by relying on the characteristic advocacy tactic of "naming and shaming"—exposing, publicizing, and condemning anti-Muslim groups as hate groups. Muslim organizations are careful to clarify that "questioning Islam or Muslims" and condemning crimes committed by individual Muslims is not Islamophobia; targeting Muslims and creating an environment that endangers their constitutional rights is. One technique anti-Muslim organizations have used is supporting legislation that directly and indirectly targets US Muslims. Since 2010, one-hundred-twenty "anti-sharia" bills have been introduced in forty-two states, and fifteen have been enacted. According to the American Bar Association, these bills "are attempting to do precisely what our founding fathers sought to prevent when they crafted our Constitution and Bill of Rights: deny fundamental rights to a group of citizens based on the vote of a state legislature."[59] Similarly, the ACLU has argued that religious laws have long been recognized in US courts and that singling out Islamic law would deny Muslim citizens the right to have important issues of marriage, divorce, adoption, and inheritance, to name a few, adjudicated in accordance with Islamic law, amounting to a violation of their First Amendment rights to freely practice their religion.

In a 2016 report, CAIR lists more than thirty groups as the "inner core" of the Islamophobia network. This inner core is funded by a small number of large donors, who collectively donated more than $200 million between 2008 and 2013 alone.[60] These donors typically present themselves as (and thus can hide behind the veneer of) not-for-profit organizations, think tanks, research centers, or blogs. They use seemingly innocuous names, such as Citizens for National Security, Center for the Study of Political Islam, and the American Freedom Law Center. The largest amongst them is ACT for America, with 635 chapters across the country and a membership base of 175,000 individuals.[61] Its stated purpose is to "educate citizens and public officials to impact policy involving national security and defeating terrorism"; however, according to the Southern Poverty Law Center (which lists ACT for America as an anti-Muslim hate group), its goal is to advance anti-Muslim legislation and flood the American public with hate speech demonizing Muslims. Its founder, Brigitte Gabriel, is known for making incendiary statements about Muslims and Islam. She has said that a "practicing Muslim cannot be a loyal citizen of the United States" and that terrorists are nothing other than "very devout followers of Mohammad."[62]

ACT for America and other anti-Muslim organizations have promoted the narrative that Uddin writes so forcefully against: that Islam is not a religion but a political ideology (and a totalitarian one, at that). This fringe and discredited claim has been echoed by individuals in President Trump's administration, including his first pick for national security adviser, General Michael Flynn, who also happens to serve on the board of ACT for America. In a speech after Trump's election in 2016, Flynn told an audience, "Islam is a political ideology. . . . It will mask itself as a religion globally and especially in the West, especially in the United States, because it can hide behind and protect itself by what we call freedom of religion."[63] Not surprisingly, the group's founder has boasted that her organization has a "direct line to Donald Trump and has played a fundamental role in shaping his views and suggest[ing] policies with respect to radical Islam."[64]

Another way Muslim organizations have sought to shame and discredit these organizations among the broader US public is by demonstrating their links to white nationalist groups. Following the 2016 elections, these links became clearer and easier to show. On June 10, 2017, ACT for America organized anti-Muslim marches across the United States to protest what they claimed was the "creeping" of sharia law into American courts and the negative impacts of Muslim immigration on the United States. The Southern Poverty Law Center reported that many of these rallies were widely attended by white supremacist and neo-Nazi groups.[65] Although ACT for America tried to distance itself from extremist groups—especially following the violent Unite the Right rally in Charlottesville, Virginia, on August 11 and 12, 2017, which ended in the death of Heather Heyer, a 32-year-old counterprotester—the anti-Muslim movement has become part and parcel of the broader white nationalist movement that helped catapult Trump into the presidency of the United States. This is not entirely surprising. Many of the themes that propelled ACT for America and other anti-Muslim organizations onto the national stage are at the core of the white nationalist movement. Chief among them are immigration and refugee resettlement.

The Prophet Was an Immigrant, Too

Immigration is an issue that affects large numbers of Muslims around the world. In the United States, two-thirds of Muslims are either immigrants or the children of immigrants. It is therefore no surprise that Muslim advocacy organizations have made the subject of immigration reform an important aspect of their domestic agendas. These advocacy organizations argue that there are economic and moral reasons for why Muslims should be at the forefront of this issue. Economically, they posit, an aging US population will require an ample supply of low-skill workers who can care for the nation's elders. Meanwhile, growing the American economy also depends on the corporations' ability to attract high-skilled workers from around the world. Their ability to do that, according to these organizations, requires reforming the current immigration system to respond to changing global dynamics. Equally important, Muslim organizations frame immigration reform as a moral issue for Muslims, claiming that "Quranic and Prophetic teachings call on us to treat our fellow human beings with respect and establish justice on earth." Finally, engagement on the issue is a way for US Muslims to demonstrate their belongingness to their nation. Simply put, "as citizens of the United States, American Muslims should have a voice in issues that affect the public interest of the nation they reside in and call home."[66]

Toward these ends, in 2013, MPAC launched a national campaign to address immigration reform and outline opportunities for Muslims to become involved in the immigration debate. The campaign, titled "A Nation of Immigrants," was promoted as a faith-based and pragmatic policy contribution that sought to uphold the "shared American and Islamic values of freedom, equality, justice and human dignity."[67] Thus, from the perspective of MPAC and other Muslim advocacy organizations, engagement on these domestic policy questions is as much about a necessary involvement with issues disproportionally affecting the Muslim community as it is about the rooting of Muslims and Islam in America. This rooting happens in two ways—first, through the discourse of commonality between the Islamic and American values these advocacy organizations rely on to explain and rationalize their involvement with immigration reform, and second, by encouraging Muslims to take action, practice their citizenship rights, and become visible voices in this debate.

"A Nation of Immigrants" encouraged individuals to call and write to their members of Congress, engage the media, write op-eds, and participate in immigration-related community events. It highlighted three talking points that Muslim constituents should address in their communications: (1) immigration is good for the economy; (2) reform should include a comprehensive path to citizenship for the eleven million undocumented immigrants in the United States; and (3) all immigrants, regardless of nationality, should be treated equally. This last point is particularly important for Muslim immigrants, who tend to be the main targets of any proposed additional screenings and background checks.

Although Muslim organizations were overwhelmingly in favor of the bipartisan comprehensive immigration plan proposed in 2013 (the Border Security, Economic Opportunity, and Immigration Modernization Act), they were troubled by a provision proposed by Senator Lindsay Graham (R-SC) that would allow additional screenings for immigrants from countries "known to pose a threat, or that contains groups or organizations that pose a threat to the national security of the United States."[68] Muslim advocacy organizations understood this as coded language referring to Muslim immigrants.

After President Trump took office—following up on campaign promises of deporting undocumented immigrants, ending DACA protections for young DREAMers, building a wall at the US-Mexico border, restricting the refugee resettlement program, and limiting immigration from Muslim-majority countries—the issue of immigration reform took on newfound urgency for Muslim organizations. They responded by intensifying their lobbying efforts on behalf of the communities they considered most vulnerable under a Trump presidency: DACA recipients and the undocumented. During the first Muslim Advocacy Day on Capitol Hill after the elections, leaders demanded action on these issues, calling on members of Congress to support two specific bills: the Bar Removal of Individuals who Dream and Grow our Economy Act (H.R. 496/S. 128), also known as the BRIDGE Act, and the No State Resources for Immigration Enforcement Act (H.R. 1446). The first bill sought to ensure the continued protection of DREAMers, even if President Trump were to discontinue their DACA status. The second would prohibit state and local officials from carrying out immigration enforcement duties under the Safe Communities program, which, according to Muslim advocacy organizations, catches non-criminals, separates families, and diverts important resources from fighting real crimes.

Hill Day participants were reminded that not only should Latinx people be considered allies but that many Latinx in the United States *are* Muslims. About 6 percent of US Muslims are now Latinx, and Latinx converts are one of the largest growing segments of the Muslim American population.[69] Further, although data on the number of Muslim DACA and Temporary Protected Status recipients are lacking, there is a growing awareness that these are not just "Latinx" issues, since many Muslims hold these liminal immigration statuses. One of the top twenty-five countries DACA recipients list as their place of birth, Pakistan, is majority Muslim; a second one, India, has a substantial Muslim population.[70] As one activist told me, "Many of our community members have DACA, but Muslims still think of immigration as a Latino issue. It's starting to change, especially among the young people. Immigration is a Muslim issue too; it's a civil rights issue." Reflecting this change, in recent years, Muslim organizations have held and joined dozens of moving interfaith rallies in support of immigrant communities and other marginalized Americans.

The leaders I spoke with stressed that protecting vulnerable communities is deeply rooted in their religious faith; it is something they are called to do. In early 2017, when Trump threatened to phase out DACA protections, sending waves of fear across immigrant communities, Muslim activists staged an interfaith act of

FIGURE 7.   MPAC Interfaith Rally for Immigrant Rights. Reproduced with the permission of the Muslim Public Affairs Council.

civil disobedience on Capitol Hill that led to their arrest. Upon their release, Omar Suleiman, a prominent imam, scholar, and activist, said, "I'm proud of the leaders who came out yesterday. . . . It was an honor to be arrested with you. I pray that millions are inspired by your leadership."[71] Linda Sarsour, also arrested at the event, shared some thoughts and images of the event in a Facebook post: "We will stand with Dreamers everyday if we have to. Proud of my leaders . . . for showing me what faith and worship look like in action. I love my beautiful faith, Islam, because it is rooted in social justice and compassion for all people. No border, no papers, just respect dignity and humanity. Honored to be arrested alongside our Jewish sisters and brothers." The hashtag #MuslimsforDreams began to trend, with Suleiman and other activists keen on showing that immigration reform and the protection of immigrants were Muslim issues, too. Videos of protests, sit-ins, and calls to actions were shared widely, as were images of activists being arrested for engaging in civil disobedience. Zaid Shakir, a prominent American Muslim imam and the cofounder of Zaytuna College, the first Muslim undergraduate institution in the nation, penned a moving poem, titled "Let them Fly: Ode to a Little Dreamer." With it, he shared a photograph of himself and the executive director of CAIR's Michigan chapter, Dawud Walid, lifting a young girl. The poem reads:

> The butterflies can no longer go home.
> We have destroyed the grounds on which they nest.
> And if this little butterfly can't roam
> Then how can we as a country be blessed?
> [. . .]
> So we say to this little girl fly high!
> And let your lovely smile serve as your guide.
> The dream inside your heart will never die,
> And we thank God He's placed us on your side.[72]

Shakir's poem echoes the themes at the heart of Muslim advocacy in the United States—protecting the vulnerable, sharing a sense of collective responsibility, being on the right side of history, and advancing what is best for the nation by advancing what is just for all who call it home.

Then, in April 2018, attorney general Jeff Sessions announced the Trump administration's "zero tolerance" policy. Any immigrant entering the United States without authorization would be referred to the Department of Justice for criminal prosecution, a policy that expanded the 2005 Operation Streamline program. More than 2,600 children were separated from their parents and placed in the custody of the Department of Health and Human Services' Office of Refugee Resettlement, which proceeded to place them in shelters across the country.[73] When news of children being systematically ripped from their parents (some of the children as young as eight months old) began to spread, people across the country took to the streets in protest. Muslim leaders joined other faith leaders to protest the policy, a policy CAIR described simply as "unconscionable." Suleiman compared the detention facilities to the Syrian refugee camps he visited twice yearly, "but there, at least we could interact with the children, provide them with some comforts," referring to the fact that his only interaction with the detained migrant children at the border was through the tinted, soundproof windows of the bus on which they were being transported—an experience that, he said, left him deeply shaken.

Muslim organizations rely on a wide range of advocacy strategies—working with the federal government as advisors and liaisons, taking the government to court, engaging in public outreach campaigns, and naming and shaming the peddlers of Islamophobia. The strategy varies with the issue and the responsiveness of the party in office. CAIR litigator Gadeir Abbas sums it up as follows:

> There was a debate as to what is the appropriate relationship to have with an Obama administration that, you know, isn't saying pejorative things about the Muslim community, but is droning people all the time, it's exploding the size of the watchlist, . . . it's his FBI that is trafficking in anti-Muslim training materials. In the face of that, what should the Muslim community's relationship be with the Obama administration? The issues are really easy under the Trump administration. There's no room for engagement. . . . And I think because there's no inside game anymore, there's really not much space to engage with the Trump administration on many issues because they use the Muslim community as a target to express general racial animus. So I think it has made the advocacy more adversarial. . . . It's also, I think, added an edge to Muslim advocacy generally, like large-scale mobilization . . . and that's great.[74]

Muslim American advocacy is no longer constrained to traditionally "Muslim issues"—if such issues ever existed. Instead, it is in flux, growing and responding to what society demands of it. As one leader told me, "The things we, as Muslims, care about are the same things that the rest of Americans care about: health care for our families, education for our children, being able to put food on the table, living with dignity." New generations of Muslims are continuing to push the envelope and expand that list to be ever more reflective of their concerns. Indeed, it is increasingly common to see topics such as gun control, access to adequate and affordable health care, and the environment discussed in Muslim American advocacy circles. A 2018 survey conducted by the Islamic Society of North America finds that more than 90 percent of US Muslims are concerned about climate change and believe they have a religious obligation to care about the issue.[75] Survey data also show that American Muslims are deeply concerned about transnational issues and US foreign policy, particularly toward Muslim-majority parts of the world. And Muslim organizations and their leaders are not as afraid as they once were to follow their lead and become involved in these issues.

ADVOCATING FOR THE MUSLIM *UMMAH*

The protection of religious freedoms at home and abroad are connected. It is part of who we are as American Muslims.

—Lori Saroya, author interview, December 18, 2017

Roughly two-thirds of Muslims in the United States say they feel a strong sense of belonging to the *ummah*, the global Muslim community.[1] This view is more common among Muslims born in the United States than it is among first-generation immigrants. This is not particularly unusual. For many ethnic groups, symbolic and emotional attachments to a homeland (real or imagined) continue to influence the process of settlement and integration into the host society, relations with so-called ethnic kin, and behavior toward both the places of origin and of settlement long after the act of migration.[2] For Muslims, the sense of belonging can be to a country of origin but it is also to the larger, global Muslim community and to the religious symbols of Islam. And, even though the majority of Muslims in the United States are not from the Middle East, the region holds particular significance for Muslims as "the origin of Islam" that houses Mecca and Medina, "the holy sites that Muslims are required to visit."[3] This often translates into a degree of emotional affiliation and, consequently, an interest in events and policies perceived to impact the region.

Equally significant is the fact that the line dividing foreign and domestic issues for Muslims (and many other ethnic and religious minorities) is not clear.[4] For American Muslims, the war on terror and the perception that Muslims (inside and outside the United States) are targets has meant that US foreign policy is not foreign to Muslims but part of their daily realities and experiences.[5] This is not an altogether new phenomenon. Since the era of Western colonialism, Muslims have been discursively associated with Arabs and the Middle East and depicted as violent, irrational, and backward, as manifested in the discourse surrounding Muslim Americans' foreignness and potential risk since September 11, 2001.[6] Not surprisingly, Muslim organizations are quick to emphasize that any domestic counterterrorism initiative must consider how US foreign policy helps fuel extremism and radicalism. According to CAIR, for example, "any honest discussion about countering the appeal of violent extremism must include a very public component addressing some U.S. foreign policy choices."[7]

Polling data corroborates these observations and underscores the overwhelming emphasis that Muslims place on questions of US foreign policy, particularly when compared to the rest of the American public.[8] In fact, in a 2012 exit poll conducted by CAIR, 92 percent of American Muslims said issues related to international relations were important to them.[9] This is not only true of foreign-born Muslims, since nonimmigrant Muslims also follow international news disproportionately and show a higher level of knowledge regarding US foreign policy.[10] But what about their opinions on specific foreign policy issues? And, how do their opinions compare to those held by the broader American public? Even the scant data available on these questions provide some glimpse into what American Muslims think of some of these issues. The first thing the existing data make clear is that Muslims are as concerned as the rest of Americans about the threat of "Islamic extremism" at home and abroad. However, the vast majority (79 percent) say there is little support for extremism among the Muslim American community. And, although Muslims have been consistently more opposed to the war in Afghanistan than the general public (48 percent versus 35 percent), their opinions regarding the Palestinian-Israeli conflict are largely on par with the rest of Americans: 62 percent say there is a way for Israel and Palestinian rights to coexist, and 81 percent support a two-state solution.[11]

These and other transnational concerns and attachments are reflected in the work of Muslim advocacy organizations and their engagement on a variety of issues related to US foreign policy. But it would be a mistake to view their advocacy in this area merely as an attempt to represent the community's interests. Instead, foreign policy advocacy is part of their overall mission to integrate and normalize Muslims and Islam in the United States, as it allows them to signal support for fundamental American values and demonstrate their commitment to US national interests above all else. The importance of this becomes clearer if we remember that the loyalty of US Muslims and the compatibility of Islam and democracy have been increasingly questioned in the post-9/11 context. Whether working to build a mosque, praying in public, or calling out Israel's human rights violations against the Palestinians, Muslims' constitutionally protected behavior is viewed as somehow subversive by a significant number of their American compatriots. As an illustration, in 2004, almost half of Americans believed the civil rights of US Muslims should be restricted, and 27 percent believed they should be asked to register with the federal government.[12]

Fast forward to 2009, when 46 percent of all Americans—and 55 percent of conservative Republicans—believed that Islam was more likely than other faiths to encourage violence. Only 22 percent believed that Islam and their own religions had a lot in common.[13] By 2017, 49 percent still believed "at least some" of their fellow Muslim citizens were "anti-American." In this context of heightened suspicion regarding the belongingness of American Muslims, it could be reasonably expected that the interest groups that claim to represent the community would focus their policy engagement solely on domestic issues and recoil from engaging in US foreign policy debates, particularly when their views ran counter to those espoused by the official US foreign policy establishment. Nonetheless, engagement on foreign policy issues perceived to affect the *ummah* has remained an important aspect of their work.

This is puzzling, since their foreign policy activism seems to contradict their interests, helping fuel perceptions of Muslims as outsiders concerned not with American interests but with those of other nations. CAIR explicitly stated that many attacks against it refer "to foreign affairs issues, particularly the Palestinian-Israeli conflict,"[14] and many of the people I spoke with told me that after 9/11, getting involved in issues related to foreign policy was risky business. As one respondent put it, "We didn't even know what evidence the government could use against us. Donating to causes we cared about became dangerous. We were not unafraid."

In such circumstances why would an organization choose to bear the cost of involvement? Think of it this way: Rather than a sign of the community's "divided loyalties," foreign policy advocacy provides Muslim organizations with an opportunity to present themselves as valuable "insider" experts to the US policy establishment, particularly on issues related to the Middle East. Consequently, involvement in foreign policy issues provides a number of purposive benefits through which to access the policy dialogue as an American minority concerned with protecting the national security and long-term interests of the United States. In so doing, these organizations communicate the belongingness of Muslims in America and advance their integration in the United States.

As scholars of ethnic lobbying tell us, interest groups play an important role in engendering ethnic solidarity and translating group grievances into legitimate collective demands. Standard techniques are to establish a commonality of concerns between group members and the broader society and to rely on a discourse of historical trauma and/or injustice to legitimize their claims.[15] Whether supporting a just resolution to the Palestinian-Israeli conflict, promoting democratization in the Middle East, or highlighting the plight of targeted minorities, such as the Rohingya in Myanmar, Muslim advocacy organizations frame their engagement in foreign policy issues around a discourse of justice and human rights. Through this framework, they present Islamic and American values as synergetic and communicate what it means to be an American Muslim. Accordingly, the values of social justice, mercy, equity, freedom (including freedom of religion), and moderation are at the core of the American Muslim identity, as advanced through these organizations' foreign advocacy efforts. In the following section, I delve more deeply into this argument by examining some of the foreign policy issues these advocacy organizations are most actively engaged in: (1) the Palestinian-Israeli conflict, (2) democratization in the Muslim-majority world, (3) religious freedoms and the plight of Muslim minorities around the world, and (4) US policy toward Iran.

Palestine: The "Heart" of the Muslim *Ummah*

American Muslims consistently rank the Palestinian-Israeli conflict as their most important foreign policy issue. When vetting candidates during the 2012 presidential election, for example, two-thirds said the conflict was "very important" in their selection.[16] Not surprisingly, they have strong attitudes regarding the United States' role and responsibility in solving the conflict. The overwhelming majority, 85 percent, favor a two-state solution and envision an independent Palestinian state coexisting alongside its Israeli neighbor. Their position seems to be in agreement with that of American Jews, 78 percent of whom also support a two-state solution.[17]

Especially for those familiar with the historical and cultural significance of the Palestinian-Israeli conflict, Muslim advocacy groups' involvement speaks to a broader sense of identification with Palestine and its people. According to Shibley Telhami, a Palestinian scholar of the Middle East, "it is not uncommon for a people to have a significant historical experience, intense and painful enough to help shape perception."[18] For many in the Jewish community, the memory of the Holocaust continues to be the lens through which they perceive current events and experiences. Similarly, for many Muslims, Palestine has come to symbolize the West's greed and deceit, as well as the painful history of failure, defeats, and humiliation Muslims have suffered, not only at the hands of the West but also because of the corruption and ineptness of their own leaders. Aware of these religious and symbolic attachments, Muslim American interest groups have mobilized around the question of Palestine as a strategy to attract support, secure some degree of group cohesion, and make themselves relevant to the policy establishment, thus legitimizing their position as the representatives of this larger collective.

The conflict provides Muslim advocacy organizations with a unifying grievance—the United States' biased support of Israel—in which they locate the culpable (US policymakers) and prescribe a remedy (pressuring policymakers to shift their strategy and focus on promoting the values that *we*, as a society, hold dear). Indeed, Muslim American organizations are seeking a *just* resolution, not simply an end to the conflict. As Salam Al-Marayati explains, "Palestine is an issue that unites Muslims because the issue goes back to the beginning of colonial rule in the Muslim world and is the longest ongoing occupation of our time. The conflict also relates to Jerusalem, a city that historically has been shared by and is significant to Muslims, Christians and Jews. Now its shared status is threatened by occupation and the incessant desire of the West to control the Muslim world by striking at its heart, Palestine."[19] Thus, Palestine is represented as "the heart" of the Muslim *ummah*—its most vital and important part. The Palestinian-Israeli conflict, a symbol of the long history of Western colonial meddling: its last visible, palpable, unapologetic remainder.

Muslim advocacy leaders I spoke with consistently highlighted the conflict's centrality. Al-Marayati was direct, referring to it as "one of the most important to us." CAIR's former legislative director, Corey Saylor, emphasized its impact on US national security: "We [CAIR] tend to talk about the conflict from the angle of American national interests. . . . If America were to be seen as the party that brought a just and lasting peace to that situation, that would just obliterate one of those arguments that our enemies use against us." I heard Saylor's comment echoed by many others who emphasized that terrorist organizations exploit the conflict to stir resentments and incite violence. The plight of the Palestinians was the first foreign policy issue that came up in my conversation with Rameez Abid, the communication director for the Islamic Circle of North America's social justice division. When I asked him why that was, he told me,

> The conflict is settled into our consciousness because it is one of the oldest in the Middle East and it is what gave rise to a lot of extremist groups in the Muslim world. . . . So it is kind of engrained into our consciousness, generationally . . . that's the thing that started it all. Even though a lot of young kids may not know it today, but we know that when Israel was first formed, [Israelis] were behaving like terrorists. They were basically bombing places trying to claim the land for themselves. . . . This was a colonial project. It still is. . . . It's one of the oldest conflicts, and it's what gave rise to everything else afterwards. Even Osama Bin-Laden, when he was asked, he brought up Palestine, he brought up U.S. support for [Israel]. So, I think this causes a lot of problems in the Middle East, and so much could be resolved if you just solved this problem.[20]

Muslim advocates have thus framed the Palestinian-Israeli conflict (and the United States' involvement in it) as a denial of group rights, or, as MPAC's Haris Tarin put it, one of "the great moral failures of our generation." Through this frame, mobilizing around the conflict is legitimized as a way to rectify a historical injustice and hold the United States accountable to its claims of the core values of justice, liberty, and the protection of human rights. Most importantly, these organizations link their advocacy for a just resolution to long-term US security interests. This strategic framing is significant because "ethnic minority interests are successful to the extent that they advance policies that are supported by the general public."[21]

In other words, advocacy regarding this conflict, and toward US foreign policy in general, is framed primarily around US national interests. As the "leader of the free world," the argument goes, the United States has a vested interest in upholding international law and supporting a two-state solution. Not doing so erodes US legitimacy at home and abroad and fuels anti-American sentiments around the world. Furthermore, although MPAC agrees that protecting and promoting Israel's security is in the national interest of the United States, it also claims that: "There is no U.S. national interest in expanding Israel's borders beyond those of 1967. In fact, our complicity with Israel's attempt to do just that through war, settlements, and annexation has been one of the main sources of resentment and anger in the Arab and Muslim world toward the United States. We gain nothing and lose much from this misbegotten policy."[22]

Through such framings, these advocacy organizations perform their roles as defenders of the nation, driven by their duties as citizens to promote the best interests of their homeland. They criticize US policy toward the conflict not because it does not benefit the Palestinian cause but because it hurts the American one. Maher Hathout explained it to me this way: "As Muslims, we are supposed to be persons of integrity and of truth and so we are very critical about the blind support of the United States to Israel, and we always clarify: not the support, the *blind* support. You support a country against the interests and the values of the United States, so somebody should have to say, 'Stop it,' for the sake of America."

Advocating for the "Right of Return" and the Right to Resist

Since their early days, Muslim advocacy organizations have consistently lobbied in favor of the two-state solution based on United Nations Resolutions 242 and 338, which call for Israel's withdrawal from territory captured during the 1967 war. They have used a combination of tactics, contesting official US policy through public opinion campaigns, publicizing the plight of the Palestinians and the violations committed by the state of Israel, holding vigils and rallies, testifying in congressional hearings, and writing policy briefs and reports for elected officials—even though few have heeded their advice.

They have also proposed concrete steps for the United States, the most basic and reiterated of which are calls for "mutual recognition" and the creation of a viable Palestinian state along the 1967 borders, with East Jerusalem as its capital. These are challenges to the discourse that demands unilateral Palestinian recognition of Israel, calling instead for the United States and the international community to recognize both states' (Israel's and Palestine's) right to exist. For a two-state solution to be feasible, they further argue, the United States must demand the dismantling of all settlements in the West Bank, Jerusalem, and the Golan Heights.[23] Although the United States has, for years, been unable or unwilling to pressure Israel to meet these demands, President Trump's election and the policies he enacted during his first year in office have essentially upended official US policy toward the conflict. In particular, his decision on December 6, 2017, to recognize Jerusalem as Israel's capital and to begin the process of moving the US embassy from its current location in Tel Aviv not only reverses seventy years of international consensus regarding the city's status but also threatens the United States' future ability to serve, and be viewed, as a legitimate peace broker.

Not surprisingly, Muslim organizations were highly critical of the decision. Emphasizing the historical and religious significance of the city for all three Abrahamic faiths, MPAC argued that the United States was "violating the religious freedom of Palestinians by recognizing Jerusalem as the capital of the Jewish state." American Muslims for Palestine wrote that the decision "could potentially inflame the Muslim world, unleash unrest in the Holy Land, and endanger our national security."[24] In a statement issued on December 7, the US Council of Muslim Organizations called Trump's decision "offensive and provocative,"[25] adding that "it harms American interests worldwide and puts beyond the pale the role of the United States as an honest broker of peace in the Middle East." A week later, Muslim organizations planned a rally to protest the declaration, which was attended by hundreds of American Muslims and others opposed to the decision. The rally's slogan was a direct repudiation of the president's announcement: "Jerusalem Forever Capital of Palestine."

Muslim organizations are acutely aware of the conflict's symbolism and the emotional attachments US Muslims feel toward it. Presenting current US policy as biased and dangerous cues their audience to the fact that a grave injustice has been committed, engendering a sense of moral outrage. This is an important legitimation tactic, for just as emotional incentives can motivate individuals to join movements, they can also motivate people to support the groups that claim to be working on their behalf.[26]

There is perhaps no better example of the reliance on symbolism and moral claims than MPAC's stance toward the Israeli West Bank Barrier, or Separation Wall, which the organization condemns as a grave violation of Palestinians' human rights and an obstruction to any peace prospects. Although Israel and the United States justify the wall as a security barrier against acts of terrorism, MPAC claims that its real purpose is to "annex large tracts of Palestinian land . . . the wall separates people from their land [and] severely breaches their right to freedom of movement, their right to property and their right to gain a livelihood."[27] What stronger way to speak as an American group, making American demands, than to echo that most American of sentiments—that all people are created equal, with inherent rights? The discursive construction of the wall as a threat to the inalienable rights articulated in the US Constitution, and granted to all people, signals that this is not a foreign concern; it is one that should concern all Americans.

CAIR's strategy has tended to focus on Israel's more immediate violations of US law, including against American citizens living in the region, at once contesting Israel's narrative of victimization and presenting Israel not as an indispensable ally of the United States but as a foreign country pursuing its own interests. This strategy was evident in the organization's response to the Israel-Gaza war in 2014. Speaking at a DC rally to protest the war, Nihad Awad declared, "I am upset with my government, because my government does not represent the values of America of peace, justice, and equality for all." He further proposed that the Israeli Defense Force should be renamed the "Israeli offensive against civilian population forces," declaring that Israel's targeting of civilians and civilian infrastructure was a "defiance to what we stand for as Americans."[28] Awad also argued that Israel was "a strategic liability on the United States," the implicit message being that our government is putting the interests of Israel ahead of those of the United States.

In a similar narrative thread, CAIR has "repeatedly questioned Israel's apparent violation of America's Arms Exports Control Act of 1978," arguing that the act requires "foreign governments receiving American weaponry" to use those weapons only for internal security and legitimate self-defense. Why would our elected officials support Israel at the expense of American interests? Ironically, the answer lies in the corrupting role of interest groups on the policy process: "AIPAC should have its hand off the United States congress," Awad said at the rally, because "they have corrupted our foreign policy. They have corrupted our political leaders." The only way to remedy the situation is for political leaders to "reclaim their allegiance to America and American values" (as opposed, it is to be assumed, to AIPAC and Israel).[29] This narrative positions CAIR, Muslim Americans, and others who criticize unconditional US support of Israel as American patriots seeking what is best for their country—countering frequent narratives that such criticism is un-American.

Muslim advocacy efforts also link US policy toward the Palestinian-Israeli conflict to one of the gravest threats to US national security: violent religious extremism. As Al-Marayati told me, "Longstanding conflicts, and particularly the Israeli-Palestinian conflict, [are] the main source of anti-American feelings in the Muslim world."[30] Drawing on the frame of US national security is an important legitimation tactic that challenges perceptions of Muslims as the source of the threat and presents them as patriotic fellow citizens working to advance their nation's interests. This reframing highlights Israel as the main source of threat and presents American citizens as direct targets of Israeli violence. During the 2006 Israel-Hezbollah War, for example, CAIR called on the United States to safeguard the lives of more than twenty-five thousand of its citizens living in Lebanon: "If a call for the full cessation of attacks on the civilian population of a U.S. ally is too much to ask for, at least we can demand that Israel stop its bombing campaign long enough to evacuate American citizens. The highest duty of any president is to protect the lives of Americans." Demanding this protection not only challenges the all-too-common portrayal of Palestinians and Muslims as inherently violent but also makes Muslim American citizens *visible*. In other words, claiming that "our" main duty is to protect "our" own citizens against a foreign threat shifts the source of danger from Palestinian (and Muslim) violence to Israeli violence waged upon American civilians living in the region—decisively asserting the belongingness of US Muslims to their nation.

Although CAIR focuses more of its advocacy on Israel's direct violations of US law, all of the US Muslim advocacy organizations I examined agree upon, and pursue, the major positions espoused by international law: the establishment of a viable Palestinian state alongside Israel, the right of return for all Palestinian refugees and their descendants, and the rights of occupied people to resist their occupiers. MPAC is clear in referring to the right of return as a nonnegotiable principle "in accordance with UN resolution 194."[31] CAIR describes the right of return as "a common position among those seeking justice for Palestinians." And American Muslims for Palestine movingly advocate for it in a 2016 video promoting the organization's annual conference. The video shows a young man packing a suitcase. He packs a Palestinian flag and an old key, like the thousands that Palestinian refugees carried with them for decades, believing they would one day use them to reenter their homes. The clip closes with three shots of white text on a black background:

> RETURN IS OUR RIGHT
> AND OUR DESTINY
> NEVER FORGET PALESTINE[32]

Such appeals uphold the right of return as a principle at the core of international law, a fundamental human right, legitimized on both legal and moral grounds.

Muslim advocacy groups generally support the Fourth Geneva Convention, "the right of occupied people to resist occupation."[33] As MPAC explains, "Palestinians have a right, derived from international law, to resist the Israeli occupation." However, this support extends only to what these organizations perceive as legitimate types of resistance, emphasizing nonviolent resistance, which MPAC promotes as "the most recommended course of action." The types of resistance they recommend are, inevitably, reflective of their position as American institutions, embedded in American civil life and influenced by the narrative of the country's civil rights movements.

I do not mean to suggest that nonviolent resistance is an exclusively American form of resistance. This sentiment does suggest, however, that these advocacy groups are quintessential American institutions, working within the American political system and making American policy demands. The limits of what they envision and promote as legitimate are thus determined by the specific institutional context in which they function. And so, even while aiming to challenge and ultimately change US policy, their very participation in the policy process serves to guarantee that the broader frameworks for seeing, interpreting, and speaking about the Palestinian-Israeli conflict are maintained and reproduced. Being aspiring policy "insiders," even insiders seeking change, influences their organizational identities and establishes the limits of what they can reasonably demand, while preventing other alternatives from being imagined. And so, while their policy demands seek to alter the status quo, they also reinscribe relatively stable proposals for bringing about change.

Boycott, Divestment, and Sanctions

The Boycott, Divestment, Sanctions (BDS) movement—a grassroots and Palestinian-led campaign to economically pressure Israel to meet its obligations under international law—has wide support among US Muslim advocacy groups, which describe it as "the most American way to resist."[34] CAIR's Legal Defense Fund has engaged in litigation on the issue, filing suits against state governments that have passed, or attempted to pass, legislation intended to make participating in BDS illegal. (Many public institutions around the country have included "No Boycotts of Israel" clauses in their employment contracts in an attempt to ban the award of state contracts to people or entities that support or engage in the BDS movement.)

For example, in December 2018, CAIR filed a lawsuit challenging Texas's Anti-BDS Act (H.B. 89) on behalf of Bahia Amawi, a speech pathologist who lost her job at a public school because she refused to sign such a contract. Amawi not only refused to sign the clause; she decided to sue, claiming the clause amounted to a violation of her constitutionally protected right to free speech. "I felt like my rights were taken away and that I had no choice in what products I could purchase," Amawi told the *Dallas Observer*, explaining her decision to go to court.[35] In April 2019, a district judge ruled in her favor, arguing that the statute served no purpose other than to "silence speech with which Texas disagrees."[36] The law was struck down as unconstitutional, and CAIR celebrated the decision as a landmark victory. It was, according to CAIR's national litigation director, Lena Masri, "a victory for the First Amendment."[37] Gadeir Abbas, one of the lead attorneys on the case, echoed Masri's comments, saying the decision was "a complete victory of the First Amendment against Texas's attempts to suppress speech in support of Palestine."[38]

When I sat down to speak with Abbas a few months before the ruling, anti-BDS legislation was weighing heavily on him. He was genuinely worried about the plaintiffs he and CAIR's legal team were representing, and he indicated that he sometimes found the whole thing disheartening. But, he told me, he was certain of two things: first, that the anti-BDS clauses were clearly unconstitutional; and second, that the courts would determine this to be the case. His faith in the courts was resolute and contagious. He spent much of our conversation explaining how anti-BDS laws were being introduced and passed in legislatures across the country—the result of a concerted effort by a small number of committed, right-wing, pro-Israel, and anti-Muslim groups that had garnered the support of Republican politicians for whom support of Israel is sacrosanct.

As I listened to him, I found myself thinking that, for American Muslims, the binary between domestic and foreign policy is simply nonexistent. They do not have the luxury of being removed from foreign policy considerations, of not paying attention; foreign policy finds its way into the most ordinary aspects of their lives, like signing an employment contract. Abbas's voice reverberated, bringing me back to the hotel lobby and the anti-BDS lawsuit we were discussing:

> Israel and its allies in the United States are trying to head off a well-orchestrated campaign. They are having states pass these laws that forbid state entities from contracting with people who are participating in BDS. It's an interesting area, where there are domestic efforts that seek to enforce foreign policy choices, or dissuade, or put obstacles in the way of Muslim Advocacy for Palestine. . . . Twenty-some states have passed laws like this. There has been a bunch of executive orders from governors. . . . Arizona is really kind of an extreme case. It required *any* public entity, in *every* contract that it submits with anybody, for the counterparty to certify that they do not engage in any kind of BDS activity. . . . So, the Muslim Student Association and Arizona State Uni-

versity said they wanted to invite American Muslims for Palestine . . . and Hatem Bazian to come to ASU and speak about BDS activism. . . . And then they had to send all these contracts requiring the participants to certify that they [did] not engage in any BDS activism, which, obviously, they can't do! [laughs] So, you know, we sued!

In line with the mainstream, Muslim advocacy organizations view litigation as a deeply American activity—a means of demonstrating that no one is above the law, holding government accountable to the people, and safeguarding the institutions of democracy. These are issues at the forefront of the Muslim American experience. Whether at home in the United States or abroad in the countries where many Muslim immigrants have roots, Muslims are continuously forced to think about democracy—and democracy promotion.

Democratization in the Muslim-Majority World

Aside from the Palestinian-Israeli conflict, the most lasting US involvement in the Middle East has revolved around regime change. Following the post-9/11 US invasions of Afghanistan and Iraq, the themes of democracy promotion and democratization gained increased political and international significance, with the US government attempting to legitimize its wars as steps in its broader strategy of bringing democracy and freedom to the region. The Bush administration drummed up support for the Iraq invasion by lying to the American people, telling them that Saddam Hussein possessed weapons of mass destruction. Deposing Hussein and establishing the foundations of a democratic state, the argument went, was necessary to ensure the safety of the United States and the world.[39] It would also make Iraq a beacon of democracy that other countries in the region would seek to emulate. That US-led invasion and subsequent occupation became an important focus of Muslim American advocacy, engendering a lively debate regarding the role US Muslims should play in advising, informing, and resisting their government's democratization efforts in the Arab and Muslim world.

On the surface, the policy reports, analyses, and recommendations these organizations produced were attempts to inform and influence the US foreign policy establishment. But, similar to their positions on the Palestinian-Israeli conflict, they were also negotiating and delimiting what could be legitimately argued and demanded. Their participation in foreign policy advocacy—attending government panels on democracy promotion, presenting their recommendations to elected officials, and producing foreign policy reports aimed at representatives of government—relied on a particular understanding of dissent and opposition from within, which they both reflected and helped reproduce through their engagement.[40]

Following the fall of Saddam Hussein, for example, MPAC released a statement declaring that it "wished Saddam Hussein had avoided this war by heeding our call . . . to step down from power."[41] MPAC was referring to demands it had made at the organization's annual convention on December 22, 2002, but it was also linking its demands to those of the United States. After all, who could forget former president George W. Bush's ultimatum on March 17, 2003: "Saddam Hussein and his sons must leave Iraq within 48 hours. Their refusal to do so will result in military conflict, commenced at a time of our choosing."[42] Some readers might be surprised to learn of a Muslim American organization's apparent support for President Bush's rationale for invading Iraq. If we approach advocacy as not just a claims-making practice but as a discursive site where Muslim American identity is performed and negotiated, MPAC's behavior is easier to understand. Even when critical of US policy, MPAC and other groups are speaking, first and foremost, as American organizations, driven by their duty to protect American interests and, consequently, by a desire to demarcate themselves and the communities they represent as "insiders."

Support should not be confused with acquiescence, however. Even though MPAC agreed with a limited intervention in Iraq, it remained critical and apprehensive of the scope of the mission, recommending the invasion be as short as possible to complete "our" responsibilities. Further, its initial agreement with the basic US policy goals of deposing Hussein and establishing the foundations of a functioning democratic state did not translate into support for subsequent US policy, particularly the long-term military occupation of Iraq. MPAC became increasingly critical of the prolonged conflict. Nevertheless, its initial agreement with a limited US mission to depose Hussein was remarkable, considering that at the time 75 percent of American Muslims were against the war.[43]

Their position becomes even less surprising when we consider the multiple audiences to which national Muslim American organizations are trying to appeal: fellow Muslim Americans, the broader American public, and the US policy establishment including policymakers and institutions such as the military, intelligence, and security. As Al-Marayati told me,

> Half of our [national] budget is on national security. We cannot deny the importance of security and national security to the country. And we cannot deny that a lot of it is detrimental to us [Muslims], so we have to engage. That's why part of our strategy is not just to engage Congress, or

even the White House. But we should start engaging the Pentagon more. Because . . . the reality is they wield a lot of influence in Washington. A lot. Probably the most. They get most out of the budget, so we need to start engaging people in the Pentagon, to start talking about policies in Muslim majority countries that end up coming back here.[44]

Supporting the policy establishment in this case, which strongly favored a limited intervention to depose Hussein, became an important way for MPAC to seek the access and legitimacy it needed to have a modicum of influence on an outcome the organization viewed as inevitable—despite the unpopularity of that position among Muslim Americans. Unlike purely grassroots organizations, interest groups cannot rely solely on oppositional strategies to achieve their goals, because their goals are fundamentally different. Al-Marayati was blunt on this point, arguing that the community's interests cannot be met by protesting but by claiming access to decision makers and making the community's demands heard where it mattered—in the centers of power.[45] Dr. Hathout elaborated this point further:

We need to make our voice heard as much as we can, and we do that by being around the table. We don't want to stand out and shout and protest. We are a non-protesting group; we want to engage. All I want from you, Mr. Policymaker, is [for you] to listen to the other side of the story. I have a narrative that you didn't have a chance to hear, so let me give it to you, and *alsalam alaikum* [peace be upon you]. We found that this is much more effective than all the demonstrations and picketing and shouting and screaming. We want to engage, educate, empower. . . . None of [these goals] is [to] protest or object.[46]

Organizations are driven by different goals, resulting in different strategic calculations. And although organizations usually have a choice about their strategies, they are also shaped, constrained, and influenced by the very strategic choices they make. A tactic of policy engagement presents opportunities to reach the upper echelons of the policy establishment, with potentially immeasurable impact. At the same time, such a strategy delimits the boundaries of what can be legitimately said and done, influencing the kinds of discursive practices that become privileged and the identities that are consequently favored, performed, and communicated.

This does not mean that these groups are homogenous or that no dissonance exists. What it does suggest is that these organizations are constantly negotiating the expectations of their varied audiences. To illustrate this point, it is useful to examine CAIR's stance toward the war on Iraq, which differed significantly from

MPAC's, at least initially. In a statement a few days before the US invasion, CAIR stated its unequivocal opposition to the war: "[An] American attack on Iraq would almost certainly lead to the death of many innocent civilians, further destabilize an already unstable region, harm international efforts to combat terrorism, drain much-needed financial resources from our struggling economy, and set a dangerous precedent for unilateral intervention in the affairs of other nations. Any American invasion and occupation of Iraq will fuel anti-American sentiment and would thereby harm our nation's image and interests in areas outside the Middle East."[47]

Nevertheless, the differences in these organizations' positions should be seen as differences of degree rather than principle. Both considered promoting and defending American interests and security to be their primary goals. They each made claims to the same guiding principles of justice, human dignity, and freedom, basing those claims on Islamic jurisprudence and American values. Where they differed was in the questions of *how*—how to realize these principles and how US interests could best be served. Whereas MPAC envisioned the possibility of a limited US intervention as potentially beneficial to US interests, CAIR saw any intervention in the Muslim world as harmful to America's long-term security and economic interests.

Regardless of their differences, these organizations recognize the importance of promoting substantive democracy to US interests. They are also unafraid to hold the United States accountable to the principles it purports to export to other parts of the world. And so they have continued to call on the United States to own up to the fact that its past policies toward the Middle East, its support of dictatorships, and its biased support of Israel have been primary factors in the instability of the region and, consequently, in the weakening of US interests. Framing their demands around an Islamic discourse of justice, righteousness, and dignity, they argue that *because* they are Muslims—not in spite of that fact—they are best able to promote and protect key American democratic values. Their religion is an asset, not a liability. Islam is thus transformed from a threat to American democracy, as often depicted, to one of its guardians and guarantors.

Democracy and the Historical Narrative of Islam's Founding

All discourse relies on a historical narrative to produce meaning. To understand and accurately examine a particular discourse, one must account for its sociohistorical context and the historical narratives on which it relies, explicitly or implicitly.[48] The role of democracy in the history of Islam's founding is a major theme for Muslim organizations in the United States.

The leaders I interviewed often emphasized Islam's democratic foundation and its resulting natural place in American democracy. Saylor described what he perceived to be the role of Muslim Americans post-9/11 as follows: "Maybe this is conceit on my part, but I honestly and sincerely believe that in many ways the American Muslim community is now at the frontline of defending the Constitution from the forces that would erode it. We have our African American brothers and sisters to thank for the Civil Rights Act of 1965, but the struggle continues. Now it's on us to continue to defend the gains made by those who struggled before us. We must continue to push forward for the sake of all Americans."[49]

Laying claim to America's racial history and discursively placing Muslim Americans within that history is one way the discourse of democratization draws on history and social context to produce its meaning. This is what the linguistic scholar Norman Fairclough refers to as "interdiscursivity"—the reliance on previous discourses in the articulation of a communicative act. All communicative events, he argues, draw on previous events, thus rearticulating and redrawing the boundaries of any specific discourse.[50] In other words, history is inescapable. By positioning Muslim American claims making within the broader framework of the American civil rights movement, Saylor places Muslim American advocacy in the spectrum of minority activism, thus contesting the common misconceptions of Muslims as both foreign to America and a threat to its social fabric.

The discourse of democratization draws on a particular historical construction of Islam's founding and the roles democracy and consultation played in its establishment. Speaking about how to reconcile Islamic theology with secular forms of government, Al-Marayati argued that Muslims must understand that the combination of religion and government is a bad mix—something, he claimed, early Muslim theologians were acutely aware of, going on to say that classic Islamic jurisprudence calls for the separation of religion and state: "Imam Ja'far, who was a great scholar of Islam, declined taking any power. He said the *'ulema* [religious scholars] should be separate from the state. That classical Islamic jurisprudence understanding is missing today, that there needs to be a separation, a wall of separation, between religion and the state."[51]

This narrative, at least in our historical context, is not one that is universally accepted. Reflecting on this point, Saylor told me that although the great majority of his values as an American were in agreement with his values as a Muslim, there were "small differences," such as the fact that "in Islam there is not so much of an embrace of secularism." Nevertheless, he argued, secularism is the right form of government, because when faith communities run governments, "they don't really have a good track record, no matter what the faith."[52] Although CAIR and MPAC both embrace the dual discourse of democracy and secularism, it is interesting to see the different ways they justify that support. Al-Marayati presents secularism as central to an accurate understanding of Islamic theology, whereas Saylor argues that even though secularism is not necessarily strongly embraced in Islam, it is nevertheless the right form of governance.

In a March 2014 speech titled "Is Sharia Compatible with Democracy?" Saylor delved into this theme, in particular how the term *sharia* has been hijacked by a popular discourse that erroneously defines it in opposition to American law.[53] He began by quoting the definition of sharia law proposed by Muslim American legal scholar Asifa Quraishi-Landes: "*Sharia* refers to the way that god has advised Muslims to live, as documented in the Quran and exemplified in the practices of Prophet Muhammad. In other words, *sharia* can be understood as the Islamic recipe for living a good life. But of course, no one can taste a recipe. We can only taste the product of a chef's efforts to follow one. In addition, different chefs can follow the same recipe and still come up with quite varied results." He then argued that Muslims understand that "the process of understanding God's will is ongoing" and that "there is the ideal of divine law, and the reality of human interpretation." Relying on Quraishi-Landes's metaphor, he described sharia as a recipe from which different people create different dishes. He emphasized that the term *democracy* is similarly contested and open for interpretation, but that if one examines the basic guiding principles of both terms, one finds sharia and democracy to be not only compatible but equivalent. In fact, Saylor claimed, the same guiding principles are present in Islamic jurisprudence and the Declaration of Independence:

> The right to the protection of life.
> The right to the protection of family.
> The right to the protection of education (intellect).
> The right to the protection of property (access to resources).
> The right to the protection of human dignity.
> The right to the protection of religion.

Accordingly, there is no dissonance between sharia and democracy, and, in fact, both are fighting the same enemy—the "extremists who claim Islam motivates them" and who "provide the breeding ground for much of the anti-Muslim extremism we are living through today." By linking Islamic extremists to the anti-Muslim extremism they engender, Saylor is contesting the image of Muslims as perpetrators of extremism, presenting them, instead, as its victims (presumably of Western Islamophobia). Rather than "adopting an 'us [Americans] vs. them [Muslims]' attitude," he reasons, "we can adopt a 'we are all in the struggle against violent extremism together' approach."[54]

Saylor's speech reflects an important tactic of dissociating US Muslims from "them" and associating them with "us," a tactic that all the major Muslim advocacy organizations in the United States pursue—*us* being the broader American public who all strive to promote and protect American laws and principles.

Democracy Promotion 2.0: America's Role in the Arab Spring

Highly disillusioned with Bush-era policies, foreign and domestic, Muslims turned out overwhelmingly to vote for Barack Obama in November 2008. Compared to 2000, the first time US Muslims voted as a bloc, with more than 80 percent favoring George W. Bush, 93 percent voted to elect Obama.[55] This was a dramatic shift in party affiliation in less than a decade. Muslims celebrated the election of the first African American president as an affirmation of the viability of the American Dream, their own place in the American Public Square, and the endless capacity of people to effect change. In retrospect, however, many considered their expectations of President Obama to have been unrealistic, as they went largely unmet.

Domestically, the new president continued many of the programs American Muslims had so staunchly opposed, overseeing the expansion of NSA surveillance and the covert monitoring of prominent American Muslims.[56] Internationally, he committed to withdrawing US troops from Iraq and Afghanistan but hesitated to intervene in support of the mass uprisings that began to sweep the Middle East in late 2010. The Obama administration's dithering strategy toward the Syrian crisis and the inability to enforce its 2012 "red line" against Bashar al-Assad's use of chemical weapons dealt a heavy blow to US standing in the region. Obama's approach toward the Arab Spring was all the more puzzling for US Muslims, since they, like many others across the country and the world, had reasons to be hopeful, particularly after the president's "Arab Spring" speech on May 19, 2011.

"We have a chance to show that America values the dignity of the street vendor in Tunisia more than the raw power of the dictator," President Obama had said.[57] He had outlined a three-pronged approach for the US response to the uprisings: standing up firmly for democratic values, helping the countries' struggling economies, and engaging directly with Arab citizens, as opposed to the dictators they were attempting to topple. However, as the uprisings in Libya and Syria turned violent, the president followed a strategy of extreme caution, or, as critics called it, US retrenchment. More than anything else, his response reflected his (and the American electorate's) disillusionment with the project of democracy promotion in the region, a view deeply shaped by the US experience in Iraq.

As a candidate, Obama had emphasized his belief that the United States was too involved in the Middle East, to the detriment of America and the region. This belief influenced his presidential response to the Arab Spring and the Syrian civil war.[58]

Following President Obama's "Arab Spring" speech, CAIR—in conjunction with other representatives of the Muslim and Arab American community—released a statement applauding the president's stance but cautioning that the principles he had delineated must be translated into "actions and concrete policies."[59] Especially because of its history in supporting the region's dictators, the statement argued, the United States could not remain neutral but must support the people's demands for freedom and human dignity. By making reference to US policy in the region, Muslim organizations emphasized that the United States was partly responsible for the current state of affairs; US neutrality was no longer an option.

Calling for the United States to support the "masses' demands for human dignity and freedom" is not a controversial position, but calling for direct US intervention is, particularly in a post–Iraq war context. Indeed, CAIR and MPAC both called for the United States to "act" and bring an end to Syrian president Bashar al-Assad's regime. Whereas CAIR called for the Obama administration to "act without delay,"[60] MPAC favored a limited US intervention in Syria. However, Muslim Americans were divided regarding what actions, if any, the United States should take in response to the Arab Spring. According to a 2011 Pew Research Center poll, they were evenly split, with 44 percent saying it was more important to have democratic governments and another 44 percent saying stability was more important.[61]

In a policy paper MPAC presented on Capitol Hill in September 2013, the organization called for "decisive and quick support for military intervention in Syria with important conditions," including putting no troops on the ground, executing the military strike in a way that would minimize civilian casualties, and securing a commitment from the international community to rebuild Syria after the conflict ended.[62] MPAC legitimized its recommendations as based on "the Islamic value of establishing justice and preserving human life," arguing that the United States could not stand by and allow the Assad regime to continue its gross violation of international law. In other words, as the world's superpower, the United States had a duty to uphold international law, which al-Assad was flagrantly violating by using chemical weapons against his own people and thereby crossing Obama's "red line." The United States was therefore called to act in order to fulfill its duties and bring an end to the suffering of the Syrian people. Perhaps aware of how unpopular their recommendation might be among both US Muslims and the broader American public, the paper differentiates the Syrian situation: "We must be clear: Syria is not Iraq. The Iraq war was based on a fabrication. . . . With Syria, there are no such questions. The evidence has been clear and compelling."[63]

How do Muslim advocacy groups rationalize and legitimize their calls for the United States to intervene in a Muslim-majority country? To answer this question, we must account for the ways in which Islamic values and jurisprudence are interpreted through these organizations' discourse. Arab dictators who oppress their people, violate their human rights, and deny their freedoms and dignity are presented as being in stark violation of the basic precepts of Islam, which call, above all else, for respecting the sanctity of life. "Basing our decision on the Islamic value of establishing justice and preserving human life," MPAC stated, "we support conditional military intervention in Syria." Similarly, in a press release following the December 2016 bombing of civilian areas in Aleppo by Syrian and Russian forces, the USCMO called for US action with the argument that "no people should suffer or be denied the basic rights of freedom and democracy."[64] Islamic and American principles are thus established as being one and the same. Emphasizing the Arab Spring as driven by people's yearning for freedom and justice—rather than as the geostrategic calculations of regional powers—allows Muslim American groups to more easily legitimize their calls for intervention as part of a moral cause against injustice and oppression. Indeed, they seem to make an important distinction between violence used to oppress (what Arab dictators have done, and what the United States has done in Iraq) and violence used to end suffering and oppression (in a US intervention in Syria).

Support for US intervention in the region was also influenced by the rise and brutality of the self-proclaimed Islamic State (IS). CAIR, which describes IS as "un-Islamic and morally repugnant," backed the 2014 US decision to begin bombing IS fighters in northern Iraq, asserting their support not only for this "limited" intervention but also for further US "actions" in the Muslim world: "We applaud the humanitarian effort to assist those surrounded by [IS] extremists in Iraq and hope the compassion expressed for Iraqi civilians will lead to similar actions to alleviate the suffering of civilian populations of Gaza, Burma (Myanmar), Syria, and the Central African Republic."[65] Whether the actions envisioned and encouraged are military or political is unclear, but since the statement encourages "similar actions" as the US bombings in northern Iraq, it is reasonable to deduct that further "limited" US bombings for "humanitarian" purposes would not be opposed. The United States is simultaneously commended for intervening on behalf of Iraq's non-Muslim minorities and chastised for not doing so on behalf of Muslims in other ongoing crises. Thus, while IS and extremist groups like it are presented as grave threats to international security and human rights, the lack of a US response to end the suffering that authoritarian regimes impose on their people is presented as an equally dangerous threat to international security.

In addition to advising US policy officials, these organizations were reaching out to officials of foreign governments who were seeking the Muslim American perspective. In March 2013, the Moroccan government—perhaps as a way of precluding mass discontent in the kingdom from following the path of neighboring countries—invited a delegation of Muslim and Arab American organizations, scholars, and religious figures to advise them on political reforms and democracy. CAIR was among those invited. According to Omar Zaki, one of CAIR's representatives, the goal was to "share what we have learned with our community and the larger [American] society."[66] Members of the Muslim American community were clearly perceived as having something meaningful to contribute regarding democratization and the role that Islam and Muslims can play in a democracy. This perception is internalized by Muslim American elites who, by agreeing to advise the Moroccan government about "political reforms and the process of strengthening democracy," are signaling that their position as American Muslims gives them a unique and potentially helpful perspective on issues of democratization.[67]

Defending the *Ummah*'s Religious Freedom and Human Rights

As with their engagements on Syria and the Arab Spring, Muslim advocacy groups in the United States have not recoiled from calling on their government to intervene in other cases where they believe the lives and fundamental rights of Muslims are under threat. Three recent cases concern the Kashmir dispute, the plight of the Rohingya Muslims in Myanmar, and the systemic human rights violations China has committed against its Uighur population, a predominantly Muslim ethnic minority. Despite their vastly different contexts, Muslims in the United States have tended to focus their advocacy concerning these conflicts on similar themes of protecting religious freedom and human rights. The territorial dispute over Kashmir is a legacy of the Partition of India that accompanied the British withdrawal in 1947. India and Pakistan have both made claims on the region and have fought three wars since 1947 to advance those claims, resulting in grave human rights abuses. Amnesty International estimates that from 1990 to 2011 alone, more than forty-seven thousand people lost their lives in the conflict and that cases of torture, rape, and other human rights abuses are rampant and underreported.[68]

The plight of the Rohingya can be similarly traced to British colonial rule in Burma (now Myanmar). British colonial policies encouraged migrant labor to

Burma in order to increase cultivation and profits. Ethnic Rohingya have been in the country since the twelfth century, when many migrants entered from Bangladesh through these policies. Indeed, the Muslim population in Burma tripled between 1871 and 1911.[69] The long-standing persecution of Rohingya Muslims was institutionalized with the passage of the Citizenship Act of 1982, which formally stripped the Rohingya of citizenship rights, making them the largest stateless community in the world today.

In the summer of 2017, the Burmese military began a vicious campaign against what they called a terrorist threat by a Rohingya militant group (the Arakan Rohingya Salvation Army). More than four hundred thousand Rohingya civilians were forced to flee to neighboring Bangladesh, prompting the United Nations human rights chief to describe it as a "textbook example of ethnic cleansing."[70] As the plight of the Muslim Rohingya became front-page news and audiences were exposed to devastating images of civilians fleeing the violence, Muslim organizations began calling for a US-led humanitarian intervention on their behalf. Again, their rationale was the need to defend religious liberties, which should not stop at our borders: "As American Muslims, we support the strongest possible protections for religious liberties here in the United States and vigorously defend the rights of religious minorities abroad, including in Muslim majority countries."[71] That fall, Muslim American organizations launched an assertive lobbying campaign on behalf of the Rohingya. In a letter to Nikki Haley, then US ambassador to the United Nations, CAIR asked for "immediate and decisive action" in defense of the Rohingya, including reinstating economic and political sanctions on the government of Myanmar; investigating the "extremist Burmese monk Ashin Wirathu . . . who has reportedly described himself as the "Buddhist Bin Laden"; and pressuring Myanmar's political leader, Aung San Suu Kye, to "live up to her democratic ideals."[72]

Leaders staged protests and public prayers in front of the embassy of Myanmar in Washington, DC. Simultaneously, they asked Congress to support Senate Resolution 250 and House Resolution 528, which called for an end to the violence, the restoration of citizenship for the Rohingya, and the protection of their economic and social well-being. CAIR also lobbied the senate to support a bipartisan amendment (SA 607) to the 2018 National Defense Authorization Act which would ensure that the US military would not provide any direct military assistance to the government of Burma.[73] These measures were required, according to CAIR, to "uphold the United States' position as a leading advocate for human rights."[74] MPAC put it more bluntly, stating that, as Americans: "We cannot allow any ethnic or religious minority to be attacked simply because of who they are and what they believe."[75] Once again, Muslim American advocacy organizations legitimized their concern about issues affecting Muslims overseas and their calls for US intervention in terms of US interests and the need to defend America's standing in the world.

Following a different strategy, in September 2017, Oussama Jamal, the secretary general of the USCMO, launched an "international diplomatic campaign" to end the persecution and ethnic cleansing of the Rohingya. His organization met with the ambassadors of Myanmar, Turkey, and the Organization of Islamic Cooperation to discuss both short-term humanitarian assistance efforts and a long-term political resolution to the crisis. In describing the meetings, Jamal stated: "We focused on common ground to establish channels for American Muslims to help the Rohingya survive the catastrophe they face now and to undo the insupportable conditions that have allowed it for their future. . . . Our push is to open a direct door for American Muslims to help alleviate the Rohingya's literally life-and-death needs now, to become first-hand observers of their conditions, and to advocate for their human rights and political enfranchisement into the future."[76] The USCMO was not only working to advise and pressure its own government regarding foreign policy affecting the *ummah* but also directly lobbying foreign officials in an attempt, as Jammal claimed, to "open a direct door for American Muslims" to be involved in issues affecting the global Muslim community.

Those issues abound. However, Muslim American organizations often lack the capacity and political capital to be meaningfully involved. And, unlike the cases of the Palestinian-Israeli conflict and democratization in the Middle East, many of these issues, particularly those related to human rights violations around the world, cannot be as easily interpreted through a lens of US national interests, further limiting the ability to mobilize around them. Often, the only feasible option is to react as they occur or intensify. Such was the case in mid-2019, when the Indian government announced it was revoking Article 370 of its Constitution, which granted Jammu and Kashmir special status and some degree of autonomy. "There is a humanitarian crisis brewing in the Kashmir valley," Nihad Awad said at a rally following the announcement. "The State Department should urge the Indian government to immediately reinstate the protected status, lift the siege, and enter into peaceful negotiations to determine the future of the Indian-controlled state of Jammu and Kashmir."[77] Advocacy on Kashmir is thus also framed around a number of themes that are at the center of Muslim American advocacy: protecting national security and human rights; promoting freedom, democracy, and justice; and speaking truth to power at home and abroad.

This was not the first time American Muslims had mobilized around Kashmir. In 2008, protests demanding self-determination broke out in the region. The

Indian government responded by sending thousands of troops in an attempt to quell the unrest.[78] As the situation escalated, MPAC called on the US government to support the people's right to self-determination. Blaming both Pakistan and India for their handling of the conflict and their record of grave human rights violations against civilians, MPAC called on the United States to bring the two governments together "to address the core issue of the right to Kashmiri self-determination" and thus "bring stability to this region."[79] CAIR was also clear that the question of Kashmir raises resentment among Muslims around the world. During an event organized in conjunction with the University of Chicago, CAIR described the conflict "as one of the two major sources of what has been euphemistically labeled the Muslim angst. There are national security implications for the U.S. as well, as the road to peace in Afghanistan is widely believed to go through Kashmir."[80]

Similarly, in a 2002 speech to the State Department, Al-Marayati noted that Kashmir "deserves our attention," since "it is a potential flashpoint for nuclear conflict." Thus, the United States is not only morally obliged to defend the Kashmiri people's right to self-determination but also required to do so to protect US national security interests and support counterterrorism efforts by addressing the root causes of radicalization around the world. The framing is familiar, even if the rationale is not altogether direct.

As the Kashmir conflict took yet another violent turn in 2016, MPAC was more direct in pointing the finger at the Indian government, blaming the latest wave of unrest on the Indian military's killing of Burhan Wani, a twenty-two-year-old Kashmiri separatist militant. The organization also accused India of committing widespread human rights crimes in the name of order and security, including the de facto suspension of religious freedoms for Kashmiri Muslims by canceling religious celebrations and enacting strict curfews during Eid al-Adha, one of the most important holidays celebrated by Muslims worldwide. Critiquing President Obama's description of the conflict as "an internal issue," MPAC called on the international community and the United States to pressure the Indian government to change its policies.[81]

Importantly, MPAC has relied on foreign policy issues, including the Kashmiri and Palestinian-Israeli conflicts to attract support from the Muslim American community, even listing its advocacy on the Kashmir conflict as a reason for qualifying to receive zakat (charitable giving to the poor or needy, and one of the five pillars of Islam) because zakat "should be used to help eliminate all forms of oppression."[82] Acutely aware of the symbolic significance of these conflicts and the narrative of oppression against the *ummah*, many Muslim organizations seeking to represent their community's interests (and attract their support) have strategically focused part of their advocacy efforts on these issues. Even while advocating on behalf of the *ummah*, however, they rely on frameworks that clearly position them as an American minority making uniquely American claims.

Nuclear Nonproliferation and US Policy toward Iran

No other foreign policy issue embodies the performative aspect of Muslim American advocacy like Iran's nuclear weapons program. Advocacy group efforts on this issue have centered on two goals: achieving a nonmilitary solution to the threat of nuclear proliferation and opposing the "theocratic nature" of the Iranian regime. In fact, American Muslim organizations heavily lobbied for and supported the 2015 Iran nuclear deal, which the Obama administration brokered. During the 2012 election campaigns, several Republican presidential candidates expressed support for a military strike on Iran. Others, including President Obama, expressed a desire to "keep all options on the table," a strategy many viewed as a euphemism for a military strike.[83] Concerned about the prospects of yet another US military intervention in a Muslim-majority country, Muslim advocacy organizations began to lobby in favor of a political resolution to the impasse. Haris Tarin put it as follows: "With Arab Spring changes sweeping the Middle East and just winding down our mission in Iraq, the last thing our nation and the region needs is another war based on questionable premises."[84] In January 2014, Muslim groups joined dozens of other faith-based and advocacy organizations in urging the Senate to vote against imposing new sanctions on Iran, which they described as "a poison pill for negotiations."[85] When the Iran nuclear deal was signed in Geneva later that year, US Muslim advocacy organizations welcomed it unanimously.

Under the deal, Iran agreed to extensive limitation of its nuclear energy program in return for the lifting of economic sanctions. According to the Council on Foreign Relations, Iran restricted its nuclear program following passage of the act and granted international inspectors unprecedented access, even though it had yet to see the economic recovery predicted with the lifting of sanctions.[86] Within a few years, even as the full impacts and implications of the deal were still being shaped, the Trump administration was working to dismantle it. In early May 2018, the president announced that the United States would be quitting the deal, calling it a "horrible one-sided deal that should have never, ever been made."[87] Muslim organizations opposed the move and rang alarm bells about Trump's behavior. "Trump's tweets at #Iran could trigger WWIII," MPAC tweeted, with an image of its "#No War with Iran" campaign.[88] Drawing parallels with the war on Iraq,

CAIR called on Congress and the American people to stand up to Trump to prevent another future endless and meaningless war. "We must not once again go to war based on the claims of a White House that lies about anything and everything," their action alert to Congress reads. "Congress must stop this march to war. The media must challenge the narrative leading us to war. The American people must speak up against war. Not again. Not on our watch."

Such strong opposition to a potential war with Iran and overwhelming support for the nuclear deal, however, should not be read as support for the Iranian regime. On the contrary, these organizations are highly critical of what they refer to as a "theocratic," "authoritarian," and "un-Islamic" regime. Even while promoting a nonmilitary response to Iran's nuclear program as part of its "vision for a more secure and safe American and global society," MPAC has made its distaste for the Iranian regime clear for years: "We oppose, on religious grounds, the theocratic and authoritarian nature of the current Iranian political system."[89] Similarly, CAIR has lambasted Iran for its role in the Syrian civil war, commenting in 2013 that: "While we welcome this move toward international peace and stability, we must also call on Iranian leaders to realize the un-Islamic nature of their massive political, military and financial support for the brutal Syrian dictatorship. Iranian support for the Assad regime has contributed to the killing of more than 120,000 Syrians, including some 11,000 children. No government that claims Islamic legitimacy can continue to back those who are massacring Muslims."[90]

Given all this, how should the United States deal with the threat posed by Iran? The answer, according to MPAC's communications director, Marium Mohiddin, is simple: support and empower the Iranian people, and engage in people-to-people diplomacy. Al-Marayati elaborated this point during one of our interviews, arguing that much of Iran and the region's problems can be traced to a deep lack of confidence by the United States and other world powers in the Iranian people's capacity to solve their own problems: "Whether we are talking about Syria, Egypt, or Iran, people have to be empowered to make the decisions about what is happening in their countries. This is what people have demanded time and time again. Why is it that we are unable to hear them, to support them? We must do better."[91]

Through their advocacy on US foreign policy issues, Muslim organizations are actively communicating, negotiating, and performing what it means to be an American Muslim. The act of engaging policymakers to present the Muslim American perspective is an act of establishing and grounding Muslims as an important American minority with something meaningful to contribute to policymakers and to the national dialogue alike. These organizations claim their belonging by presenting themselves as a constructive voice and an important part of the solution to the foreign policy problems plaguing the United States rather than as a source of those problems, as they are so often depicted.

However, the identity these organizations are constructing through their foreign policy discourse is one that, like all identities, privileges certain subgroups of Muslims and marginalizes others. Some may embrace the secular, liberal, and democratic Muslim American identity these organizations tend to emphasize, while those who cannot accommodate that narrative find it alienating. Most minority groups must grapple with this tension, but the scrutiny that Muslim Americans face makes it a particularly challenging—and increasingly relevant—issue to address.

WHO SPEAKS FOR AMERICAN MUSLIMS?

Don't assume any person claiming to represent Muslim Communities really does.

Don't use fringe Muslims as representatives for diverse Muslim communities.

Don't say the "Muslim world." There is no "Muslim World."

Don't assume all Muslims can speak accurately about Islam.

—Institute for Social Policy and Understanding, Tips for Improving Depth of Coverage, "Covering American Muslims Objectively and Creatively: A Guide for Media Professionals"

In the summer of 2013, the Jerusalem-based Shalom Hartman Institute launched the Muslim Leadership Initiative (MLI), inviting "Muslims in North America" to "explore how Jews understand Judaism, Israel, and Jewish peoplehood" and "how Palestinians identify themselves." Spearheaded by Imam Abdullah Antepli, Duke University's first Muslim chaplain, and Yossi Klein Halevi, an American Israeli journalist and political activist, the MLI's stated mission was to encourage participants to develop a critical understanding of the complexities of the Palestinian-Israeli conflict and its impacts on the Palestinian and Israeli people. Although not the first of its kind, the program, and those invited to participate in it, engendered a heated debate about leadership and the politics of representation within the Muslim American community. Who speaks, or should speak, for American Muslims? What grants them the legitimacy to do so? What issues should they mobilize around, and why?

It is no coincidence that an initiative related to the Palestinian-Israeli conflict would catapult this internal and often contentious debate. As the previous chapter shows, American Muslim organizations have long tried to position themselves as relevant voices in the Palestinian-Israeli conflict, even though the vast majority of US Muslims are from neither Palestine nor Israel. And although these organizations unanimously define the conflict in territorial terms, they have also highlighted Palestine's religious significance for Muslims around the world, including those in the United States. Critics of the MLI accused it of conflating Zionism with Judaism, overstating the religious dimensions of the conflict, and whitewashing Israeli apartheid.[1] In an open letter signed by more than fifty organizations, signatories called on American Muslims to boycott the initiative and pledged to "not give a platform to any MLI participant to speak about their experiences at our community centers, places of worship, and campuses."[2]

The discussion among the Muslim community soon turned from the MLI's merits and purpose to the divisions that it had sowed among US Muslims and their leaders: "We have seen how this program has fractured American Muslim communities and institutions and has mobilized selective American Muslim leaders as tools to further conceal rather than challenge the oppression of the Palestinian people,"[3] reads a petition drafted by Yale University Professor Zareena Grewal and Duke University Professor Omid Safi, among others. Discord over individuals' decisions to participate soon slipped into personal attacks. In a Facebook post on August 22, 2015, Linda Sarsour criticized MPAC's president, Salam Al-Marayati, for what she considered to be his implicit support for the initiative: "Salam Al-Marayati just wrote this on my status [about the MLI], 'The enemies of Islam do not need to divide us. We are doing a good job for them ourselves.'"[4]

The responses to Sarsour's post reflect not just divisions but deep chasms between Muslim American leaders and the communities they seek to represent. "If Muslims worked better in Shura [consultation] with their own community rather than get their marching orders from law enforcement and government agencies, we may have better unity," one person wrote in response, along with a link to a *Patheos* article that makes reference to MPAC's Safe Spaces Initiative.[5] Another claimed, "This, right here, is something that the charlatan sell out Uncle(/Auntie) Tom self appointed leaders will never comprehend"; in other words, the leaders could never grasp Sarsour's critique because they had been "corrupted by power." Al-Marayati responded more than once, attempting to clarify his stance: "I am not part of MLI. My point has been that the infighting over it has been counterproductive." His statements were drowned out by a cacophony of accusations against him, his organization's engagement with government agencies, and "Muslim sell-outs."

Advocacy Groups and the Right of Representation

Questions and contention over the right of representation are, of course, not exclusive to the Muslim American community. Interest groups have a long history in American politics, although those representing marginalized groups, such as women, racial minorities, and low-income people, are relative newcomers. As previously discussed, most of these have emerged since the 1960s, in the era of civil rights, and have become important conduits for the articulation and representation of the interests of the marginalized.[6] Regardless, the debate over who can legitimately speak for underrepresented groups is one that advocacy organizations have grappled with for decades, particularly those that claim to represent intersectionally marginalized groups.[7] This debate is amplified because many such organizations seek their legitimacy from their stated mission to advance social justice and equality rather than from a direct mandate from the individuals they claim to represent.[8] Crucially, although there is broad agreement that the mushrooming of these organizations has helped marginalized groups in general, concerns remain about how well they actually represent their constituents.

The concerns can be divided into three main critiques. First, some scholars argue that organizations advocating for marginalized groups have tended to focus on middle-class, "post-materialist" issues, such as identity or the environment, that affect more advantaged subgroups at the expense of economic justice.[9] A second, similar critique is that in order to avoid alienating potential members, donors, and government officials, advocacy organizations tend to sideline contentious issues—particularly those dealing with race, gender, and sexuality—in favor of more mainstream ones.[10] In other words, organizations generally tend to ignore issues they perceive as "narrow" in favor of those they consider to affect a broader segment of their constituents, thus guaranteeing the continuing support of a majority. The third critique often waged against these organizations is that they choose to focus on policy "niches" that can be easily recognized as "theirs" in order to make themselves more attractive to policymakers, even if doing so leaves many everyday issues affecting their communities unaddressed.[11]

Compounding these universal critiques of interest group representation is the fact that few American Muslims believe that the existing national advocacy organizations represent their interests. As a reminder, only 30 percent of those polled by Gallup in 2011 claimed that *any* of the major national Muslim advocacy organizations represented their interests, and 55 percent of men and 42 percent of women claimed that no single organization represented their interests.[12] Notably, as we have seen in previous chapters, some of the specific policy positions these organizations espouse also seem to reflect a level of dissonance between them and the constituencies they seek to represent, further buttressing the perception that these groups are out of touch with the concerns of the average American Muslim.

Muslim Advocacy and Policy Framing

What I hope this book has made exceedingly clear is that, as all advocacy groups are, Muslim American advocacy organizations are framers. According to Robert Entman, one of the most cited scholars of framing in the literature on interest groups, "To frame is to select one aspect of a perceived reality and make them more salient in a communicating text in such a way as to promote a particular problem definition, causal interpretation, moral evaluation, and/or treatment recommendation for the item described."[13] In this respect, what Muslim advocacy organizations do is wholly typical of the mainstream.[14] When calculating their framing decisions, they, like other advocacy groups, respond to two different types of logic: "the logic of membership" and "the logic of influence."[15] The first entails groups behaving in accordance with their constituents in order to ensure their continued legitimacy and access to resources; the second demands that groups rely on frames that enable them to exercise influence over policy outcomes. Sometimes the two overlap, but not always.

In some areas of Muslim American interest group advocacy, notably in regard to domestic civil rights, these two types of logic seem to be in alignment. Islamophobia and anti-Muslim discrimination are at the forefront of most Muslim Americans' concerns. For example, when asked in Pew's 2017 survey, "Is there a lot of discrimination against Muslims in the United States?" 75 percent of respondents answered affirmatively. Further, almost half of those polled, 49 percent, reported having personally experienced a discriminatory incident in the past year. Interest groups have responded to this reality by focusing the majority of their resources and advocacy work on these issues, relying on a framework of constitutional rights to attract support for their cause and pursue their demands. Can the same be said of their advocacy on issues related to US foreign policy? Is foreign policy engagement merely an elite concern? The answer, at least from the available polling data, is a resounding no. In fact, American Muslims care about foreign policy *far more* than is reflected in the work of their national advocacy organizations. Regardless of country of origin, age, or economic status, American Muslims collectively demonstrate a high degree of interest and engagement on issues related to US foreign policy.

But national advocacy organizations are attempting to balance the need to respond to their constituents' concerns about foreign policy (the logic of membership) with the need to speak to the policy establishment as a legitimate group concerned with issues of relevance to not only American Muslims but all Americans (the logic of influence). In a post-9/11 context of increased suspicion, these organizations have even sought to distance themselves from foreign policy advocacy in an attempt to forestall the accusations of "dual loyalties" that are commonly waged against ethnic interest groups, especially in times of war.[16] Almost every individual leader I interviewed highlighted that most of their advocacy efforts were focused on constitutional rights and domestic policy engagement. Corey Saylor, currently CAIR's director of the Department to Combat Islamophobia, tried to make this point forcefully by showing me an internal report indicating that in the past fifteen years, only 10 percent of CAIR's work has related to US foreign policy. And Salam al-Marayati told me the following, reflecting on the dissonance between the level of attention Muslim Americans place on foreign policy and the domestic orientation of his organization:

> At the end of the day you have to ask yourself: How are you demonstrating that you are part of the American fabric, or is it just what people think it is? They think it is just lip service; that you're saying it, but you're not *really* a part of America. We have to demonstrate that we are part of America. I feel that sometimes we are not honest with ourselves as far as where home is. Is home where my children and grandchildren are going to live, or is home where my grandparents lived? Home should be where our kids are going to live, but I don't think people think of that. They say: "I'm from Syria. My family is from Iraq." But that's not home. So there needs to be a reorientation of the American Muslim community that America is home.[17]

For the vast majority of American Muslims, America is indeed home, even if they are still negotiating their places within it. We know from the existing data that US Muslims proudly embrace the "Muslim" and the "American" part of their identities.[18] What the data cannot tell us, however, is what they mean by this, and whether the articulation of Muslim American identity being advanced by the interest groups I have examined is one that conforms to how the majority of US Muslims understand their experiences. The majority of those polled in 2017 said that believing in God, loving the prophet Mohammad, working for social justice, and protecting the environment were essential elements of what it meant to be Muslim. This may well give us a glimpse into how American Muslims see themselves, since, after all, religious values do not exist outside of the specific social and historical contexts in which they are practiced. Moreover, most Muslims in the United States do not spend their waking moments thinking about belonging and questioning their identities and what it means to be Muslim, American, or both. Nor should they be expected to do so. They, like most of us, probably relate to their religious and national identities as two of the many descriptors (including class, gender, professional affiliation, and marital status, among many others) that make them who they are.

"They are Islamists!" and Other Such Accusations

Undoubtedly, many readers will disagree with the arguments I have laid out. Some will continue to doubt that observant, practicing Muslims can follow the precepts of their religion and be loyal, patriotic American citizens at the same time. Others may question whether Muslim advocacy organizations are hiding their true motives behind a veneer of American values and civil rights talk. Political scientists Peter Skerry and Gary Schmitt summarized this critique in a 2011 piece they wrote for Brookings, in which they argued that CAIR and other mainstream Muslim American organizations were best understood through the lens of Islamism[19] rather than civil rights:

> Here, as in Egypt, Islamism has importantly shaped the discourse and the organizations that Muslims are now using to carve out civil and political space for their religion. Does this mean that America's freedoms are in danger from these same Islamists? We think not. But we are struck as well by the tendency of many in the United States, including the media and various government agencies, to ignore the Islamist influences on established Muslim American organizations and their leaders. For example, the Council on American-Islamic Relations (CAIR), which has origins and ties to the Muslim Brotherhood and Hamas, is routinely described and treated as though it were just another civil rights or advocacy organization.[20]

The conclusion readers are meant to draw is that the organizations advocating for the rights of American Muslims are different from those that advocate on behalf of other minority groups. Their main difference? Their "Islamism," which Muslims are called to confront if they want to be accepted by their fellow Americans. Accordingly, Schmitt and Skerry conclude by asking American Muslims to try to appease the fears and anxieties of their fellow Americans: "At a time when Americans, including some Muslims, are in combat overseas against *Muslim* adversaries, Muslim Americans cannot afford to consider themselves a community apart. If they are to realize full citizenship, it is not enough for Muslims here simply to assert their rights but also to address questions whose continued neglect fuels understandable anxieties about Islam among their fellow citizens."[21] In this iteration, integration and "full citizenship" result from the choices that individuals and groups make (in this case Muslims), not the policies and practices that governments enact and help facilitate. The burden is laid squarely at the feet of American Muslims, who are expected to appease, to confront, to disavow. Only then can they begin to realize full citizenship, as the authors argue—seeming to concede that this is something Muslim citizens lack. Hence, claiming belonging is something Muslim citizens are allowed to do *only after* disavowing a particular set of political ideologies and distancing themselves from "our Muslim adversaries" overseas.

Yet, this, too, is not enough. The authors also call on American Muslims to "face up to the full implications of the Islamist origins and history of their leadership."[22] However, those whom US Muslims consider to be their leaders, and how well (or whether) those leaders represent their perspectives, is far more ambiguous and contested than Schmitt and Skerry seem to assume. Indeed, criticism toward Muslim American organizations and their leaders comes not only from the outside but also from within the Muslim American community. As I have discussed, a strong majority of US Muslims do not consider *any* existing Muslim organization in America to represent their interests. Many openly and vehemently disagree with the positions these organizations have taken on a variety of issues, criticize what they see as their dogmatism, and reject them as outdated institutions run by a predominantly Arab immigrant cohort of middle-class professionals who implicitly discriminate against poor, black, and working-class Muslims. Wajahat Ali, a Muslim American journalist, writer, and lawyer, has summarized many of these criticisms on social media, particularly in a post that became the basis of an essay he wrote for *The Atlantic* on being disinvited from the Islamic Society of North America's fifty-fifth annual convention.[23]

One basis for his "ex-communication," as he facetiously puts it, appears to be an essay he wrote in which he recounts his experiences visiting Israeli settlements and engaging with some of the ardent Zionists who reside in them through the Shalom Hartman Institute's Muslim Leadership Initiative. ISNA's official letter disinviting him (which Ali posted on Facebook) states, "Our Muslim speakers . . . are supposed to support broadly our values as a unifying Islamic organization. Other than our creed as Muslims, there is perhaps nothing more exemplifying and unifying than our community's support for the Palestinian people of all faith traditions in their struggles against occupation and disposition." Ali's response to the letter is as illuminating as ISNA's position. "Why is the issue of Palestine next to 'creed'? . . . Who decided and when? What happens if people disagree?"

The ensuing commentary and responses to the post are equally revealing. "Disappointed but not surprised," reads one response, adding that "lack of consistent moral leadership is the bane [of] ISNA and CAIR's existence." Another respondent commends Ali's stance: "You articulate exactly what is wrong with Muslims and 'Islam' and organizations claiming to represent them/it in this country." More surprisingly, some commenters accuse ISNA and CAIR of being beholden to Saudi Arabia: "ISNA is funded by the Saudis . . . ISNA and CAIR have not been able to change the Muslim narrative." This is an accusation these organizations have faced for decades, and one they vehemently deny, but it is usually made in an attempt to delegitimize and discredit not only the organizations but also Muslims and Islam in general. The fact that these critiques are being voiced by American Muslims themselves is an important reminder about the diversity of Muslim American life and the complexity of Muslim American political identity.

The Future of Muslim American Advocacy

Muslim advocacy organizations are attempting to accurately and vociferously represent their constituents' preferences and concerns—but not all preferences and concerns. They are also emphasizing and dedicating limited resources to issues that the majority of their US Muslim constituents do not deem important but which legitimize their existence and ensure their continued survival—the primary goals of any interest group. And they are acutely aware of the need to expand their advocacy efforts beyond civil rights.

These organizations face a difficult conundrum, in that achieving their policy goals may make them increasingly irrelevant. In other words, if they succeed in their efforts to combat Islamophobia and anti-Muslim discrimination so that Muslims do become fully and meaningfully integrated into US society, politics, and culture, then their primary raison d'être would cease to exist. But questions of economic justice, employment, and the environment are increasingly becoming part of the national Muslim American advocacy agenda. Like an overwhelming majority of young Americans, for example, Muslim youth care deeply about the environment. Indeed, 35 percent of US Muslims are under the age of thirty, and 62 percent of this cohort say protecting the environment is an essential part of what being Muslim means to them.[24] The Muslim American community is changing, and the advocacy concerns of their organizations are reflecting that.

Whether mobilizing on issues of domestic policy (such as religious profiling, surveillance, and immigration) or US foreign policy (such as the Palestinian-Israeli conflict and democratization in the Muslim-majority world), Muslim American advocacy organizations are drawing from and relying on rights claims, working to advance American values, and grounding their arguments on the Constitution and the Bill of Rights. Knowing that, my point is a rather simple one: Muslim American advocacy groups are quintessentially *American* organizations. They rely on traditional interest group tactics to make their claims on the state and to demand their constituents' individual and collective rights. In so doing, they are articulating what it means to be an *American* Muslim and helping draw the contours of a distinctly liberal, inclusive, and civically engaged Muslim American political identity.

Notes

INTRODUCTION

1. Third United National Muslim National Day on Capitol Hill, training webinar, April 25, 2017.

2. Executive Order 13769 barred entry into the United States for ninety days of nationals of seven Muslim-majority countries (Iran, Iraq, Libya, Somalia, Syria, Sudan, and Yemen). It also banned the entry of refugees for 120 days, and it indefinitely banned the entry of Syrian refugees. Faced with mounting legal challenges, the administration implemented two additional iterations of the ban. On June 26, 2018, the US Supreme Court allowed the third iteration (Presidential Proclamation 9645) to go into full effect. Under this version, most people from Chad, Iran, Libya, Somalia, Syria, Yemen, and North Korea, as well as some government officials from Venezuela, are indefinitely banned from obtaining most immigrant and nonimmigrant visas to the United States, unless they obtain a consular "waiver"—a provision Supreme Court Justice Stephen Breyer described as "window dressing." Amy Howe, "Opinion Analysis: Divided court upholds Trump travel ban," Supreme Court of the United States (blog), June 26, 2018, https://www.scotusblog.com/2018/06/opinion-analysis-divided-court-upholds-trump-travel-ban/.

3. David Bier, "Trump Cut Muslim Refugees 91%, Immigrants 30%, Visitors by 18%," *Cato at Liberty* (blog), The Cato Institute, December 7, 2018, https://www.cato.org/blog/trump-cut-muslim-refugees-91-immigrants-30-visitors-18.

4. Author interview with Robert McCaw, CAIR director of the Department of Government Affairs, July 28, 2016.

5. Author interview with Corey Saylor, CAIR director of the Department to Monitor and Combat Islamophobia, June 22, 2014.

6. Author interview with Jaylani Hussein, director of CAIR-Minnesota, October 20, 2018.

7. Maha Hilal (speaking at CAIR's 2018 National Policy and Leadership Conference, Arlington, VA, October 19, 2018).

8. Khaled A. Beydoun, *American Islamophobia: Understanding the Roots and Rise of Fear* (Oakland, CA: University of California Press, 2019), 28–29.

9. Beydoun, *American Islamophobia*, 28–29.

10. For more on the historical roots of Orientalism, see Edward W. Said, *Orientalism* (New York: Vintage, 1978) and *Covering Islam: How the Media and the Experts Determine How We See the Rest of the World* (New York: Vintage, 1981).

11. United States Congress, Freedom of Religion Act of 2017, H.R. 852, 115th Cong. (2017), https://www.congress.gov/115/bills/hr852/BILLS-115hr852ih.pdf; United States Congress, No Religious Registry Act of 2017, H.R. 489, 115th Cong. (2017), https://www.congress.gov/115/bills/hr489/BILLS-115hr489ih.pdf.

12. *Liminal* legality refers to an in-between status in which immigrants have been granted some form of formal documentation (most commonly, a social security number and work permit) and temporary relief from deportation but have no long-term security or pathway to acquire citizenship. For more on the subject, see Cecilia Menjívar, "Liminal Legality: Salvadoran and Guatemalan Immigrants' Lives in the United States," *American Journal of Sociology* 111, no. 4 (January 2006): 999–1037.

13. United States Congress, BRIDGE Act, H.R. 496, 115th Cong. (2017), https://www.congress.gov/115/bills/hr496/BILLS-115hr496ih.pdf.

14. Sam Sanders, "Ted Cruz Criticized After Suggesting Law Enforcement Patrol Muslim Areas," NPR, March 23, 2016, https://www.npr.org/2016/03/23/471600823/ted-cruz-faces-criticism-after-suggesting-law-enforcement-patrol-muslim-areas.

15. Theodore Schleifer, "Ted Cruz: Muslim Refugees from Syria Should Go to Other Islamic Countries," CNN, November 17, 2015, https://www.cnn.com/2015/11/17/politics/ted-cruz-refugees-syria/index.html.

16. Katie Leslie, "Ted Cruz Strongly Backs Trump Travel Ban, While John Cornyn More Cautious," *Dallas News*, January 30, 2017, https://www.dallasnews.com/news/politics/2017/01/30/ted-cruz-strongly-backs-trump-travel-ban-john-cornyn-cautious.

17. Gallup Research Center, *Muslim Americans: Faith Freedom and the Future: Examining U.S. Muslims Political Social, and Spiritual Engagement 10 Years after September 11*, August 2, 2011, 25, http://www.gallup.com/poll/148931/presentation-muslim-americans-faith-freedom-future.aspx.

18. Pew Research Center, *U.S. Muslims Concerned about Their Place in Society, But Continue to Believe in the American Dream: Findings from Pew Research Center's 2017 Survey of U.S. Muslims*, July 26, 2017, 42, https://www.pewresearch.org/wp-content/uploads/sites/7/2017/07/U.S.-MUSLIMS-FULL-REPORT.pdf.

19. Youssef Chouhoud, "What's the Hidden Story Behind American Muslim Poverty?" Institute for Social Policy and Understanding, October 2, 2018, https://www.ispu.org/whats-the-hidden-story-behind-american-muslim-poverty/.

20. Beydoun, *American Islamophobia*.

21. Throughout this book, I use the terms *advocacy organizations*, *lobby organizations*, and *interest groups* interchangeably.

22. Howard Zinn and Anthony Arnove, eds., *Voices of a People's History of the United States*, 2nd ed. (New York: Seven Stories Press, 2009).

1. DISCRIMINATION, ADVOCACY, AND COLLECTIVE IDENTITY

1. For more on Orientalism as the precursor of American Islamophobia, see Erik Love, *Islamophobia and Racism in America* (New York: New York University Press, 2015) and Khaled Beydoun, *American Islamophobia* (Oakland: University of California Press, 2019).

2. Khaled Beydoun, "Between Muslim and White: The Legal Construction of Arab American Identity," *New York University Annual Survey of American Law* 69, no. 29 (2013): 1–35.

3. Nazita Lajevardi, Melissa R. Michelson, and Marianne Marar Yacobian, "The Unbearable Whiteness of Being Middle Eastern: Causes and Effects of the Racialization of Middle Eastern Americans," in *Understanding Muslim Political Life in America: Contested Citizenship in the Twenty-First Century*, ed. Brian R. Calfano and Nazita Lajevardi (Philadelphia: Temple University Press, 2019), 52–68.

4. Kerem Ozan Kalkan, Geoffrey C. Layman, and Eric M. Uslaner, "'Bands of Others'? Attitudes Toward Muslims in Contemporary American Society," *Journal of Politics* 71, no. 3 (July 2009): 847–62.

5. Nazita Lajevardi and Kassra A. R. Oskooii, "Old-Fashioned Racism, Contemporary Islamophobia, and the Isolation of Muslim Americans in the Age of Trump," *Journal of Race, Ethnicity, and Politics* 3 (February 2018): 119.

6. Lajevardi and Oskooii, "Old-Fashioned Racism," 128–29.

7. United States Department of Justice, Federal Bureau of Investigation (FBI), "2017 Hate Crime Statistics," Uniform Crime Reporting (UCR), November 13, 2018, https://ucr.fbi.gov/hate-crime/2017.

8. John Zaller, *The Nature and Origins of Mass Opinion* (New York: Cambridge University Press, 1992).

9. David Lopez and Yen Espiritu, "Panethnicity in the U.S.: A Theoretical Framework," *Ethnic and Racial Studies* 13, no. 2 (2010); Dina G. Okamoto, "Toward a Theory of Panethnicity: Explaining Asian American Collective Action, *American Sociological Review* 68, no. 6 (November 2003).

10. See Felix Padilla, *Latino Ethnic Consciousness: The Case of Mexican Americans and Puerto Ricans in Chicago* (Notre Dame, IN: Notre Dame University Press, 1985).

11. Michael Omi and Howard Winat, *Racial Formations in the United States*, 3rd ed. (New York: Routledge, 2015).

12. Mehdi Bzorgmehr, Paul Ong, and Sarah Tosh, "Panethnicity Revisited: Contested Group Boundaries in the Post-9-11 Era," *Ethnic Racial Studies* 39, no. 5 (2016): 727–45.

13. Bzorgmehr, Ong, and Tosh, "Panethnicity Revisited," 727–45. See also Yen Le Espiritu, *Asian American Panethnicity: Bridging Institutions and Identities* (Philadelphia: Temple University Press, 1992); Yen Le Espiritu and Paul Ong, "Class Constraints on Racial Solidarity Among Asian Americans," in *The New Immigration in Los Angeles and Global Restructuring*, ed. Paul Ong, Edna Bonacich, and Lucie Cheng (Philadelphia: Temple University Press, 1994), 295–321.

14. Henri Tajfel and John C. Turner, "An Integrative Theory of Intergroup Conflict," *Social Psychology of Intergroup Relations* 33, no. 47 (1979): 74–89.

15. Kalkan, Layman, and Uslaner, "'Band of Others'?" 2.

16. Sahar Aziz, "Countering Religion or Terrorism? Selective Enforcement of Material Support Laws against Muslim Charities," Institute for Social Policy and Understanding, Policy Brief #47, September 2011; Sahar Aziz, "Caught in a Preventive Dragnet: Selective Counterterrorism in a Post-9/11 America," *Gonzaga Law Review* 47 (2012): 1–71.

17. Abu-Ras Wahiba and Zulema Suarez, "Muslim Men and Women's Perception of Discrimination, Hate Crimes and PTSD Symptoms Post 9/11," *Traumatology* 15, no. 3 (September 1, 2009); Patricia M. Rodriguez Mosquera, Tasmiha Khan, and Arielle Selya, "American Muslims' Anger and Sadness about In-Group Social Image," *Frontiers in Psychology* 7 (2017).

18. Saher Selod and David Embrick, "Racialization and Muslims: Situating the Muslim Experience in Race Studies," *Social Compass* 7, no. 8 (2013): 651.

19. Matt Barreto and Karam Dana, "Muslim and American: Transnational Ties and Participation in American Politics" (paper presented at the Midwest Political Science Association Conference, Chicago, 2008).

20. Benjamin Radcliff and Martin Saiz, "Race, Turnout, and Public Policy in the American States," *Political Research Quarterly* 48, no. 4 (1995); Adrian Pantoja and Gary Segura, "Fear and Loathing in California: Contextual Threat and Political Sophistication among Latino Voters," *Political Behavior* 25, no. 3 (2003); Matt Barreto, Gary M. Segura, and Nathan D. Woods, "The Mobilizing Effect of Majority-Minority Districts on Latino Turnout," *American Political Science Review* 98, no. 1 (2004).

21. Anny Bakalian and Medhi Bozorgmehr, *Backlash 9/11: Middle Eastern and Muslim Americans Respond* (Berkeley: University of California Press, 2009); Mucahit Bilici, *Finding Mecca in America: How Islam Is Becoming an American Religion* (Chicago: The University of Chicago Press, 2012), 132.

22. Bzorgmehr, Ong, and Tosh, "Panethnicity Revisited."

23. Monisha Das Gupta, *Unruly Immigrants: Rights, Activism, and Transnational South Asian Politics in the United States* (Durham, NC: Duke University Press, 2006).

24. Emily Cury, "How Muslim Americans Are Fighting Islamophobia and Securing Their Civil Rights," *The Conversation* (September 4, 2017).

25. Bert Klandermans, "Collective Political Action," in *Oxford Handbook of Political Psychology*, ed. D. O. Sears, L. Huddy, and R. Jervis (Oxford: Oxford University Press, 2003), 687.

26. Benedict Anderson, *Imagined Communities: Reflections on the Origins and Spread of Nationalism* (London: Verso, 1983).

27. Roger Brubaker, *Ethnicity without Groups* (Cambridge, MA: Harvard University Press, 2004), 13.

28. Brubaker, *Ethnicity without Groups*, 13.

29. Muslim Public Affairs Council (MPAC), *I Am Change*, April 14, 2010, https://www.mpac.org/programs/i-am-change/mpac-hosts-i-am-change-leadership-program.php.

30. Salam Al-Marayati, "My Faith. My Vote. My Future," Muslim Public Affairs Council (MPAC), 2012, https://www.mpac.org/myfaithmyvote.

31. Islamic Circle of North America (ICNA), "Historic First National Muslim Advocacy Day," April 17, 2015, http://www.icna.org/historic-first-national-muslim-advocacy-day.

32. Erica L. Ciszek, "Advocacy Communication and Social Identity," *Journal of Homosexuality* 64, no. 14 (2017).

33. Bilici, *Finding Mecca in America*, 133.

34. See Richard P. Bagozzi, Utpal M. Dholakia, and Lisa R. Klein Pearo, "Antecedents and Consequences of Online Social Interactions," *Media Psychology* 9, no. 1 (2007); Jillianne R. Code and Nicholas E. Zaparyniuk, "Social Identities, Group Formation, and the Analysis of Online Communities," in *Social Computing: Concepts, Methodologies, Tools, and Applications*, ed. Subhasish Dasgupta, 1346–61 (New York: IGI Global, 2010).

35. Caren Neal, "A Social Movement Online Community," *Media Movements and Political Change* 33 (2012): 163–93, https://sociology.unc.edu/files/2016/12/Gaby-SMOC-Caren-Et-al.pdf.

36. Pew Research Center, *Muslim Americans: No Sign of Growth in Alienation or Support for Extremism*, August 2011, 70, https://www.people-press.org/2011/08/30/muslim-americans-no-signs-of-growth-in-alienation-or-support-for-extremism/.

37. See Dispelling Rumors About CAIR at https://www.cair.com/about_cair/dispelling-rumors-about-cair/.

38. Ervin Goffman, *Frame Analysis: An Essay on the Organization of Experience* (Boston: Northeastern University Press, 1974).

39. CAIR, *Challenging Islamophobia Pocket Guide*, accessed April 3, 2020, https://d3n8a8pro7vhmx.cloudfront.net/cairhq/pages/2005/attachments/original/1504011059/Islamophobia-Pocket-Guide.pdf?1504011059.

40. CAIR, MPAC, and other organizations also allow individuals to report personal incidents of Islamophobia on their websites.

41. Muslim stand-up comedy has burgeoned in the post-9/11 era, with comedy troupes such as Axis of Evil (which began touring in 2005 and gained national recognition with an appearance on Comedy Central) and Allah Made Me Funny.

42. Bilici, *Finding Mecca in America*, 196.

43. Quoted in Bilici, *Finding Mecca in America*, 196.

44. Muslim Public Affairs Council (MPAC), "MPAC Launches #ISpeakOutBecause Campaign," August 7, 2014, http://www.mpac.org/issues/civil-rights/mpac-launches-ispeakoutbecause-campaign1.php#.VA5SFEu5fwI.

45. "MPAC Launches #ISpeakOutBecause Campaign."

46. MPAC (@mpac_national), Twitter, August 13, 2014, 11:41 a.m., https://twitter.com/mpac_national/status/499626778718380034.

47. Daniel Eisenbud, "Tariq Abu Khdeir Cleared of Wrongdoing," *Jerusalem Post*, January 28, 2015, http://www.jpost.com/Arab-Israeli-Conflict/Tariq-Abu-Khdeir-cleared-of-wrongdoing-389198.

48. Council on American Islamic Relations (CAIR), "Demand Israel Free and Return Tariq Khdeir to the U.S.," 2014, https://www.cair.com/action_alerts/demand-israel-free -and-return-tariq-khdeir-to-the-u-s/.

2. FROM MUSLIMS IN AMERICA TO AMERICAN MUSLIMS

1. Bill Ong Hing, "Vigilante Racism: The De-Americanization of Immigrant America," *Michigan Journal of Race and Law* 3, no. 7 (2002): 444.

2. Hing, "Vigilante Racism," 444.

3. Paul Ricoeur, *Time and Narrative*, trans. Kathleen Blamey and David Pellauer (Chicago: Chicago University Press, 1988), 247.

4. Ricoeur, *Time and Narrative*, 247.

5. For more on claims making by collective actors, see David Collier and Ruth Collier, *Shaping the Political Arena* (Notre Dame, IN: University of Notre Dame Press, 1991); Kathleen Thelen, "Historical Institutionalism in Comparative Politics," *Annual Review of Political Science* 2 (1999): 369–404; and Theda Skocpol, *Social Policy in the United States* (Princeton, NJ: Princeton University Press, 1995).

6. Tim Buthe, "Taking Temporality Seriously: Modeling History and the Use of Narratives as Evidence," *American Political Science Review* 96, no. 3 (2002): 487.

7. Besheer Mohamed, "New Estimates Show U.S. Muslim Population Continues to Grow," Pew Research Center, January 3, 2018, https://www.pewresearch.org/fact-tank /2018/01/03/new-estimates-show-u-s-muslim-population-continues-to-grow/.

8. Pew Research Center, "U.S. Muslims Concerned about Their Place in Society, But Continue to Believe in the American Dream," July 26, 2017, https://www.pewforum.org /2017/07/26/findings-from-pew-research-centers-2017-survey-of-us-muslims/.

9. Julianne Hammer and Omid Safi, *The Cambridge Companion to American Islam* (Cambridge: Cambridge University Press, 2013), 29–44.

10. However, their theological beliefs differ vastly from those of mainstream Muslims and are thus better understood as a uniquely indigenous American religion that borrowed from Islam. For more on this subject, see Kambiz Ghanea Bassiri's excellent book, *A History of Islam in America* (Cambridge: Cambridge University Press, 2010), 193–227.

11. Southern Poverty Law Center (SPLC), "Nation of Islam," Extremist Files, accessed March 18, 2020, https://www.splcenter.org/fighting-hate/extremist-files/group/nation -islam.

12. Pew Research Center, *U.S. Muslims Concerned*, 37.

13. Karen Leonard, *Muslims in the United States: The State of Research* (New York: Russell Sage Foundation, 2003); Yvonne Yazbeck Haddad, *Becoming American? The Forging of Arab and Muslim Identity in Pluralist America* (Waco, TX: Baylor University Press, 2011).

14. Haddad, *Becoming American?*; Yvonne Haddad, Jane Smith, and John Esposito, *Religion and Immigration: Christian, Jewish and Muslim Experience in the United States* (Oxford: Altamira Press, 2003).

15. Gustavo López and Jynnah Radford, "2015, Foreign-Born Population in the United States Statistical Portrait," Hispanic Trends, Pew Research Center, May 3, 2017, http:// www.pewhispanic.org/2017/05/03/facts-on-u-s-immigrants-current-data/.

16. Pew Research Center, "Facts on U.S. Immigration, 2017: Statistical Portrait of the Foreign-Born Population in the United States," June 3, 2019, https://www.pewresearch .org/hispanic/2019/06/03/facts-on-u-s-immigrants/.

17. Samuel Huntington, *Who Are We? The Challenges to America's National Identity* (New York: Simon & Schuster, 2004); Haddad, Smith, and Esposito, *Religion and Immigration*.

18. Caroline R. Nagel and Lynn A. Staeheli, "'We're Just Like the Irish': Narratives of Assimilation, Belonging and Citizenship amongst Arab-American Activists," *Citizenship Studies* 9, no. 5 (2005): 485–98.

19. For more on the Americanization movement at the turn of the twentieth century, see Katharyne Mitchell, "Education for Democratic Citizenship: Transnationalism, Multiculturalism, and the Limits of Liberalism," *Harvard Educational Review* 71, no. 1 (2001): 51–79; Frank Van Nuys, *Americanizing the West: Race, Immigrants, and Citizenship, 1890–1930* (Lawrence: University Press of Kansas, 2002); and Aneta Pavlenko, "'We Have Room for But One Language Here': Language and National Identity in the US at the Turn of the 20th Century," *Multilingua* 21 (2002): 163–96.

20. Howard C. Hill, "The Americanization Movement," *American Journal of Sociology* 25, no. 6 (1919): 609–42.

21. With its large immigrant workforce at the turn of the twentieth century, Ford Motor Company was at the forefront of the Americanization movement. For an excellent analysis on the subject, see Stephen Meyer, "Adapting the Immigrant to the Line: Americanization in the Ford Factory, 1914–1921," *Journal of Social History* 14, no. 1 (1980): 71.

22. Quoted in Meyer, "Adapting the Immigrant to the Line," 73.

23. Yvonne Yazbeck Haddad, *Not Quite American? The Shaping of Arab and Muslim Identity in the United States* (Waco, TX: Baylor University Press, 2004), 4.

24. Haddad, *Not Quite American?* 4.

25. Haddad, *Not Quite American?* 24. See also Leonard, *Muslims in the United States*; Bakalian and Bozorgmehr, *Backlash 9/11*.

26. Jill Johnson, *Lesbian Nation: The Feminist Solution* (New York: Simon and Schuster, 1973); Luce Irigaray, *Je, Tu, Nous: Toward a Culture of Difference* (New York: Routledge, 1993).

27. Leonard, *Muslims in the United States*.

28. For a summary of this perspective, see Huntington, *Who Are We?*

29. Peggy Levitt, "Transnational Migrants: When 'Home' Means More Than One Country," Migration Policy Institute, October 1, 2004, https://www.migrationpolicy.org/article/transnational-migrants-when-home-means-more-one-country.

30. For more on transnationalism and its positive impact on the process of immigrant settlement and integration, see Alvaro Lima, "Transnationalism: A New Mode of Immigrant Integration" (paper presented at Securing the Dream: Power, Progress, Prosperity, the Statewide Latino Public Policy Conference, The Mauricio Gastón Institute, University of Massachusetts, Boston, September 17, 2010), http://www.bostonplans.org/getattachment/b5ea6e3a-e94e-451b-af08-ca9fcc3a1b5b/; Alejandro Portes and Rubén Lambaut, *Immigrant America: A Portrait* (Berkeley: University of California Press, 2006); Laura Morales and Miruna Morariu, "Is 'Home' a Distraction? The Role of Migrants' Transnational Practices in Their Political Integration into Receiving-Country Politics," in *Social Capital, Political Participation and Migration in Europe: Making Multicultural Democracy Work?* ed. Laura Morales and Marco Giugni (London: Palgrave Macmillan, 2011), 140–71; Ewa Morawska, "Immigrant Transnationalism and Assimilation: A Variety of Combination and the Analytic Strategy It Suggests," in *Toward Assimilation and Citizenship: Immigrants in Liberal Nation-States*, ed. Christian Joppe and Ewa Morawska, 133–76 (Basingstoke, UK: Palgrave-Macmillan, 2003); and Steven Vertovec, "Migration and Other Modes of Transnationalism: Towards Conceptual Cross-Fertilization," *International Migration Review* 37, no. 3 (2003): 951–73.

31. Aslam Abdullah and Gasser Hathout, *The American Muslim Identity: Speaking for Ourselves* (Los Angeles: Multimedia Vera International, 2003); Haddad, *Not Quite American?*

32. Nadine Naber, "'Look, Mohammed the Terrorist Is Coming!' Cultural Racism, Nation-Based Racism, and the Intersectionality of Oppressions after 9/11," in *Race and Arab Americans before and after 9/11: From Invisible Citizens to Visible Subjects*, ed. Amaney Jamal and Nadine Naber (Syracuse, NY: Syracuse University Press, 2003), 276–304.

33. Haddad, *Not Quite American?* 6.

34. Haddad, *Becoming American?*; Bilici, *Finding Mecca in America*.

35. Bilici, *Finding Mecca in America*, 92.

36. Stuart Hall, "The Question of Cultural Identity," in *Modernity: An Introduction to Modern Societies*, ed. Stuart Hall, Don Huber, and Thomson Kenneth (Cambridge: Cambridge University Press, 1996); Ruth Wodak, "The Discourse-Historical Approach," in *Methods of Critical Discourse Analysis*, ed. Ruth Wodak and Michael Meyer (London: Sage, 2001).

37. For an excellent introduction to Islam's early history and principles, see John Esposito, *The Oxford History of Islam* (Oxford: Oxford University Press, 1999).

38. Bilici, *Finding Mecca in America*.

39. Christoph Schumann, "A Muslim Diaspora in the United States?" *Muslim World* 97, no. 11 (2007): 11, 32.

40. Syed Abul Hassan Ali Nadwi, *Muslims in the West: The Message and Mission* (Leicester, UK: The Islamic Foundation, 1983), 111.

41. Bilici, *Finding Mecca in America*.

42. Charles Hirschman, "The Origins and Demise of the Concept of Race," *Population and Development Review* 30, no. 3 (2004): 6.

43. For the role of the church in mobilizing African Americans and other minority groups, see Sidney Verba, Kay Lehman Schlozman, and Henry E. Brady, *Voice and Equality: Civic Voluntarism in American Politics*, vol. 4 (Cambridge, MA: Harvard University Press, 1995); Allison Calhoun-Brown, "African American Churches and Political Mobilization: The Psychological Impact of Organizational Resources," *Journal of Politics* 58, no. 4 (1996): 935–53; and Michael Jones-Correa and David L. Leal, "Political Participation: Does Religion Matter?" *Political Research Quarterly* 54, no. 4 (2001): 751–70. Amaney Jamal was the first scholar to extend these studies to examine the role of mosque participation on Muslim Americans' political mobilization; see Amaney Jamal, "The Political Participation and Engagement of Muslim Americans: Mosque Involvement and Group Consciousness," *American Politics Research* 33, no. 4 (2005): 521–44.

44. Karam Dana, Bryan Wilcox-Archuleta, and Matt Barreto, "The Political Incorporation of Muslims in the United States: The Mobilizing Role of Religiosity in Islam," *Journal of Race, Ethnicity, and Politics* 2, no. 2 (September 2017): 170–200.

45. The mosque, established in Detroit by Imam Hussein Karoub, an immigrant from Syria who arrived in Michigan in 1914 to work at the Ford plant, did not survive long, most likely due to lack of funding. Imam Karoub established another mosque in 1937, known as the Dix Mosque, which still exists today.

46. Ihsa Bagby, *The American Mosque 2011: Basic Characteristics of the American Mosque, Attitude of Mosque Leaders*, US Mosque Study Report 1, January 2012.

47. Akel Ismail Kahera, *Deconstructing the American Mosque: Space, Gender and Aesthetics* (Austin: University of Texas Press, 2002).

48. Leonard, *Muslims in the United States*.

49. Omar Khalidi, "Mosques in North America," *American Studies Journal* 52 (2008), http://www.asjournal.org/52-2008/mosques-in-north-america/.

50. Women's Mosque of America, "FAQ," accessed March 19, 2020, http://womensmosque.com/faq/.

51. Muslim Students Association, "Who We Are," https://www.msanational.org.

52. Islamic Society of North America, "About," http://www.isna.net/about/.

53. See Why Islam, "About Us," https://www.whyislam.org/about/.

54. Benedict Anderson, *Imagined Communities: Reflections on the Origins and Spread of Nationalism* (London: Verso, 1993).

55. Robert Putnam, *Bowling Alone: The Collapse and Revival of American Community* (New York: Simon and Schuster, 2000).

56. Larry Poston, *Islamic Da'wah in the West: Muslim Missionary Activity and the Dynamics of Conversion to Islam* (New York: Oxford University Press, 1992), 32.

57. Author interview with Corey Saylor, CAIR director of the Department to Monitor and Combat Islamophobia, June 22, 2014.

58. Tom Gjelten, *A Nation of Nations: A Great American Immigration Story* (New York: Simon & Schuster, 2015).

59. Bilici, *Finding Mecca in America*, 126.

60. Eric Lichtblau, "Arrests Tie Charity Group to Palestinian Terrorists," *New York Times*, July 28, 2004, https://www.nytimes.com/2004/07/28/us/arrests-tie-charity-group-to-palestinian-terrorists.html.

61. Christoph Schumann, "Muslim Diaspora in the United States?" 11–32; Peter Mandaville, "Reimagining Islam in Diaspora: The Politics of Mediated Community," *International Communication Gazette*, 2001; Haddad, *Becoming American?*; Bilici, *Finding Mecca in America*.

62. Among the most important Muslim intellectuals writing on issues of democracy and pluralism from an Islamic perspective prior to 9/11 were Fathi Osman, a Princeton University–educated scholar born in Egypt, and Abdulaziz Sachedina, the current chair of George Mason University's Islamic Studies Program. For an excellent analysis on the topic, see Abdulaziz Sachedina, *The Islamic Roots of Democratic Pluralism* (New York: Oxford University Press, 2001).

63. Author interview with Salam Al-Marayati, president of MPAC, July 2, 2013.

3. FROM THE PATRIOT ACT TO THE "MUSLIM BAN"

1. Author interview with Corey Saylor, July 22, 2014.

2. Author interview with Sarwat Hussain, president of CAIR-San Antonio, May 2, 2017.

3. Author interview with Khaled Beydoun, July 8, 2019.

4. Glenn Greenwald and Murtaza Hussain, "Meet the Muslim American Leaders the FBI and NSA Have Been Spying On," *Intercept*, July 9, 2014, https://firstlook.org/theintercept/2014/07/09/under-surveillance.

5. For more on the subject, see Louise Cainkar, "Post 9/11 Domestic Policies Affecting U.S. Arabs and Muslims: A Brief Review," *Comparative Studies of South Asia, Africa and the Middle East* 24, no. 1 (2005): 245–48; Leti Volpp, "The Citizen and the Terrorist," *UCLA Law Review* 49 (2001): 1576–601; John W. Whitehead and Steven H. Aden, "Forfeiting Enduring Freedom for Homeland Security: A Constitutional Analysis of the USA Patriot Act and the Justice Department's Anti-Terrorism Initiatives," *American University Law Review* 51 (2002): 1081; Vijay Sekhon, "The Civil Rights of 'Others': Antiterrorism, The Patriot Act, and Arab and South Asian American Rights in Post-9/11 American Society," *Texas Forum on Civil Liberties & Civil Rights* 8 (2003); Aziz, "Countering Religion or Terrorism?"

6. Exec. Order No. 13769, "Executive Order Protecting the Nation from Foreign Terrorist Entry into the United States," March 6, 2017, https://www.whitehouse.gov/the-press-office/2017/03/06/executive-order-protecting-nation-foreign-terrorist-entry-united-states.

7. Article II of the Constitution and §212f of the Immigration and Nationality Act give the executive broad powers over immigration policy and enforcement.

8. Louise Cainkar and Sunaina Maira, "Targeting Arab/Muslim/South Asian Americans: Criminalization and Cultural Citizenship," *Amerasia Journal* 31, no. 3 (2005): 1–28.

9. Ibrahim Al-Marashi, "Travel Bans in Historical Perspective: Executive Orders Have Defined 'Terrorists' Since Nixon," *Perspectives on History*, November 2017, https://www.historians.org/publications-and-directories/perspectives-on-history/november-2017/travel-bans-in-historical-perspective-executive-orders-have-defined-terrorists-since-nixon.

10. Richard Nixon, "Memorandum Establishing a Cabinet Committee to Combat Terrorism," September 25, 1972 (available at The American Presidency Project, UC Santa Barbara, https://www.presidency.ucsb.edu/documents/memorandum-establishing-cabinet-committee-combat-terrorism).

11. Haddad, *Not Quite American?* 21.

12. Paul Magnusson, "FBI Reveals FBI Tapping of Sirhan Lawyer's Calls," *Washington Post*, August 3, 1997, https://www.washingtonpost.com/archive/politics/1977/08/03/fbi-reveals-nsa-tapping-of-sirhan-lawyers-calls/044c120f-a22f-449a-b175-62f424a06378/.

13. President George W. Bush proposed the Uniting and Strengthening America by Providing Appropriate Tools Required to Intercept and Obstruct Terrorism Act on September 24, 2001. It passed almost unanimously, and without debate, in the Senate (98–1) and the House of Representatives (357–66) and was signed into law on October 26, 2001. President Barack Obama extended the act on May 26, 2011.

14. Susan Herman, "Taking Liberties: The ACLU and the War on Terror," ACLU, June 12, 2011, https://www.aclu.org/other/taking-liberties-aclu-and-war-terror.

15. Herman, "Taking Liberties."

16. Darren K. Carlson, "Far Enough? Public Wary of Restricted Liberties," Gallup, January 20, 2004, http://news.gallup.com/poll/10324/far-enough-public-wary-restricted-liberties.aspx.

17. Carlson, "Far Enough?"

18. Pew Research Center, *United in Remembrance, Divided over Policies: Ten Years after 9/11*, U.S. Politics & Policy, September 1, 2011, http://www.people-press.org/2011/09/01/united-in-remembrance-divided-over-policies/.

19. American Civil Liberties Union (ACLU), "ACLU Files First-Ever Challenge to USA Patriot Act, Citing Radical Expansion of FBI Powers," July 30, 2003, https://www.aclu.org/news/aclu-files-first-ever-challenge-usa-patriot-act-citing-radical-expansion-fbi-powers.

20. United States Congress, Uniting and Strengthening America by Providing Appropriate Tools Required to Intercept and Obstruct Terrorism Act of 2001 (USA PATRIOT Act). Pub. L. No. 107–56, 115 Stat. 272 (2001). http://www.gpo.gov/fdsys/pkg/PLAW-107publ56/pdf/PLAW-107publ56.pdf.

21. Sekhon, "The Civil Rights of 'Others.'"

22. USA PATRIOT Act §102(5).

23. USA PATRIOT Act §102(4).

24. ACLU, *Unpatriotic Acts: The FBI's Power to Rifle through Your Records and Personal Belongings without Telling You*, July 2003, 3, https://www.aclu.org/other/unpatriotic-acts-fbis-power-rifle-through-your-records-and-personal-belongings-without-telling.

25. Sekhon, "The Civil Rights of 'Others,'" 126.

26. US Department of Justice, Office of the Inspector General, *The September 11 Detainees: A Review of the Treatment of Aliens Held on Immigration Charges in Connection with the Investigation of the September 11 Attacks*, June 2003, https://oig.justice.gov/special/0306/chapter2.htm#II.

27. Ziglar v. Abbasi, 582 U.S. ___ (2017), https://supreme.justia.com/cases/federal /us/582/15-1358/opinion3.html.

28. US Department of Justice, FBI, *Domestic Investigations and Operations Guide*, December 16, 2008, https://vault.fbi.gov/FBI%20Domestic%20Investigations%20and%20 Operations%20Guide%20(DIOG).

29. ACLU, *Unleashed and Unaccountable: The FBI's Unchecked Abuse of Authority*, September 2013, 16, https://www.aclu.org/sites/default/files/assets/unleashed-and-unaccoun table-fbi-report.pdf.

30. ACLU, *Unleashed and Unaccountable*, 17.

31. ACLU, *Blocking Faith, Freezing Charity: Chilling Muslim Charitable Giving in the "War on Terrorism Financing,"* June 2009, 59, https://www.aclu.org/files/pdfs/humanrights /blockingfaith.pdf.

32. Barbara Bradley Hagerty, "Muslims Face Risk in Giving to Charities," *Morning Edition*, NPR, June 16, 2009, http://www.npr.org/templates/story/story.php?storyId =105449968.

33. ACLU, *Blocking Faith, Freezing Charity*, 48.

34. ACLU, *Blocking Faith, Freezing Charity*, 62.

35. ACLU, "ACLU Challenges Government Stigmatization of Mainstream Muslim Groups in Holy Land Case," June 18, 2018, https://www.aclu.org/press-releases/aclu-chal lenges-governments-stigmatizing-mainstream-muslim-groups-holy-land-case.

36. ACLU, "Statements of Support for UCC Clients," accessed March 20, 2020, https://www.aclu.org/other/statements-support-ucc-clients.

37. United States of America v. Holy Land Foundation for Relief and Development et al. North American Islamic Trust (5th Cir. Oct. 20, 2010), http://caselaw.findlaw.com /us-5th-circuit/1541982.html.

38. Ashcroft announced NSEER in November 2002. The program consisted of two parts: the first entailed registration of immigrants through ports of entry; the second called for "voluntary" registrations of nonresident immigrants. See Maia Jachimowicz and Ramah McKay, "'Special Registration' Program," Migration Policy Institute, April 1, 2003, http://www.migrationpolicy.org/article/special-registration-program#1.

39. BBC News, "Mass Arrests of Muslims in LA," December 19, 2002, http://news .bbc.co.uk/2/hi/americas/2589317.stm.

40. US Department of Justice, Immigration and Naturalization Service, "Department of Justice Proposes New Rule for Nonimmigrant Aliens," June 13, 2002 (available at US Department of State Archive, http://2001-2009.state.gov/s/ct/rls/fs/2002/11409.htm).

41. Naber, "'Look, Mohammad the Terrorist Is Coming!'" 285.

42. Bill Ong Hing, "Misusing Immigration Policies in the Name of Homeland Security," *CR: The New Centennial Review* 6, no. 1 (2006): 195–224; Bakalian and Bozorg-mehr, *Backlash 9/11*.

43. Alexander Cockburn, "Obama and the Indefinite Detention of U.S. Citizens," *Nation*, January 4, 2012, https://www.thenation.com/article/obama-and-indefinite-detention -us-citizens/.

44. Maha Hilal, "When Life Is Disposable: Muslim Bodies as Precarious in the War on Terror," Amnesty International, accessed March 20, 2020, https://www.amnestyusa.org /when-life-is-disposable-muslim-bodies-as-precarious-in-the-war-on-terror/.

45. ACLU, "ACLU Says Bush Administration Should Not Allow Operation TIPS to Become an End Run around Constitution," July 15, 2002, https://www.aclu.org/news /aclu-says-bush-administration-should-not-allow-operation-tips-become-end-run -around.

46. §880 of the Homeland Security Act, signed into law on November 25, 2002, specifically forbade the creation of the TIPS program.

47. Greenwald and Hussain, "Meet the Muslim American Leaders."

48. Petra Bartosiewicz, "Deploying Informants, the FBI Stings Muslims," *Nation*, June 14, 2012, https://www.thenation.com/article/deploying-informants-fbi-stings-muslims/.

49. ACLU, "Factsheet: The NYPD Muslim Surveillance Program," accessed March 20, 2020, https://www.aclu.org/other/factsheet-nypd-muslim-surveillance-program.

50. Mitchell D. Silber and Arvin Bhatt, *Radicalization in the West: The Homegrown Threat*, Intelligence Division, New York Police Department (NYPD), 2007, 8; https://info .publicintelligence.net/NYPDradicalization.pdf.

51. Silber and Bhatt, *Radicalization in the West*, 12.

52. In June 2013, the ACLU, the NYCLU, and the CLEAR Project at CUNY Law School filed a lawsuit challenging the NYPD's surveillance program.

53. US Department of Justice, FBI, "Response to Media Reporting Regarding Counterterrorism Training," FBI National Press Office, September 15, 2011, https://archives .fbi.gov/archives/news/pressrel/press-releases/response-to-media-reporting-regarding -counterterrorism-training.

54. Although my research is concerned with the effects of othering the Muslim American out-group, internal *others* are fundamental for the construction of any national identity. Through the (re)presentation of the other, the identity of the in-group is also (re)produced.

55. US Government Printing Office (GPO), *Compilation of Hearings on Islamist Radicalization—Volume 1* (Washington, DC: GPO, 2012), 3, https://www.gpo.gov/fdsys /pkg/CHRG-112hhrg72541/pdf/CHRG-112hhrg72541.pdf.

56. CNN, "Emotions Fly at Controversial Hearing on Muslim Americans," March 10, 2011, https://www.cnn.com/2011/POLITICS/03/10/radicalization.hearings/index.html.

57. CNN, "Emotions Fly."

58. Pew Research Center, *Muslim Americans: Middle Class and Mostly Mainstream*, May 22, 2007, https://www.pewresearch.org/2007/05/22/muslim-americans-middle-class -and-mostly-mainstream/.

59. Pew Research Center, *Muslim Americans: Middle Class and Mostly Mainstream*, 7.

60. "Peter King's Obsession," *New York Times*, March 7, 2011, http://www.nytimes .com/2011/03/08/opinion/08tue1.html.

61. Daniel W. Reilly, "Rep. Peter King: There Are 'Too Many Mosques in This Country,'" *Politico Now* (blog), Politico, September 19, 2007, https://www.politico.com/blogs /politico-now/2007/09/rep-peter-king-there-are-too-many-mosques-in-this-country -003213. See also WorldNetDaily (WND), "Congressman: Muslims 'Enemy amongst Us,'" February 13, 2004, http://www.wnd.com/2004/02/23257/.

62. Suzanne Ito, "ACLU Lens: King Hearings Relies on False Premises, Discriminatory Attitudes," *Speak Freely* (blog), ACLU, March 11, 2011, https://www.aclu.org/blog /national-security/aclu-lens-king-hearing-relies-false-premises-discriminatory-attitudes.

63. Author interview with John Robbins, July 29, 2016.

64. Elsadig Elsheikh, Basima Sisemore, and Natalia Ramirez Lee, *Legalizing Othering: The United States of Islamophobia* (Berkeley, CA: Haas Institute for a Fair and Inclusive Society, 2017), https://haasinstitute.berkeley.edu/sites/default/files/haas_institute_legalizing _othering_the_united_states_of_islamophobia.pdf.

65. Azmat Khan, "Pamela Geller: 'This Is a Clash of Civilizations,'" *Frontline*, PBS, September 27, 2011, http://www.pbs.org/wgbh/frontline/article/pamela-geller-this-is-a -clash-of-civilizations/.

66. Elsheikh, Sisemore, and Lee, *Legalizing Othering*, 20.

67. Pew Research Center, "Controversies over Mosques and Islamic Centers Across the U.S.," Religion & Public Life, September 27, 2012, http://www.pewforum.org/2012 /09/27/controversies-over-mosques-and-islamic-centers-across-the-u-s-2/.

68. Laurie Goodstein, "Across Nation, Mosque Projects Meet Opposition," *New York Times*, August 7, 2010, http://www.nytimes.com/2010/08/08/us/08mosque.html ?pagewanted=all&mcubz=3.

69. ACLU, "Nationwide Anti-Mosque Activity," updated December 2019, https://www .aclu.org/issues/national-security/discriminatory-profiling/nationwide-anti-mosque -activity.

70. Othering and Belonging Institute, UC Berkeley, "Islamophobia," accessed March 23, 2020, https://belonging.berkeley.edu/global-justice/islamophobia.

71. SPLC, "David Yerushalmi," Extremist Files, accessed March 23, 2020, https://www .splcenter.org/fighting-hate/extremist-files/individual/david-yerushalmi#.UalaAK VfmCI.

72. US Department of Justice, FBI, *Hate Crime Statistics, 2001*, Uniform Crime Reporting (UCR), accessed March 23, 2020, https://ucr.fbi.gov/hate-crime/2001.

73. Dalia Mogahed, "Islamophobia Is Made Up," *Islamic Monthly*, September 25, 2013, http://www.theislamicmonthly.com/islamophobia-is-made-up/.

74. Jeffrey Kaplan, "Islamophobia in America? September 11 and Islamophobic Hate," *Terrorism and Political Violence* 18, no. 1 (2007): 24.

75. The FBI's Hate Crime Statistics annual reports (starting with 1996) are available at https://www.fbi.gov/services/cjis/ucr/publications#Hate-Crime%20Statisticshttps:// www.fbi.gov/services/cjis/ucr/publications#Hate-Crime%20Statistics.

76. Mark Potok, "DOJ Study: More Than 250,000 Hate Crimes a Year, Most Unreported," Southern Poverty Law Center, March 26, 2013, https://www.splcenter.org /hatewatch/2013/03/26/doj-study-more-250000-hate-crimes-year-most-unreported.

77. Michael Tesler, "The Conditions Ripe for Racial Spillover Effect," *Political Psychology* 36 (2015): 101–17.

78. Scholars from across disciplines have examined the process of public opinion formation and the role elites play in that process. For some of this literature, see P. E. Converse, "The Nature of Belief Systems in Mass Publics," in *Ideology and Discontent*, ed. D. Apter (New York: Free Press, 1964); Zaller, *Nature and Origins of Mass Opinion*; J. Karp, "The Influence of Elite Endorsements in Initiative Campaigns," *Citizens as Legislators* 3 (1998): 149–65; Adam Berinsky, *In Time of War: Understanding American Public Opinion from World War II to Iraq* (Chicago: University of Chicago Press, 2009); and G. L. Cohen, "Party over Policy: The Dominating Impact of Group Influence on Political Beliefs," *Journal of Personality and Social Psychology* 85, no. 5 (2003).

79. Zaller, *Nature and Origins of Mass Opinion*, 13–14; Teun A. Van Dijk, "Principles of Critical Discourse Analysis," *Discourse & Society* 4, no. 3 (1993): 249–83.

80. Jessica Autumn-Brown, "The New Southern Strategy: Immigration, Race and "Welfare Dependency" in "Contemporary US Republican Political Discourse," *Geopolitics, History and International Relations* 8, no. 2 (2016): 22–41; Eduardo Bonilla-Silva, "What We Were, What We Are, and What We Should Be: The Racial Problem of American Sociology," *Social Problems* 64, no. 2 (2017): 79–87.

81. Antoine J. Banks and Nicholas A. Valentino, "Emotional Substrates of Racial Attitudes," *American Journal of Political Science* 56, no. 2 (2012): 286–97.

82. Tyler Reny, Ali Valenzuela, and Loren Collingwood, "'No, You're Playing the Race Card': Testing the Effects of Anti-Black, Anti-Latino and Anti-Immigrant Appeals in the Post-Obama Era," *Journal of Political Psychology* 42, no 2 (2020): 283–302.

83. Mahzarin R. Banaji and Anthony G. Greenwald, *Blindspot: Hidden Biases of Good People* (New York: Bantam, 2013).

84. Donald Kinder and Lynn Sanders, *Divided by Color: Racial Politics and Democratic Ideals* (Chicago: University of Chicago Press, 1996).

85. Brian Levin, *Special Status Report: Hate Crimes in the Cities and Counties of the U.S.: Compilation of Official Data (15 Jurisdictions)* (California State University, San Bernardino, Center for the Study of Hate and Extremism, 2017), 5, https://mynewsla.com/wp-content/uploads/2017/04/Special-Status-Report-Metro-Areas-2017-Final-Draft-32517.pdf.

86. Joshua Blank, "When Evaluating Public Support for Immigration Ban, Look beyond National Polling" (Texas Politics Project at the University of Texas at Austin, January 30, 2017), https://texaspolitics.utexas.edu/blog/when-evaluating-public-support-immigration-ban-look-beyond-national-polling.

87. Benjamin Page and Robert Shapiro, *The Rational Public: Fifty Years of Trends in American Policy Preferences* (Chicago: University of Chicago Press, 1992).

88. Loren Collingwood, Nazita Lajevardi, and Kassra Oskooii, "A Change of Heart? Why Individual-Level Public Opinion Shifted against Trump's 'Muslim Ban,'" *Political Behavior* 40, no. 4 (2018): 1035–72.

4. THE RISE OF THE MUSLIM AMERICAN LOBBY

1. Jana Winter, "Welcome to the Quiet Skies," *Boston Globe*, July 28, 2018, http://apps.bostonglobe.com/news/nation/graphics/2018/07/tsa-quiet-skies/?p1=HP_SpecialTSA.

2. Author interview with Salam Al-Marayati, June 22, 2013.

3. Author interview with Hassan Shibly, July 6, 2019.

4. Author interview with Al-Marayati.

5. Author interview with Al-Marayati.

6. J. Craig Jenkins, "Resource Mobilization Theory and the Study of Social Movements," *Annual Review of Sociology* 9 (1983): 527–53; Lorraine Minnite, "Outside the Circle: The Impact of Post-9/11 Responses on Immigrant Communities in New York City," in *Contentious City: The Politics of Recovery in New York City*, ed. John H. Mollenkopf (New York: Russell Sage Foundation, 2005): 165–204.

7. Although most scholarship on lobbying tends to emphasize the role of political entrepreneurs and the selective benefits that enable them to pursue political ends, lobbying is also often articulated as the pursuit of a set of strategic interest and policy preferences. See David Truman, *The Governmental Process*, 2nd ed. (New York: Knopf, 1971); Alexander L. George, *Presidential Decisionmaking in Foreign Policy: The Effective Use of Information and Advice* (Boulder, CO: Westview, 1980); Roger Hilsman, Laura Gaughran, and Patricia A. Weitsman, *The Politics of Policy Making in Defense and Foreign Affairs: Conceptual Models and Bureaucratic Politics* (Englewood Cliffs, NJ: Prentice-Hall, 1987); Mark Hansen, *Gaining Access: Congress and the Farm Lobby, 1919–1981* (New York: Cambridge University Press, 1991); Anthony J. Nownes and Patricia Freeman, "Interest Group Activity in the States," *Journal of Politics* 60 (1998): 86–112; Gene Grossman and Elhanah Helpman, *Special Interest Politics* (Cambridge, MA: MIT Press, 2002); Thomas Holyoke, "Interest Group Competition and Coalition Formation," *American Journal of Political Science* 53 (2009): 360–75.

8. Robert Salisbury et al., "Who Is at War with Whom? Interest Group Alliances and Opposition," *American Political Science Review* 81 (1987): 1217–34; Jeffrey Berry, *Lobbying for the People: The Political Behavior of Public Interest Groups* (Princeton, NJ: Princeton University Press, 1997); Jack L. Walker, *Mobilizing Interest Groups in America: Patrons, Professions and Social Movements* (Ann Arbor: University of Michigan Press, 1991).

9. Robert Salisbury, "An Exchange Theory of Interest Groups," *Midwest Journal of Political Science* 13 (1969): 1–32; Donatella della Porta and Mario Diani, *Social Movements:*

An Introduction (Oxford: Blackwell, 2009); Elisabeth Jean Wood, *Insurgent Collective Action and Civil War in El Salvador* (Cambridge: Cambridge University Press, 2003).

10. On the role of social networks and their influence on interest-group decision making, see Scott McClurg and Jeremy Philips, "A Social Network Analysis of Interest Group Contributions and Partisan Behavior in the 2006 House of Representatives" (proceedings of the Political Network Summer Conference, Southern Illinois University Carbondale, 2011); Michael Heaney, "Multiplex Networks and Interest Group Influence Reputation: An Exponential Random Graph Model," *Social Networks* 36 (2014): 66–81.

11. For an account of CAIR's legal advocacy work, see http://www.cair.com/civil-rights/in-the-courts.html.

12. Author interview with Corey Saylor, June 22, 2013.

13. See the Muslim Legal Fund's website, https://www.mlfa.org/about/.

14. Muslim Legal Fund of America, "Muslim Leaders Convene in Dallas for National Leadership Conference," October 6, 2017, https://www.mlfa.org/news/muslims-leaders-convene-in-dallas-for-national-leadership-conference/.

15. See US Department of Homeland Security, Countering Violent Extremism Taskforce, https://www.dhs.gov/cve/what-is-cve.

16. Author interview with Saylor.

17. Author interview with Saylor.

18. Author interview with Roula Allouch, April 17, 2019.

19. Nihad Awad, "Muslim Leader: Homophobia and Islamophobia Are Connected Systems of Oppression," *Time*, June 14, 2016, http://time.com/4367554/muslim-leader-on-orlando-shooting/.

20. Jaweed Kaleem, "How the Orlando Attack Could Mark a Shift for Gay Muslims," *Los Angeles Times*, June 14, 2016, https://www.latimes.com/nation/la-na-gay-muslim-20160614-20160612-snap-story.html.

21. David C. King and Jack L. Walker, "The Provision of Benefits by Interest Groups in the United States," *Journal of Politics* 54 (1992): 406; Wood, *Insurgent Collective Action*.

22. Salisbury, "Exchange Theory"; Della Porta and Diani, *Social Movements*; Wood, *Insurgent Collective Action*.

23. Anthony J. Nownes, "The Population Ecology of Interest Group Formation: Mobilizing for Gay and Lesbian Rights in the United States," *British Journal of Political Science* 34 (2003): 49–67.

24. Wood, *Insurgent Collective Action*.

25. Ileana Najarro, "Man Who Threatened Muslim Is Sentenced to 13 Months," *New York Times*, July 7, 2015, https://www.nytimes.com/2015/07/08/nyregion/no-jail-term-for-threats-against-a-muslim-man.html?_r=0.

26. Nihad Awad, "I am a Muslim American Leader, and the NSA Spied on Me," *Time*, July 9, 2014, https://time.com/2970573/muslim-american-nsa-spies.

27. Deposition of Hassan Shibly, p. 175, February 12, 2018, in the Matter of Elhady vs. Kable, 391 F. Supp. 3d 562 (E.D. Va. 2019).

28. Author Interview with Al-Marayati.

29. Quoted in Bilici, *Finding Mecca in America*, 128.

30. Anti-Defamation League (ADL), "ADL Joins Groups Calling on Mayors to Disavow Anti-Muslim Marches," June 9, 2017, https://www.adl.org/news/press-releases/adl-joins-groups-calling-on-mayors-to-disavow-anti-muslim-marches. For a critique of ADL's actions, see Zionist Organization of America (ZOA), "ZOA Criticizes ADL, AJC, Reform, for Joining Anti-Israel CAIR, MPAC, Presby. in Letter Supporting Syrian Refugees," December 8, 2015, https://zoa.org/2015/12/10306402-zoa-dont-bring-isisterrorist-infiltrated-hamas-supporting-jew-hating-syrian-muslims-into-the-u-s/.

31. David Austen-Smith and John R. Wright, "Counteractive Lobbying," *American Journal of Political Science* 38, no. 1 (1994): 25–44; Frank Baumgartner and Beth L. Leech, "Interest Niches and Policy Bandwagons: Patterns of Interest Group Involvement in National Politics," *Journal of Politics* 63, no. 4 (2001): 1191–213; C. Edwards et al., *Government in America: People, Politics and Policy* (New York: Longman, 2009).

32. MPAC, "Our Approach to Government Engagement," http://www.mpac.org/programs/government-relations.php.

33. MPAC, "Our Approach to Government Engagement."

34. Author interview with Haris Tarin, July 22, 2013.

35. Muslim Legal Fund of America, "Impact," accessed May 2, 2020, https://app.mobilecause.com/vf/MLFA.

36. MPAC, "I Am Change: Civic Leadership Program," https://www.mpac.org/programs/i-am-change/mpac-hosts-i-am-change-leadership-program.php.

37. Pew Research Center, "Most Muslim Americans Are U.S. Citizens, But Many Are Not Registered or Did Not Vote in 2016 Election," *U.S. Muslims Concerned about Their Place in Society, But Continue to Believe in the American Dream: Findings from Pew Research Center's 2017 Survey of U.S. Muslims*, July 26, 2017, http://www.pewforum.org/2017/07/26/political-and-social-views/pf_2017-06-26_muslimamericans-04new-02/.

38. Pew Research Center, "Black Voter Turnout Fell in 2016, Even as a Record Number of Americans Cast Ballots," May 12, 2017, https://www.pewresearch.org/fact-tank/2017/05/12/black-voter-turnout-fell-in-2016-even-as-a-record-number-of-americans-cast-ballots/.

39. MuslimsGOTV, https://www.muslimsgotv.com/election-resource/.

40. MPAC, "Young Leaders Summits," https://www.mpac.org/programs/young-leaders/summits.php.

41. Natasha Balwit, "For Muslim Americans, A Call to Public Service," *City Lab*, February 2, 2017, https://www.citylab.com/equity/2017/02/for-muslim-americans-a-call-to-public-service/515238/.

42. Jetpac.com, "Our Work" page, https://www.jet-pac.com/our-work/.

43. CAIR, Jetpac, and MPower Change, *The Rise of American Muslim Changemakers: Political Organizing in the Trump Era*, updated 2019, https://d3n8a8pro7vhmx.cloudfront.net/cairhq/pages/1125/attachments/original/1563848167/1_Rise_of_American_Muslim_Change_Makers_Updated_July_22_5pm_FOR_Print_and_web.pdf?1563848167.

44. Samantha Raphelson, "Muslim Americans Running for Office in Highest Numbers since 2001," NPR, July 18, 2018, https://www.npr.org/2018/07/18/630132952/muslim-americans-running-for-office-in-highest-numbers-since-2001.

45. Author interview with Allouch.

46. Jewish Telegraphic Agency, "Jewish Groups Join Call to Mayors to Denounce 'Anti-Sharia' Marches," June 9, 2017, https://www.jta.org/2017/06/09/news-opinion/politics/jewish-groups-join-call-to-mayors-to-denounce-anti-sharia-marches.

47. Brief of *Amici Curiae* Interfaith Coalition in Support of Appellees and Affirmance in Hawaii v. Trump, No. 17-15589 (9th Cir. 2017), p. 7, https://www.mpac.org/assets/docs/2017/Covington-9th-Cir-Interfaith-Amicus-Brief.pdf.

48. Author interview with Salam Al-Marayati, September 5, 2017.

49. MPAC, "Interfaith Coalition Decries Hate Group Leader's Appearance at L.A. Jewish Federation," June 23, 2012, https://www.mpac.org/issues/islamophobia/interfaith-coalition-decries-hate-group-leaders-appearance-at-l.a.-jewish-federation.php.

50. Author interview with Tarin.

51. Author interview with Salam Al-Marayati, June 22, 2013.

52. Much of the critique against these Muslim leaders tends to focus on the fact that their participation in government affairs legitimizes policies that are detrimental to the

community and whitewash the violence experienced by Muslims in the United States and around the world. For a sample of this critique, see Sahar Aziz, "The New Generation of Muslim American Leaders: The White House Iftar Controversy Signals the Next Phase of Muslim Leadership," Opinion, Al Jazeera, July 24, 2014, https://www.aljazeera.com/indepth/opinion/2014/07/new-generation-muslim-american-2014723143141881797.html.

53. Scholarship on Muslim American identity formation has flourished in recent years. For some of the earliest efforts in this area, see Leonard, *Muslims in the United States*; Lori Peek, *Behind the Backlash: Muslim Americans after 9/11* (Philadelphia: Temple University Press, 2006); Haddad, *Becoming American?*

54. F. J. Crosby et al., "The Denial of Personal Disadvantage among You, Me, and All the Other Ostriches," in *Gender and Thought*, ed. M. Crawford and M. Gentry (New York: Springer, 1989); N. R. Branscombe, M. T. Schmitt, and R. D. Harvey, "Perceiving Pervasive Discrimination among African-Americans: Implications for Group Identification and Well Being," *Journal of Personality and Social Psychology* 77 (1999): 135–49; Jolanda Jetten et al., "Rebels with a Cause: Group Identification as a Response to Perceived Discrimination from the Mainstream," *Personality and Social Psychology Bulletin* 27, no. 9 (2001): 1204–13; Michael T. Schmitt, Russell Spears, and Nyla R. Branscombe, "Constructing a Minority Group Identity out of Shared Rejection: The Case of International Students," *European Journal of Social Psychology* 33, no. 1 (2003): 1–12; Oliver Klein, Russell Spears, and Stephen Reicher, "Social Identity Performance: Extending the Strategic Side of SIDE," *Personality and Social Psychology Review* 11 (2007): 28–45.

55. Barreto et al. 2004.

56. Karen Phalet and Maykel Verkuyten, "Political Mobilization of Dutch Muslims: Religious Identity Salience, Goal Framing and Normative Constraints," *Journal of Social Issues* 66, no. 4 (2010): 761; D. Scott DeRue and Susan J. Ashford, "Who Will Lead and Who Will Follow? A Social Process of Leadership Identity Construction in Organizations," *Academy of Management Review* 35, no. 4 (2010): 627–47.

5. DOMESTIC ADVOCACY

1. Letter from Jerry McNerney, Doris Matsui, and Barbara Lee to US Secretary of State Mike R. Pompeo, December 17, 2018, https://mcnerney.house.gov/sites/mcnerney.house.gov/files/Letter%20to%20Pompeo_Reps.%20McNerney%20Matsui%20Lee_12.17.18.pdf.

2. CAIR, "Shaima and Ali Mourn the Passing of their 2-Year-Old Son," December 28, 2018, https://ca.cair.com/sacval/news/shaima-and-ali-mourn-the-passing-of-their-2-year-old-son/.

3. See, for instance, Paul Djupe, Andrew Lewis, and Ted Jelen, "Rights, Reflections, and Reciprocity: Implications of the Same-Sex Marriage Debate for Tolerance and Political Process," *Politics and Religion* 9, no. 3 (2016): 630–48.

4. Elizabeth M. Schneider, "The Dialectics of Rights and Politics: Perspectives from the Women's Movement," *NYU Law Review* 5, no. 89 (1986): 593.

5. Ruud Koopmans et al., *Contested Citizenship: Immigration and Cultural Diversity in Europe* (Minneapolis: University of Minnesota Press, 2005), 254.

6. Annenberg Public Policy Center of the University of Pennsylvania, "Americans Are Poorly Informed about Basic Constitutional Provisions," September 12, 2017, https://www.annenbergpublicpolicycenter.org/americans-are-poorly-informed-about-basic-constitutional-provisions/.

7. Asma T. Uddin, *When Islam Is Not a Religion: Inside America's Fight for Religious Freedom* (New York: Pegasus Books, 2018), 35.

8. Uddin, *When Islam Is Not a Religion*, 35.

9. White House Office of the Press Secretary, "Fact Sheet: The White House Summit on Countering Violent Extremism," February 18, 2015, https://obamawhitehouse.archives .gov/the-press-office/2015/02/18/fact-sheet-white-house-summit-countering-violent -extremism.

10. John Robbins, "CAIR Brief on Countering Violent Extremism (CVE)," CAIR-MA, July 9, 2015, http://www.cairma.org/cair-brief-on-countering-violent-extremism-cve/.

11. CAIR, "Brief on Countering Violent Extremism with Recommendations for U.S. Government," February 2015, https://www.yumpu.com/en/document/read/36943056/cair -brief-on-countering-violent-extremism.

12. MPAC, "MPAC Statement on CVE Act of 2015," July 15, 2015, https://www.mpac .org/blog/updates/speaking-out-on-cve-act-of-2015.php.

13. For an excellent discussion of the CVE program's impacts on the Muslim American community, see Beydoun, *American Islamophobia*, 144–51.

14. Author interview with Salam Al-Marayati, September 5, 2017.

15. For a critique of this "revolving door" policy, see, for instance, Ahmed Shaikh, "MPAC, Countering Violent Extremism, and American Muslim Astroturf: A Critical Review," *Altmuslim* (blog), Patheos, June 9, 2015, http://www.patheos.com/blogs/altmuslim /2015/06/mpac-countering-violent-extremism-and-american-muslim-astroturf-a -critical-review/.

16. US Council of Muslim Organizations (USCMO), "Muslim Council Adopts Points on Countering Violent Extremism," February 17, 2015.

17. Faiza Patel and Meghan Koushik, "Countering Violent Extremism," Brennan Center for Justice, New York School of Law, March 16, 2017, https://www.brennancenter .org/publication/countering-violent-extremism. For a sample of the documents obtained, see United States Department of Justice, FBI, *Decade in Review: Self-Selecting U.S. Persons Drive Post-2006 Increase in Anti-US Plotting*, https://d3gn0r3afghep.cloudfront .net/foia_files/2016/09/13/Decade_in_Review__March_7-2011__.pdf.

18. Emma Green, "What Lies Ahead for Obama's Countering Violent Extremism Program?" *Atlantic*, March 17, 2017, https://www.theatlantic.com/politics/archive/2017/03 /countering-violent-extremism/519822/.

19. Muslim Justice League, "What Is 'Countering Violent Extremism' (CVE)?" accessed March 26, 2020, https://www.muslimjusticeleague.org/cve/.

20. Muslim Justice League, "Contacted by the FBI?" accessed March 26, 2020, https:// www.muslimjusticeleague.org/when-the-fbi-knocks/.

21. For an excellent discussion on injustice narratives and terrorism, see the special issue of *Studies in Conflict and Terrorism* 41, no. 7 (2018), especially "The Complexity of Terrorism, Victims, Perpetrators and Radicalisation," 491–593.

22. Tom R. Tyler, Stephen Schulhofer, and Aziz Z. Huq, "Legitimacy and Deterrence Effects in Counterterrorism Policing: A Study of Muslim Americans," *Law & Society Review* 44 (2010): 365–402.

23. David Campbell, *Writing Security: United States Foreign Policy and the Politics of Identity* (Minneapolis: University of Minnesota Press, 1998).

24. Said, *Orientalism*; Bobby S. Sayyid, *A Fundamental Fear: Eurocentrism and the Emergence of Islamism* (London: Zed Books, 2003).

25. High-ranking members of government have attested to the importance of this counterterrorism policy paper. As quoted in a *Washington Times* article from November 2004, for instance, Attorney General John Ashcroft and FBI director Robert S. Mueller both "recognized the importance of MPAC's anti-terrorism initiatives and encouraged similar efforts to educate the Muslim community about federal counterterrorism efforts" (MPAC, *A Review of U.S. Counterterrorism Policy: American Muslim Critique &*

Recommendations, September 2003, http://www.mpac.org/assets/docs/publications/coun
terterrorism-policy-paper.pdf).

26. MPAC, *Review of U.S. Counterterrorism Policy*, 10.

27. MPAC, *Counterproductive Counterterrorism: How Anti-Islamic Rhetoric Is Impeding America's Homeland Security*, December 2004, http://www.mpac.org/assets/docs/pub
lications/counterproductive-counterterrorism.pdf.

28. MPAC, *Review of U.S. Counterterrorism Policy*, 33.

29. MPAC, *Review of U.S. Counterterrorism Policy*, 46.

30. Author interview with Corey Saylor, June 22, 2013.

31. MPAC, *Review of U.S. Counterterrorism Policy*, 78.

32. MPAC, *Review of U.S. Counterterrorism Policy*, 78–79.

33. Author interview with Maher Hathout, MPAC senior adviser, June 2, 2013.

34. Edward E. Curtis is a prominent scholar of African American Islam.

35. Edward E. Curtis, "For American Muslims, Everything Did Not Change after
9/11," *Religion & Politics*, July 5, 2012, http://religionandpolitics.org/2012/07/05/for-amer
ican-muslims-everything-did-not-change-after-911/.

36. Greg Noakes, "Coalition Criticizes Terrorism Bill," *Washington Report on Middle
East Affairs*, April/May 1995, https://www.wrmea.org/1995-april-may/american-muslim
-activism-coalition-criticizes-terrorism-bill.html.

37. CAIR, *A Decade of Growth: Tenth Anniversary Report, 1994–2004* (Washington,
DC: CAIR, 2004), 16.

38. ACLU v. NSA 467 F.3d 590 (6th Cir. 2006), https://www.aaup.org/brief/aclu-v
-nsa-493-f3d-644-6th-cir-2007.

39. MPAC, "MPAC Coordinates Meeting with FBI on Surveillance Reports," December 29, 2005, https://www.mpac.org/programs/anti-terrorism-campaign/mpac-coordinates
-meeting-with-fbi-on-surveillance-reports.php.

40. CAIR, "Legislative Fact Sheet: Extra-Judicial Exile of Americans Traveling Abroad,"
January 1, 2013, https://www.cair.com/wp-content/uploads/2017/09/Stop-the-Extrajudicial
-Exile-of-American-Citizens.pdf.

41. CAIR, "No-fly List Cases," accessed March 27, 2020, https://www.cair.com/success
_stories_qgafj_dwotsu7axdijni5w/no-fly-list-cases/.

42. Mohamed v. Holder et al., No. 1:2011cv00050 - Document 257 (E.D. Va. 2017),
https://law.justia.com/cases/federal/district-courts/virginia/vaedce/1:2011cv00050
/261940/257/.

43. Elhady v. Kable, 391 F.Supp.3d 562 (2019), https://int.nyt.com/data/documenthelper
/1689-terror-watchlist-ruling/75cd50557652ad0bfa2a/optimized/full.pdf#page=1.

44. Author interview with Salam Al-Marayati, July 2, 2013.

45. Salam Al-Marayati, "Guilty of 'Flying While Muslim'?" MPAC, December 11,
2004, https://www.mpac.org/issues/islamophobia/guilty-of-flying-while-muslim.php.

46. CAIR, "Legislative Fact Sheet: Racial and Religious Profiling Abuses at the U.S. Border," January 1, 2013, https://d3n8a8pro7vhmx.cloudfront.net/cairhq/pages/4304/attach
ments/original/1504521940/Stop-Racial-and-Religious-Profiling-Abuses-at-US-Border
.pdf?1504521940.

47. CAIR, "CAIR Files Complaint with CBP, DHS, and DOJ over Questioning of
American Muslims about Religious and Political Views," January 18, 2017, https://www
.cair.com/press-center/press-releases/14021-cair-files-complaints-with-cbp-dhs-and-doj
-over-questioning-of-american-muslims-about-religious-and-political-viewswww.html.

48. Bilici, *Finding Mecca in America*, 184.

49. The original executive order (13769) barred entry to the United States by citizens
of Iran, Iraq, Libya, Somalia, Sudan, Syria, and Yemen for ninety days. It also reduced the
number of refugees to be admitted in 2017 from one hundred thousand to fifty thousand,

suspended the US Refugee Admissions Program for 120 days, and indefinitely barred Syrian refugees.

50. Trump. v. International Refugee Assistance Project, 582 U.S. ___ (2017), http://www.scotusblog.com/wp-content/uploads/2017/09/16-1436-bsac-Clergy-Americans-United-for-Separation-of-Church-and-State.pdf.

51. Nine of the eleven countries included in the version of the Muslim Ban upheld by the Supreme Court are Muslim-majority countries. These include: Libya, Syria, Yemen, Iran, Somalia, Iraq, Sudan, Egypt and Mali. The other two countries included are North Korea and South Sudan.

52. CAIRtv, "CAIR Files Federal Suit Challenging Constitutionality of Trump's 'Muslim Ban' Executive Order," January 30, 2017, 2:35, https://www.youtube.com/watch?v=XkL1-e6cMYQ.

53. Jenn B. Caballero, "US Politicians on Immigration EO," Google spreadsheet, updated February 2017, https://docs.google.com/spreadsheets/u/1/d/1hSGjyWJZIQJpGz4V2ftX_qioCgBtL59oJkkhx146nFE/htmlview?sle=true&mc_cid=f94b7ac81f&mc_eid=64154722f1#.

54. *CAIR News Conference Responding to Today's #SCOTUS #MuslimBan Decision*, Facebook Live, June 26, 2018, https://www.facebook.com/CAIRNational/videos/101558 48247602695/.

55. Abby Phillip and Abigail Hauslohner, "Trump on the Future of Proposed Muslim Ban, Registry: 'You Know My Plans,'" *Washington Post*, December 22, 2016, https://www.washingtonpost.com/news/post-politics/wp/2016/12/21/trump-on-the-future-of-proposed-muslim-ban-registry-you-know-my-plans/.

56. "To President Elect Donald Trump: Register Me First," https://sign.moveon.org/petitions/register-me-first?

57. CAIR, *Legislating Fear: Islamophobia and Its Impact in the United States*, 2013, 17, https://www.cair.com/legislating-fear-2013-report.

58. Quoted in Patrick Strickland, "US: Are 'Anti-Sharia" Bills Legalising Islamophobia?" Al Jazeera, October 1, 2017, http://www.aljazeera.com/news/2017/09/anti-sharia-bills-legalising-islamophobia-170928150835240.html.

59. American Bar Association, *Resolution 113A*, August 8–9, 2011, 5, https://www.americanbar.org/content/dam/aba/directories/policy/2011_am_113a.authcheckdam.pdf.

60. CAIR, "New CAIR, UC Berkeley Report Reveals Funding, Negative Impact of Islamophobic Groups in America," June 20, 2016, http://www.islamophobia.org/reports/179-confronting-fear-islamophobia-and-its-impact-in-the-u-s-2013-2015.html.

61. CAIR, *Legislating Fear*, 17.

62. SPLC, "ACT for America," Extremist Files, accessed March 27, 2020, https://www.splcenter.org/fighting-hate/extremist-files/group/act-america.

63. Quoted in Peter Beinart, "The Denationalization of American Muslims," *Atlantic*, March 19, 2017, https://www.theatlantic.com/politics/archive/2017/03/frank-gaffney-donald-trump-and-the-denationalization-of-american-muslims/519954/.

64. Miranda Blue, "ACT for America Wants to Ban CAIR from Addressing State Legislatures," *Right Wing Watch*, December 13, 2016, http://www.rightwingwatch.org/post/act-for-america-wants-to-ban-cair-from-addressing-state-legislatures/.

65. SPLC, "Live-Blog: ACT for America's 'March against Sharia' Rallies," June 10, 2017, https://www.splcenter.org/hatewatch/2017/06/10/live-blog-act-americas-march-against-sharia-rallies.

66. MPAC, "A Nation of Immigrants: Realizing a Comprehensive Immigration Reform," September 17, 2013, 5, https://www.mpac.org/publications/policy-papers/a-nation-of-immigrants.php.

67. MPAC, "A Nation of Immigrants," 5.

68. Ty McCormick, "Could Lindsay Graham's Terrorism Amendment Target Immigrants from Ireland?" *Foreign Policy*, May 22, 2013, https://foreignpolicy.com/2013/05/22/could-lindsey-grahams-terrorism-amendment-target-immigrants-from-ireland/.

69. Tim Padgett, "Why So Many Latinos Are Becoming Muslims," WLRN Public Radio, October 9, 2013, http://wlrn.org/post/why-so-many-latinos-are-becoming-muslims.

70. US Citizenship and Immigration Services, "Number of Forms I-821D, Consideration of Deferred Action for Childhood Arrivals, by Fiscal Year, Quarter, Intake, Biometrics and Case Status Fiscal Year, 2012–2017 (March 31)," https://www.uscis.gov/sites/default/files/USCIS/Resources/Reports%20and%20Studies/Immigration%20Forms%20Data/All%20Form%20Types/DACA/daca_performancedata_fy2017_qtr2.pdf.

71. Sarah Sarder, "Dallas Muslim Leader Omar Suleiman Arrested during DACA Protest on Capitol Hill," *Dallas Morning News*, March 6, 2018, https://www.dallasnews.com/news/immigration/2018/03/06/dallas-muslim-leaderarrested-daca-protest-capitol-hill.

72. Zaid Shakir, "Let Them Fly: Ode to a Little Dreamer," March 6, 2018, https://www.facebook.com/imamzaidshakir/photos/a.10151919830963359/10155345424068359/?type=1&theater.

73. American Bar Association, "Family Separation and Detention," accessed March 27, 2020, https://www.americanbar.org/advocacy/governmental_legislative_work/priorities_policy/immigration/familyseparation/.

74. Author interview with Gadeir Abbas, October 19, 2018.

75. Islamic Society of North America, "New National ISNA Survey Finds Strong Support for Climate Solutions among Muslim-Americans," October 31, 2018, http://www.isna.net/new-national-isna-survey-finds-strong-support-for-climate-solutions-among-muslim-americans/.

6. ADVOCATING FOR THE MUSLIM *UMMAH*

1. Pew Research Center, "U.S. Muslims Concerned about Their Place in Society, But Continue to Believe in the American Dream: Findings from Pew Research Center's 2017 Survey of U.S. Muslims," report, July 26, 2017, http://www.pewforum.org/2017/07/26/findings-from-pew-research-centers-2017-survey-of-us-muslims/.

2. See Thomas Soehl and Roger Waldinger, "Inheriting the Homeland? Intergenerational Transmission of Cross-Border Ties in Migrant Families," *American Journal of Sociology* 118, no. 3 (2012): 778–813; Yossi Shain, "Jewish Kinship at a Crossroads: Lessons for Homelands and Diasporas," *Political Science Quarterly* 117, no. 2 (2002): 279–304.

3. Barreto and Dana, "Muslim and American," 8.

4. Thomas Ambrosio, *Ethnic Identity Groups and U.S. Foreign Policy* (Westport, CT: Praeger, 2002); David Paul and Rachel Paul, *Ethnic Lobbies and US Foreign Policy* (Boulder, CO: Lynne Rienner, 2008).

5. Barreto and Dana, "Muslim and American."

6. Nadine Naber, "'Look, Mohammed the Terrorist Is Coming!'"

7. Robbins, "Brief on Countering Violent Extremism."

8. Chris Cillizza, "Breaking: Voters (Still) Don't Care about Foreign Policy," *Washington Post*, September 10, 2014, https://www.washingtonpost.com/news/the-fix/wp/2014/09/10/breaking-voters-still-dont-care-about-foreign-policy/.

9. CAIR, *American Muslim Voters and the 2012 Elections: A Demographic Profile and Survey of Attitudes*, October 24, 2012, https://d3n8a8pro7vhmx.cloudfront.net/cairhq/pages/1986/attachments/original/1504007213/American_Muslim_Voter_Survey_2012.pdf.

10. Barreto and Dana, "Muslim and American."

11. Pew Research Center, *Muslim Americans: No Signs of Growth in Alienation or Support for Extremism*, 67, 73, 74.

12. Erik Nisbet and James Shanahan, *MSRG Special Report: Restrictions on Civil Liberties, Views of Islam, and Muslim Americans*, December 2004 (Ithaca, NY: Media and Society Research Group, Cornell University), http://arabsandterrorism.com/resources/Restrictions _on_Civil_Libe.pdf.

13. Pew Research Center, "Views of Islam and Violence," September 9, 2009, http://www.pewforum.org/2009/09/09/publicationpage-aspxid1398-3/.

14. "CAIR: Who We Are," https://www.cair.com/about_cair/cair-who-we-are/.

15. Ambrosio, *Ethnic Identity Groups*.

16. CAIR, *American Muslim Voters and the 2012 Elections*.

17. Pew Research Center, *Muslim Americans: No Signs of Growth in Alienation or Support for Extremism*, 29.

18. Shibley Telhami, *The World through Arab Eyes: Arab Public Opinion and the Reshaping of the Middle East* (New York: Basic Books, 2013), 73.

19. Salam Al-Marayati, "Colonial Baggage for America in Palestine," *Huffington Post*, August 12, 2014, http://www.huffingtonpost.com/salam-al-marayati/colonial-baggage-for -amer_b_5669087.html.

20. Author interview with Rameez Abid, October 18, 2018.

21. Trevor Rubenzer and Steven Redd, "Ethnic Minority Groups and US Foreign Policy: Examining Congressional Decision Making and Economic Sanctions," *International Studies Quarterly* 54, no. 3 (2010): 755–77; Eric Uslaner, "Does Diversity Drive Trust?" (FEEM working paper, May 22, 2006).

22. MPAC, "Envisioning Peace: The MPAC Perspective on the Israeli-Palestinian Conflict," June 8, 2007, 15, https://www.mpac.org/publications/policy-papers/envisioning -peace.php.

23. MPAC, "Welcome Palestine? An MPAC's Analysis on the UN Resolution for Palestinian Statehood," September 21, 2011, 4, https://www.mpac.org/publications/policy-papers /mpac-releases-new-policy-paper-welcome-palestine.php.

24. American Muslims for Palestine, "Tell President Trump That Declaring Jerusalem the Capital of Israel Is Bad for America," 2017, http://salsa3.salsalabs.com/o/51044/p/dia /action4/common/public/?action_KEY=21307.

25. USCMO, "Statement on President Trump's Recognition of Jerusalem as the Capital of Israel," December 7, 2017, https://uscmo.org/index.php/2017/12/07/statement-of -the-us-council-of-muslim-organizations-on-president-trumps-recognition-of -jerusalem-as-the-capital-of-israel/.

26. See Wood, *Insurgent Collective Action*; Jeff Goodwin, James Jasper, and Francesca Polletta, eds., *Passionate Politics: Emotions and Social Movements* (Chicago: University of Chicago Press, 2009).

27. MPAC, "Envisioning Peace," 6.

28. *CAIR Director Speaks at D.C. Rally for Gaza*, August 2, 2014, https://www.youtube .com/watch?v=WRvFVJiRbtY.

29. *CAIR Director Speaks at D.C. Rally for Gaza*.

30. Author interview with Salam Al-Marayati, May 3, 2017.

31. MPAC, "Welcome Palestine?"

32. American Muslims for Palestine, *Return Is Our #Right and Our #Destiny*, October 20, 2016, https://www.ampalestine.org/videos/return-our-right-and-our-destiny.

33. MPAC, "Envisioning Peace," 6.

34. Author interview with Gadeir Abbas, October 19, 2018.

35. Stephen Young, "Abbott Signs Bill Tightening Up Texas' Anti-BDS Statute," *Dallas Observer*, May 10, 2019, https://www.dallasobserver.com/news/texas-tightens-up -anti-bds-law-11661667.

36. Young, "Abbott Signs Bill."

37. CAIR, "Breaking: CAIR Wins Landmark First Amendment Victory Striking Down Texas Anti-BDS Law," April 25, 2019, https://cair-mo.org/press-center/in-the-news/577 -breaking-cair-wins-landmark-first-amendment-victory-striking-down-texas-anti-bds -law.html.

38. CAIR, "Breaking: CAIR Wins Landmark First Amendment Victory."

39. Charles Lewis and Mark Reading-Smith, "False Pretenses," Center for Public Integrity, January 23, 2008, https://publicintegrity.org/2008/01/23/5641/false-pretenses.

40. Norman Fairclough, "Intertextuality in Critical Discourse Analysis," *Linguistics and Education* 4, no. 3 (1992): 269–93.

41. MPAC, "Statement of Fall of Saddam Hussein & Post-War Iraq," April 10, 2003, http://www.mpac.org/issues/foreign-policy/statement-of-fall-of-saddam-hussein-post -war-iraq.php.

42. White House Office of the Press Secretary, "President Says Saddam Hussein Must Leave Iraq within 48 Hours," March 17, 2003, http://georgewbush-whitehouse.archives .gov/news/releases/2003/03/20030317-7.html.

43. Pew Research Center, *Muslim Americans: Middle Class and Mostly Mainstream*, 5.

44. Author interview with Salam Al-Marayati, September 5, 2017.

45. Author interview with Salam Al-Marayati, June 2, 2013.

46. Author interview with Maher Hathout, June 5, 2013.

47. CAIR, "US Muslims Say War on Iraq Not Justified," February, 27, 2003, https://sc.cair .com/press-center/press-releases/746-u-s-muslims-say-war-on-iraq-not-justified.html.

48. For an excellent analysis of critical discourse analysis, see Wodak, "Critical Discourse Analysis."

49. Author interview with Corey Saylor, June 22, 2013.

50. Fairclough, "Intertextuality in Critical Discourse Analysis."

51. Author interview with Al-Marayati.

52. Author interview with Saylor.

53. Corey Saylor, "Is Sharia Compatible with Democracy?" (speech delivered at the University of Maine, March 24, 2014).

54. Saylor, "Is Sharia Compatible with Democracy?" July 7, 2014, http://coreysaylor .blogspot.com.

55. "American Muslims Overwhelmingly Backed Obama," *Newsweek*, November 6, 2008, http://www.newsweek.com/american-muslims-overwhelmingly-backed-obama-85173.

56. Amy Davidson Sorkin, "The N.S.A.'s Spying on American Muslims," *New Yorker*, July 10, 2014, https://www.newyorker.com/news/amy-davidson/the-n-s-a-s-spying-on -muslim-americans.

57. White House Office of the Press Secretary, "Remarks by the President on the Middle East and North Africa," May 19, 2011, https://obamawhitehouse.archives.gov/the -press-office/2011/05/19/remarks-president-middle-east-and-north-africa.

58. Amy Hawthorne and Michele Dunne, "Remember That Historic Arab Spring Speech?" *Foreign Policy*, May 21, 2013, http://foreignpolicy.com/2013/05/21/remember -that-historic-arab-spring-speech/.

59. Nihad Awad, quoted in "CAIR: Obama's 'Arab Spring' Address Sets the Right Tone," Cision, PR Newswire, May 19, 2011, http://www.prnewswire.com/news-releases /cair-obamas-arab-spring-address-sets-the-right-tone-122262258.html.

60. CAIR, "CAIR Urges Obama to 'Act Without Delay' after Syria Gas Massacre," August 22, 2013, http://www.cair.com/press-center/press-releases/12097-cair-urges-obama -to-act-without-delay-after-syria-gas-massacre.html.

61. Pew Research Center, "Section 6: Terrorism, Concerns about Extremism & Foreign Policy," August 30, 2011, http://www.people-press.org/2011/08/30/section-6-terrorism -concerns-about-extremism-foreign-policy/.

62. MPAC, "Position Paper: On Intervention in Syria," September 6, 2013, http://www .mpac.org/assets/docs/publications/MPAC-Intervention-in-Syria-Position-Paper.pdf.

63. MPAC, "Position Paper: On Intervention in Syria."

64. USCMO, "USCMO Calls to Stop Genocide in Aleppo and to Immediately Protect Civilians," December 14, 2016, https://www.muslimamericansociety.org/humanitarian -crisis-in-aleppo-syria/.

65. CAIR, "CAIR Reiterates Condemnation of ISIS Violence, Religious Extremism," August 11, 2014, https://www.cairoklahoma.com/blog/cair-reiterates-condemnation-of -isis-violence-religious-extremism/.

66. CAIR, "CAIR Reiterates Condemnation of ISIS Violence, Religious Extremism."

67. Like many other immigrant-majority groups in the post-twentieth century, American Muslims retain meaningful transnational connections. For more on the networks that link US Muslims to the Middle East, see Zareena Grewal, *Islam Is a Foreign Country: American Muslims and the Global Crisis of Authority* (New York: NYU Press, 2013).

68. Amnesty International, "Denied: Failures in Accountability for Human Rights Violations by Security Force Personnel in Jammu and Kashmir," June 30, 2015, https:// www.amnestyusa.org/reports/denied-failures-in-accountability-for-human-rights -violations-by-security-force-personnel-in-jammu-and-kashmir/.

69. Engy Abdelkader, "The Rohingya Muslims in Myanmar: Past, Present and Future," *Oregon Review of International Law* 15, no. 3 (2014): 393–411, https://scholarsbank .uoregon.edu/xmlui/bitstream/handle/1794/17966/Abdelkader.pdf.

70. United Nations, "UN Human Rights Chief Points to 'Textbook Example of Ethnic Cleansing' in Myanmar," UN News, September 11, 2017, http://www.un.org/apps/news /story.asp?NewsID=57490.

71. MPAC, "Burma's Rohingya: A Slow Genocide," September 17, 2017. https://www .mpac.org/blog/policy-analysis/burmas-rohingya-a-slow-genocide.php.

72. CAIR, "CAIR Letter to U.N. Ambassador Haley: Decisive Action Needed in Response to Burma's Ethnic Cleansing of Rohingya Muslims," Facebook, September 12, 2017, https://www.facebook.com/CAIRNational/posts/rohingyamuslims-rohingyagenocide-cair -letter-to-un-ambassador-haley-decisive-act/10155149316092695/.

73. CAIR, "CAIR Action Alert: Tell U.S. Senate 'No Military Aid to Burma' Because of Genocide of Rohingya Muslims," accessed September 20, 2017, https://www.cair.com /action_alerts/cair-action-alert-tell-u-s-senate-no-military-aid-to-burma-because-of -genocide-of-rohingya-muslims/.

74. CAIR, "Support Bipartisan Efforts in Congress Condemning Genocide against Rohingya Muslims (Senate Resolution 250 and House Resolution 528)," October 10, 2017, https://oneclickpolitics.com/messages/edit?promo_id=3613.

75. MPAC, "Burma's Rohingya: A Slow Genocide," September 14, 2017, https://www .mpac.org/blog/policy-analysis/burmas-rohingya-a-slow-genocide.php.

76. USCMO, "USCMO Meets with Myanmar, OIC, Turkish Ambassador Demanding Halt to Rohingya Ethnic Cleansing," September 15, 2017, https://uscmo.org/index.php /2017/09/15/4998/.

77. CAIR, "Urge State Department to Pressure India to End Lockdown, Lift Curfew and End Siege of Kashmir Valley," Action Center, August 6, 2019, https://www.votervoice .net/CAIR/campaigns/67781/respond.

78. The so-called land row began when the Kashmiri government promised to give forestland to the trust that runs Amarnath, a Hindu shrine located in Jammu. Muslims took to the streets to oppose the decision, and the ensuing clashes soon widened into pro-independence rallies. Faced with growing unrest, the Kashmiri government rescinded the initial land transfer, a decision that angered many Hindus and led to the worst levels of violence the region had seen in the last two decades.

79. MPAC, "U.S. Should Support Kashmiri Call for Self-Determination," September 5, 2008, https://www.mpac.org/issues/foreign-policy/u.s.-should-support-kashmiri-call-for-self-determination.php.

80. CAIR, "Kashmir: History, Context, and Consequences Presentation on March 20th," March 8, 2012, http://www.cairchicago.org/blog/2012/03/kashmir-history-context-and-consequences-presentation-on-march-20th/.

81. MPAC, "Unprecedented Violence Erupts in Jammu and Kashmir," September 22, 2016, https://www.mpac.org/blog/policy-analysis/unprecedented-violence-erupts-in-jammu-and-kashmir.php.

82. MPAC, *An Islamic Perspective on Giving Zakat to the MPAC Foundation*, July 10, 2015, https://www.mpac.org/old-images/zakat-brochure.pdf.

83. Patrick O'Connor and Julian E. Barnes, "Gingrich Calls for Regime Change in Iran," *Wall Street Journal*, November 24, 2011, http://online.wsj.com/article/SB10001424052970204531404577054911628578368.html; Kimberly Schwandt, "President Obama Doesn't Rule Out Military Option in Iran," *Fox News*, November 14, 2011, https://www.foxnews.com/politics/president-obama-doesnt-rule-out-military-option-in-iran.

84. MPAC, "Action Alert: Say Yes to Diplomacy, No to War with Iran," February 20, 2012, https://www.mpac.org/take-action/action-alert-say-yes-to-diplomacy-no-to-war-with-iran.php.

85. "MPAC Urges Senate to Oppose Sanctions on Iran," January 14, 2014, https://www.mpac.org/issues/foreign-policy/mpac-urges-senate-to-oppose-sanctions-on-iran.php.

86. Zachary Laub, "The Impact of the Iran Nuclear Agreement," Council on Foreign Relations, updated May 8, 2018.

87. Kevin Liptak and Nicole Gaouette, "Trump Withdraws from Iran Nuclear Deal, Isolating Him Further from World," CNN, updated May 9, 2018, https://www.cnn.com/2018/05/08/politics/donald-trump-iran-deal-announcement-decision/index.html.

88. "Trump's tweets at #Iran could trigger WWIII. It's time to cut out the hateful rhetoric. Tell Congress that a war with Iran is both unnecessary and would subject another generation to war's depravity and devastation. Tweet. Email. Call. Raise your voice: http://mpac.org/noiranwar #NoWarWithIran" (MPAC, Facebook, July 17, 2019, https://www.facebook.com/mpacnational/photos/a.456754193393/10157600175398394/?type=3&theater).

89. MPAC, *Selecting 'Options on the Table' Carefully: The Consequences of a Military Strike on Iran*, January 30, 2012, https://www.mpac.org/assets/docs/publications/MPAC_Paper--Selecting_Options_on_the_Table_Carefully__The_Consequences_of_a_Military_Strike_on_Iran.pdf.

90. CAIR, "CAIR: U.S. Muslims Welcome Nuclear Deal with Iran," Cision, PR Newswire, November 24, 2013, https://www.prnewswire.com/news-releases/cair-us-muslims-welcome-nuclear-deal-with-iran-233247341.html.

91. Author interview with Al-Marayati.

CONCLUSION. WHO SPEAKS FOR AMERICAN MUSLIMS?

1. Sa'ed Atshan, "Faithwashing: A Reflection on Muslim Leadership Initiative," New Arab, April 7, 2015, https://www.alaraby.co.uk/english/comment/2015/4/7/faithwashing-a-reflection-on-the-muslim-leadership-initiative.

2. "Say No to Faithwashing: Boycott Muslim Leadership Initiative," January 27, 2016, https://www.amchainitiative.org/wp-content/uploads/2016/01/Say-No-to-Faithwashing_-Boycott-Muslim-Leadership-Initiative-_2.pdf.

3. Kamal Abu-Shamsieh et al., "Call for Immediate Halt to Muslim Leadership Initiative (MLI), Sponsored by Shalom Hartman Institute," Care2 Petitions, 2015, https://www.thepetitionsite.com/takeaction/927/756/193/.

4. Linda Sarsour, Facebook, August 22, 2015, https://www.facebook.com/linda.sarsour/posts/10153688511010572.

5. Shaikh, "MPAC, Countering Violent Extremism and American Muslim Astroturf."

6. Jeffrey Berry, *The New Liberalism: The Rising Power of Citizen Groups* (Washington, DC: Brookings, 1999).

7. Dara Strolovitch, "Do Interest Groups Represent the Disadvantaged? Advocacy at the Intersection of Race, Class, and Gender," *Journal of Politics* 68, no. 4 (2006): 894–910.

8. Berry, *The New Liberalism*.

9. Berry, *The New Liberalism*.

10. Ken Kollman, *Outside Lobbying: Public Opinion and Interest Group Strategies* (Princeton, NJ: Princeton University Press, 1998).

11. See, for instance, William Browne, "Organized Interests and Their Issue Niches," *Journal of Politics* 52, no. 2 (1990): 477–509; Virginia Gray and David Lowery, *The Population Ecology of Interest Representation* (Ann Arbor: University of Michigan Press, 1996).

12. More people were familiar with CAIR, mainly because of its active role in civil rights issues, having taken individuals and the government to court on discrimination cases, many of which it has won.

13. Robert Entman, "Framing: Toward Clarification of a Fractured Paradigm," *Journal of Communication* 43, no. 4 (1993): 52; Iskander De Bruycker, "Framing and Advocacy: A Research Agenda for Interest Group Advocacy," *Journal of European Public Policy* 2, no. 5 (2016): 1–13.

14. Baumgartner and Leech, "Interest Niches and Policy Bandwagons"; Frank Baumgartner and Christine Mahoney, "The Two Faces of Framing: Individual Level Framing and Collective Issues Definition in the European Union," *European Union Politics* 9, no. 3 (2008): 435–49; Frida Boräng and Daniel Naurin, "Try to See It My Way! Frame Congruence between Lobbyists and European Commission Officials," *Journal of European Public Policy* 22, 15 (2015): 499–515; Rainer Eising, Daniel Rasch, and Patrycja Rozbicka, "Institutions, Policies, and Arguments: Context and Strategy in EU Policy Framing," *Journal of European Public Policy* 22, no. 4 (2015): 516–33; Heike Klüver, Christine Mahoney, and Marc Opper, "Framing in Context: How Interest Groups Employ Framing to Lobby the European Commission," *Journal of European Public Policy* 22, no. 4 (2015): 481–98.

15. Philippe C. Schmitter and Wolfgang Streeck, "The Organization of Business Interests: Studying the Associative Action of Business in Advanced Industrial Societies," Max-Planck-Institut für Gesellschaftsforschung (MPIfG) Discussion Paper 99/1, March 1999.

16. Ambrosio, *Ethnic Identity Groups*.

17. Author interview with Salam Al-Marayati, September 5, 2017.

18. According to Pew's 2017 survey, 89 percent of US Muslims say they are proud to be both American and Muslim.

19. The label "Islamism" emerged in the 1970s to refer to the growing number of movements and organizations drawing on Islamic symbols and traditions to articulate a political agenda. The roots of Islamism, however, emerged more than a century ago as an attempt to fill the social, political, and ideological disruptions caused by the collapse of the Ottoman Empire and the ensuing colonial power struggle to carve out the region that comprises the modern Middle East. At the core of Islamism lies an idealized view of early Islamic history, a powerful critique of the West (especially its influence in and domination of Muslim societies), and a call to "return" to Islam and organize all aspects of sociopolitical life on the Qur'an and sunna (the teachings of the prophet Mohammad). The Muslim Brotherhood is the largest Islamist movement in the world today. For more on Islamism, see Guilain Denoeux, "The Forgotten Swamp: Navigating Political Islam," *Middle East Policy* 9, no. 2 (2002): 56–81. For more on the evolution of the Muslim Brotherhood,

see Mona El-Ghobashy, "The Metamorphosis of the Egyptian Muslim Brothers," *International Journal of Middle East Studies* 37, no. 3 (2005): 373–95.

20. Gary Schmitt and Peter Skerry, "On the Peter King Hearing and Islamism in America," Brookings, March 10, 2011, https://www.brookings.edu/opinions/on-the-peter-king-hearing-and-islamism-in-america/.

21. Schmitt and Skerry, "On the Peter King Hearing."

22. Schmitt and Skerry, "On the Peter King Hearing."

23. Wajahat Ali, "Ex-Communication: A Short Story," Facebook, May 30, 2018, https://www.facebook.com/photo.php?fbid=10106675418195253&set=a.765494181393&type=1&theater.

24. Pew Research Center, *U.S. Muslims Concerned about Their Place in Society, But Continue to Believe in the American Dream*, 24.

Bibliography

Abdelkader, Engy. "The Rohingya Muslims in Myanmar: Past, Present and Future." *Oregon Review of International Law* 15, no. 3 (2014): 393–411. https://scholarsbank.uoregon.edu/xmlui/bitstream/handle/1794/17966/Abdelkader.pdf.

Abdullah, Aslam, and Gasser Hathout. *The American Muslim Identity: Speaking for Ourselves*. Los Angeles: Multimedia Vera International, 2003.

Abu-Shamsieh, Kamal, Laila El-Haddad, Zareena Grewal, Hatem Bazian, and Omid Safi. "Call for Immediate Halt to Muslim Leadership Initiative (MLI), Sponsored by Shalom Hartman Institute." Care2 Petitions, 2015. https://www.thepetitionsite.com/takeaction/927/756/193/.

ACLU v. NSA 467 F.3d 590 (6th Cir. 2006). https://www.aaup.org/brief/aclu-v-nsa-493-f3d-644-6th-cir-2007.

Ahmed, Arshad, and Farid Senzai. *The USA Patriot Act: Impact on the Arab and Muslim American Community*. Clinton Township, MI: Institute for Social Policy and Understanding, 2004. http://www.ispu.org/pdfs/patriot%20act%20_2-04%20-%20with%20cover_.pdf

Ali, Wajahat. "Ex-Communication: A Short Story." Facebook, May 29, 2018. https://www.facebook.com/photo.php?fbid=10106675418195253&set=a.765494181393&type=1&theater.

Al-Marashi, Ibrahim. "Travel Bans in Historical Perspective: Executive Orders Have Defined 'Terrorists' Since Nixon." *Perspectives on History*, November 2017. https://www.historians.org/publications-and-directories/perspectives-on-history/november-2017/travel-bans-in-historical-perspective-executive-orders-have-defined-terrorists-since-nixon.

Al-Marayati, Salam. "Colonial Baggage for America in Palestine." *Huffington Post*, August 12, 2014. http://www.huffingtonpost.com/salam-al-marayati/colonial-baggage-for-amer_b_5669087.html.

——. "Guilty of 'Flying While Muslim'?" MPAC, December 11, 2004. https://www.mpac.org/issues/islamophobia/guilty-of-flying-while-muslim.php.

——. "My Faith. My Vote. My Future." Muslim Public Affairs Council (MPAC), 2012. https://www.mpac.org/myfaithmyvote.

Alsultany, Evelyn. *Arabs and Muslims in the Media: Race and Representation after 9/11*. New York: NYU Press, 2012.

Ambrosio, Thomas. *Ethnic Identity Groups and U.S. Foreign Policy*. Westport, CT: Praeger, 2002.

American Bar Association. "Family Separation and Detention." Accessed March 27, 2020. https://www.americanbar.org/advocacy/governmental_legislative_work/priorities_policy/immigration/familyseparation/.

——. *Resolution 113A*. August 8–9, 2011. https://www.americanbar.org/content/dam/aba/directories/policy/2011_am_113a.authcheckdam.pdf.

American Civil Liberties Union (ACLU). "ACLU Files First-Ever Challenge to USA Patriot Act, Citing Radical Expansion of FBI Powers." July 30, 2003. https://www.aclu.org/news/aclu-files-first-ever-challenge-usa-patriot-act-citing-radical-expansion-fbi-powers.

——. "ACLU Says Bush Administration Should Not Allow Operation TIPS to Become an End Run around Constitution." July 15, 2002. https://www.aclu.org/news/aclu-says -bush-administration-should-not-allow-operation-tips-become-end-run-around.

——. *Blocking Faith, Freezing Charity: Chilling Muslim Charitable Giving in the "War on Terrorism Financing."* June 2009. https://www.aclu.org/files/pdfs/humanrights /blockingfaith.pdf.

——. "Factsheet: The NYPD Muslim Surveillance Program." Accessed March 20, 2020. https://www.aclu.org/other/factsheet-nypd-muslim-surveillance-program.

——. "Nationwide Anti-Mosque Activity." Updated December 2019. https://www.aclu.org /issues/national-security/discriminatory-profiling/nationwide-anti-mosque -activity.

——. "Statements of Support for UCC Clients." Accessed March 20, 2020. https://www .aclu.org/other/statements-support-ucc-clients.

——. *Unleashed and Unaccountable: The FBI's Unchecked Abuse of Authority.* September 2013. https://www.aclu.org/sites/default/files/assets/unleashed-and-unaccountable-fbi -report.pdf.

——. *Unpatriotic Acts: The FBI's Power to Rifle through Your Records and Personal Belongings without Telling You.* July 2003. https://www.aclu.org/other/unpatriotic-acts-fbis -power-rifle-through-your-records-and-personal-belongings-without-telling.

American Muslims for Palestine. *Return Is Our #Right and Our #Destiny.* October 20, 2016. https://www.ampalestine.org/videos/return-our-right-and-our-destiny.

——. "Tell President Trump That Declaring Jerusalem the Capital of Israel Is Bad for America." 2017. http://salsa3.salsalabs.com/o/51044/p/dia/action4/common/public /?action_KEY=21307.

"American Muslims Overwhelmingly Backed Obama." *Newsweek,* November 6, 2008. http://www.newsweek.com/american-muslims-overwhelmingly-backed-obama -85173.

Amnesty International. "Denied: Failures in Accountability for Human Rights Violations by Security Force Personnel in Jammu and Kashmir." June 30, 2015. https://www .amnestyusa.org/reports/denied-failures-in-accountability-for-human-rights -violations-by-security-force-personnel-in-jammu-and-kashmir.

Anderson, Benedict. *Imagined Communities: Reflections on the Origins and Spread of Nationalism.* London: Verso, 1983.

Annenberg Public Policy Center of the University of Pennsylvania. "Americans Are Poorly Informed about Basic Constitutional Provisions." September 12, 2017. https://www .annenbergpublicpolicycenter.org/americans-are-poorly-informed-about-basic -constitutional-provisions/.

Anti-Defamation League (ADL). "ADL Joins Groups Calling on Mayors to Disavow Anti-Muslim Marches." June 9, 2017. https://www.adl.org/news/press-releases/adl-joins -groups-calling-on-mayors-to-disavow-anti-muslim-marches.

Atshan, Sa'ed. "Faithwashing: A Reflection on Muslim Leadership Initiative." New Arab, April 7, 2015. https://www.alaraby.co.uk/english/comment/2015/4/7/faithwashing -a-reflection-on-the-muslim-leadership-initiative.

Austen-Smith, David, and John R. Wright. "Counteractive Lobbying." *American Journal of Political Science* 38, no. 1 (1994): 25–44.

Autumn-Brown, Jessica. "The New Southern Strategy: Immigration, Race and 'Welfare Dependency' in Contemporary US Republican Political Discourse." *Geopolitics, History and International Relations* 8, no. 2 (2016): 22–41.

Awad, Nihad. "I am a Muslim American Leader, and the NSA Spied on Me." *Time,* July 9, 2014. https://time.com/2970573/muslim-american-nsa-spies.

———. "Muslim Leader: Homophobia and Islamophobia Are Connected Systems of Oppression." *Time*, June 14, 2016. http://time.com/4367554/muslim-leader-on -orlando-shooting/.

Aziz, Sahar. "Caught in a Preventive Dragnet: Selective Counterterrorism in a Post-9/11 America." *Gonzaga Law Review* 47 (2012): 1–71.

———. "Countering Religion or Terrorism? Selective Enforcement of Material Support Laws against Muslim Charities." Institute for Social Policy and Understanding, Policy Brief #47, September 2011.

———. "The New Generation of Muslim American Leaders: The White House Iftar Controversy Signals the Next Phase of Muslim Leadership." Opinion, Al Jazeera, July 24, 2014. https://www.aljazeera.com/indepth/opinion/2014/07/new-generation-muslim -american-2014723143141881797.html.

Bagby, Ihsa. *The American Mosque 2011: Basic Characteristics of the American Mosque, Attitude of Mosque Leaders*. US Mosque Study Report 1, January 2012.

Bagozzi, Richard P., Utpal M. Dholakia, and Lisa R. Klein Pearo. "Antecedents and Consequences of Online Social Interactions." *Media Psychology* 9, no. 1 (2007).

Bakalian, Anny, and Medhi Bozorgmehr. *Backlash 9/11: Middle Eastern and Muslim Americans Respond*. Berkeley: University of California Press, 2009.

Banaji, Mahzarin R., and Anthony G. Greenwald. *Blindspot: Hidden Biases of Good People*. New York: Bantam, 2013.

Banks, Antoine J., and Nicholas A. Valentino. "Emotional Substrates of Racial Attitudes." *American Journal of Political Science* 56, no. 2 (2012): 286–97.

Barreto, Matt, and Karam Dana. "Muslim and American: Transnational Ties and Participation in American Politics." Paper presented at the Midwest Political Science Association (MPSA) Conference, Chicago, 2008.

Barreto, Matt A., and Dino N. Bozonelos. "Democrat, Republican, or None of the Above? The Role of Religiosity in Muslim American Party Identification." *Politics and Religion* 2 (2002): 200–29.

Barreto, Matt A., Gary M. Segura, and Nathan D. Woods. "The Mobilizing Effect of Majority-Minority Districts on Latino Turnout." *American Political Science Review* 98, no. 1 (2004).

Bartosiewicz, Petra. "Deploying Informants, the FBI Stings Muslims." *The Nation*, June 14, 2012. https://www.thenation.com/article/deploying-informants-fbi-stings-muslims.

Baumgartner, Frank, and Beth L. Leech. "Interest Niches and Policy Bandwagons: Patterns of Interest Group Involvement in National Politics." *Journal of Politics* 63, no. 4 (2001): 1191–213.

Baumgartner, Frank, and Christine Mahoney. "The Two Faces of Framing: Individual Level Framing and Collective Issues Definition in the European Union." *European Union Politics* 9, no. 3 (2008): 435–49.

Beinart, Peter. "The Denationalization of American Muslims." *Atlantic*, March 19, 2017. https://www.theatlantic.com/politics/archive/2017/03/frank-gaffney-donald -trump-and-the-denationalization-of-american-muslims/519954.

Berinsky, Adam. *In Time of War: Understanding American Public Opinion from World War II to Iraq*. Chicago: University of Chicago Press, 2009.

Berry, Jeffrey. *Lobbying for the People: The Political Behavior of Public Interest Groups*. Princeton, NJ: Princeton University Press, 1997.

———. *The New Liberalism: The Rising Power of Citizen Groups*. Washington, DC: Brookings, 1999.

Beydoun, Khaled A. *American Islamophobia: Understanding the Roots and Rise of Fear*. Oakland: University of California Press, 2019.

——. "Between Muslim and White: The Legal Construction of Arab American Identity." *New York University Annual Survey of American Law* 69, no. 29 (2013): 1–35.

Bier, David. "Trump Cut Muslim Refugees 91%, Immigrants 30%, Visitors by 18%." *Cato at Liberty* (blog), The Cato Institute, December 7, 2018. https://www.cato.org/blog/trump-cut-muslim-refugees-91-immigrants-30-visitors-18.

Bilici, Mucahit. *Finding Mecca in America: How Islam Is Becoming an American Religion.* Chicago: The University of Chicago Press, 2012.

Blank, Joshua. "When Evaluating Public Support for Immigration Ban, Look beyond National Polling." Texas Politics Project at the University of Texas at Austin, January 30, 2017. https://texaspolitics.utexas.edu/blog/when-evaluating-public-support-immigration-ban-look-beyond-national-polling.

Blue, Miranda. "ACT for America Wants to Ban CAIR from Addressing State Legislatures." Right Wing Watch, December 13, 2016. http://www.rightwingwatch.org/post/act-for-america-wants-to-ban-cair-from-addressing-state-legislatures.

Bonilla-Silva, Eduardo. "What We Were, What We Are, and What We Should Be: The Racial Problem of American Sociology." *Social Problems* 64, no. 2 (2017): 79–87.

Boräng, Frida, and Daniel Naurin. "Try to See It My Way! Frame Congruence between Lobbyists and European Commission Officials." *Journal of European Public Policy* 22, 15 (2015): 499–515.

Branscombe, N. R., M. T. Schmitt, and R. D. Harvey. "Perceiving Pervasive Discrimination among African-Americans: Implications for Group Identification and Well Being." *Journal of Personality and Social Psychology* 77 (1999): 135–49.

Browne, William. *Ethnicity Without Groups.* Cambridge, MA: Harvard University Press, 2004.

——. "Organized Interests and Their Issue Niches," *Journal of Politics* 52, no. 2 (1990): 477–509.

Brubaker, Roger. *Ethnicity without Groups.* Cambridge, MA: Harvard University Press, 2004.

Buthe, Tim. "Taking Temporality Seriously: Modeling History and the Use of Narratives as Evidence." *American Political Science Review* 96, no. 3 (2002): 481–93.

Bzorgmehr, Mehdi, Paul Ong, and Sarah Tosh. "Panethnicity Revisited: Contested Group Boundaries in the Post-9-11 Era." *Ethnic Racial Studies* 39, no. 5 (2016): 727–45.

Caballero, Jenn B. "US Politicians on Immigration EO." Google spreadsheet, updated February 2017. https://docs.google.com/spreadsheets/u/1/d/1hSGjyWJZIQJpGz4V2ftX_qioCgBtL59oJkkhx146nFE/htmlview?sle=true&mc_cid=f94b7ac81f&mc_eid=64154722f1#.

Cainkar, Louise. "Post 9/11 Domestic Policies Affecting U.S. Arabs and Muslims: A Brief Review." *Comparative Studies of South Asia, Africa and the Middle East* 24, no. 1 (2005): 245–48.

Cainkar, Louise, and Sunaina Maira. "Targeting Arab/Muslim/South Asian Americans: Criminalization and Cultural Citizenship." *Amerasia Journal* 31 no. 3 (2005): 1–28.

CAIR TV. "CAIR Director Speaks at D.C. Rally for Gaza." August 2, 2014. https://www.youtube.com/watch?v=WRvFVJiRbtY.

——. "CAIR Files Federal Suit Challenging Constitutionality of Trump's 'Muslim Ban' Executive Order." January 30, 2017. https://www.youtube.com/watch?v=XkL1-e6cMYQ.

Calhoun-Brown, Allison. "African American Churches and Political Mobilization: The Psychological Impact of Organizational Resources." *Journal of Politics* 58, no. 4 (1996): 935–53.

Campbell, Christopher. *Race, Myth and the News.* Thousand Oaks, CA: Sage, 1995.

Campbell, David. *Writing Security: United States Foreign Policy and the Politics of Identity*. Minneapolis: University of Minnesota Press, 1998.

Carlson, Darren K. "Far Enough? Public Wary of Restricted Liberties." Gallup, January 20, 2004. http://news.gallup.com/poll/10324/far-enough-public-wary-restricted-liberties.aspx.

Chouhoud, Youssef. "What's the Hidden Story Behind American Muslim Poverty?" Institute for Social Policy and Understanding, October 2, 2018. https://www.ispu.org/whats-the-hidden-story-behind-american-muslim-poverty/.

Cillizza, Chris. "Breaking: Voters (Still) Don't Care about Foreign Policy." *Washington Post*, September 10, 2014. https://www.washingtonpost.com/news/the-fix/wp/2014/09/10/breaking-voters-still-dont-care-about-foreign-policy/.

Ciszek, Erica L. "Advocacy Communication and Social Identity." *Journal of Homosexuality* 64, no. 14 (2017).

Cockburn, Alexander. "Obama and the Indefinite Detention of U.S. Citizens." *The Nation*, January 4, 2012. https://www.thenation.com/article/obama-and-indefinite-detention-us-citizens/.

Code, Jillianne R., and Nicholas E. Zaparyniuk. "Social Identities, Group Formation, and the Analysis of Online Communities." In *Social Computing: Concepts, Methodologies, Tools, and Applications*, edited by Subhasish Dasgupta, 1346–61. New York: IGI Global, 2010.

Cohen, G. L. "Party over Policy: The Dominating Impact of Group Influence on Political Beliefs." *Journal of Personality and Social Psychology* 85, no. 5 (2003).

Collier, David, and Ruth Collier. *Shaping the Political Arena*. Notre Dame, IN: University of Notre Dame Press, 1991.

Collingwood, Loren, Nazita Lajevardi, and Kassra Oskooii. "A Change of Heart? Why Individual-Level Public Opinion Shifted against Trump's 'Muslim Ban.'" *Political Behavior* 40, no. 4 (2018): 1035–72.

Converse, P. E. "The Nature of Belief Systems in Mass Publics." In *Ideology and Discontent*, edited by D. Apter, 206–61. New York: Free Press, 1964.

Council on American-Islamic Relations (CAIR). *American Muslim Voters and the 2012 Elections: A Demographic Profile and Survey of Attitudes*. October 24, 2012. https://d3n8a8pro7vhmx.cloudfront.net/cairhq/pages/1986/attachments/original/1504007213/American_Muslim_Voter_Survey_2012.pdf.

——. "Breaking: CAIR Wins Landmark First Amendment Victory Striking Down Texas Anti-BDS Law." April 25, 2019. https://cair-mo.org/press-center/in-the-news/577-breaking-cair-wins-landmark-first-amendment-victory-striking-down-texas-anti-bds-law.html.

——. "Brief on Countering Violent Extremism with Recommendations for U.S. Government." February 2015. https://www.yumpu.com/en/document/read/36943056/cair-brief-on-countering-violent-extremism.

——. "CAIR Action Alert: Tell U.S. Senate 'No Military Aid to Burma' Because of Genocide of Rohingya Muslims." Accessed September 20, 2017. https://www.cair.com/action_alerts/cair-action-alert-tell-u-s-senate-no-military-aid-to-burma-because-of-genocide-of-rohingya-muslims/.

——. "CAIR-FL Files 10 Complaint with CBP After the Agency Targeted and Questioned American Muslims about Religious and Political Views." January 18, 2017. https://www.cairflorida.org/newsroom/press-releases/720-cair-fl-files-10-complaints-with-cbp-after-the-agency-targeted-and-questioned-american-muslims-about-religious-and-political-views.html.

——. "CAIR Letter to U.N. Ambassador Haley: Decisive Action Needed in Response to Burma's Ethnic Cleansing of Rohingya Muslims." Facebook, September 12, 2017.

https://www.facebook.com/CAIRNational/posts/rohingyamuslims-rohingyageno-cide-cair-letter-to-un-ambassador-haley-decisive-act/10155149316092695/.

———. "CAIR: Obama's 'Arab Spring' Address Sets the Right Tone." Cision, PR Newswire, May 19, 2011. http://www.prnewswire.com/news-releases/cair-obamas-arab-spring-address-sets-the-right-tone-122262258.html.

———. "CAIR Reiterates Condemnation of ISIS Violence, Religious Extremism." August 11, 2014. https://www.cairoklahoma.com/blog/cair-reiterates-condemnation-of-isis-violence-religious-extremism/.

———. "CAIR Urges Obama to 'Act Without Delay' after Syria Gas Massacre." August 22, 2013. http://www.cair.com/press-center/press-releases/12097-cair-urges-obama-to-act-without-delay-after-syria-gas-massacre.html.

———. "CAIR: U.S. Muslims Welcome Nuclear Deal with Iran." Cision, PR Newswire, November 24, 2013. https://www.prnewswire.com/news-releases/cair-us-muslims-welcome-nuclear-deal-with-iran-233247341.html.

———. *A Decade of Growth: Tenth Anniversary Report, 1994–2004.* Washington, DC: CAIR, 2004.

———. "Demand Israel Free and Return Tariq Khdeir to the U.S." 2014. https://www.cair.com/action_alerts/demand-israel-free-and-return-tariq-khdeir-to-the-u-s/.

———. "Kashmir: History, Context, and Consequences Presentation on March 20th." March 8, 2012. http://www.cairchicago.org/blog/2012/03/kashmir-history-context-and-consequences-presentation-on-march-20th/.

———. *Legislating Fear: Islamophobia and Its Impact in the United States.* 2013. http://cair.com/images/islamophobia/Legislating-Fear.pdf.

———. "Legislative Fact Sheet: Extra-Judicial Exile of Americans Traveling Abroad." January 1, 2013. https://www.cair.com/wp-content/uploads/2017/09/Stop-the-Extrajudicial-Exile-of-American-Citizens.pdf.

———. "Legislative Fact Sheet: Racial and Religious Profiling Abuses at the U.S. Border." January 1, 2013. https://d3n8a8pro7vhmx.cloudfront.net/cairhq/pages/4304/attachments/original/1504521940/Stop-Racial-and-Religious-Profiling-Abuses-at-US-Border.pdf?1504521940.

———. "New CAIR, UC Berkeley Report Reveals Funding, Negative Impact of Islamophobic Groups in America." June 20, 2016. http://www.islamophobia.org/reports/179-confronting-fear-islamophobia-and-its-impact-in-the-u-s-2013-2015.html.

———. "No-fly List Cases." Accessed March 27, 2020. https://www.cair.com/success_stories_qgafj_dwotsu7axdijni5w/no-fly-list-cases/.

———. "Shaima and Ali Mourn the Passing of their 2-Year-Old Son." December 28, 2018. https://ca.cair.com/sacval/news/shaima-and-ali-mourn-the-passing-of-their-2-year-old-son/.

———. "Support Bipartisan Efforts in Congress Condemning Genocide against Rohingya Muslims (Senate Resolution 250 and House Resolution 528)." October 10, 2017. https://oneclickpolitics.com/messages/edit?promo_id=3613.

———. "Urge State Department to Pressure India to End Lockdown, Lift Curfew and End Siege of Kashmir Valley." Action Center, August 6, 2019. https://www.votervoice.net/CAIR/campaigns/67781/respond.

———. "US Muslims Say War on Iraq Not Justified." February 27, 2003. https://www.cair.com/press_releases/u-s-muslims-say-war-on-iraq-not-justified/.

Crosby, F. J., A. Pufall, R. C. Snyder, M. O'Connell, and P. Whalen. "The Denial of Personal Disadvantage among You, Me, and All the Other Ostriches." In *Gender and Thought*, edited by M. Crawford and M. Gentry, 79–99. New York: Springer, 1989.

Curtis, Edward E. "For American Muslims, Everything Did Not Change after 9/11." *Religion & Politics*, July 5, 2012. http://religionandpolitics.org/2012/07/05/for-american-muslims-everything-did-not-change-after-911/.

———. *Islam in Black America: Identity, Liberation, and Difference in African American Islamic Thought*. New York: Albany State University Press, 2002.

———. *Muslims in America: A Short History*. New York: Oxford University Press, 2009.

Cury, Emily. "Contesting Islamophobia and Securing Collective Rights: Muslim American Advocacy in the 2016 Elections." *Politics and Religion* 12, no. 4 (2019): 710–35.

———. "How Muslim Americans Are Fighting Islamophobia and Securing Their Civil Rights." *The Conversation*, September 4, 2017.

Dahl, Robert A. *Who Governs? Democracy and Power in an American City*. New Haven, CT: Yale University Press, 2005.

Dana, Karam, Bryan Wilcox-Archuleta, and Matt Barreto. "The Political Incorporation of Muslims in the United States: The Mobilizing Role of Religiosity in Islam." *Journal of Race, Ethnicity, and Politics* 2, no. 2 (September 2017): 170–200.

Das Gupta, Monisha. *Unruly Immigrants: Rights, Activism, and Transnational South Asian Politics in the United States*. Durham, NC: Duke University Press, 2006.

De Bruycker, Iskander. "Framing and Advocacy: A Research Agenda for Interest Group Advocacy." *Journal of European Public Policy* 24, no. 5 (2016): 1–13.

Della Porta, Donatella, and Mario Diani. *Social Movements: An Introduction*. Oxford: Blackwell, 2009.

Denoeux, Guilain. "The Forgotten Swamp: Navigating Political Islam." *Middle East Policy* 9, no. 2 (2002): 56–81.

DeRue, D. Scott, and Susan J. Ashford. "Who Will Lead and Who Will Follow? A Social Process of Leadership Identity Construction in Organizations." *Academy of Management Review* 35, no. 4 (2010): 627–47.

Djupe, Paul, Andrew Lewis, and Ted Jelen. "Rights, Reflections, and Reciprocity: Implications of the Same-Sex Marriage Debate for Tolerance and Political Process." *Politics and Religion* 9, no. 3 (2016): 630–48.

Edwards, C., George Martin, P. Wattenberg, and Robert L. Lineberry. *Government in America: People, Politics and Policy*. New York: Longman, 2009.

Eisenbud, Daniel. "Tariq Abu Khdeir Cleared of Wrongdoing." *Jerusalem Post*, January 28, 2015. http://www.jpost.com/Arab-Israeli-Conflict/Tariq-Abu-Khdeir-cleared-of-wrongdoing-389198.

Eising, Rainer, Daniel Rasch, and Patrycja Rozbicka. "Institutions, Policies, and Arguments: Context and Strategy in EU Policy Framing." *Journal of European Public Policy* 22, no. 4 (2015): 516–33.

El-Ghobashy, Mona. "The Metamorphosis of the Egyptian Muslim Brothers." *International Journal of Middle East Studies* 37, no. 3 (2005): 373–95.

Elsheikh, Elsadig, Basima Sisemore, and Natalia Ramirez Lee. *Legalizing Othering: The United States of Islamophobia*. Berkeley, CA: Haas Institute for a Fair and Inclusive Society, 2017. https://haasinstitute.berkeley.edu/sites/default/files/haas_institute_legalizing_othering_the_united_states_of_islamophobia.pdf.

Entman, Robert. "Framing: Toward Clarification of a Fractured Paradigm." *Journal of Communication* 43, no. 4 (1993).

Espiritu, Yen Le. *Asian American Panethnicity: Bridging Institutions and Identities*. Philadelphia: Temple University Press, 1992.

Espiritu, Yen Le, and Paul Ong. "Class Constraints on Racial Solidarity among Asian Americans." In *The New Immigration in Los Angeles and Global Restructuring*, edited by Paul Ong, Edna Bonacich, and Lucie Cheng, 295–321. Philadelphia: Temple University Press, 1994.

Esposito, John. *The Oxford History of Islam*. Oxford: Oxford University Press, 1999.

Executive Order No. 13769. "Executive Order Protecting the Nation from Foreign Terrorist Entry into the United States." March 6, 2017. https://www.whitehouse.gov/the-press-office/2017/03/06/executive-order-protecting-nation-foreign-terrorist-entry-united-states.

Fairclough, Norman. "Intertextuality in Critical Discourse Analysis." *Linguistics and Education* 4, no. 3 (1992): 269–93.

Gallup Research Center. *Muslim Americans: Faith, Freedom and the Future: Examining U.S. Muslims' Political, Social, and Spiritual Engagement 10 Years after September 11*. August 2, 2011. http://www.gallup.com/poll/148931/presentation-muslim-americans-faith-freedom-future.aspx.

———. "Muslim Americans: A National Portrait: An In-Depth Analysis of America's Most Diverse Religious Community." 2009. https://news.gallup.com/poll/116260/muslim-americans-exemplify-diversity-potential.aspx.

George, Alexander L. *Presidential Decisionmaking in Foreign Policy: The Effective Use of Information and Advice*. Boulder, CO: Westview, 1980.

GhaneaBassiri, Kambiz. *A History of Islam in America*. Cambridge: Cambridge University Press, 2010.

Ginger, Jeff. "The Facebook Project: Performance and Construction of Digital Identity." Master's paper, University of Illinois, 2008. https://www.ideals.illinois.edu/bitstream/handle/2142/8818/FacebookProjectMastersPaperR4.pdf?sequence.

Gjelten, Tom. *A Nation of Nations: A Great American Immigration Story*. New York: Simon and Schuster, 2015.

Goffman, Ervin. *Frame Analysis: An Essay on the Organization of Experience*. Boston: Northeastern University Press, 1974.

Goodstein, Laurie. "Across Nation, Mosque Projects Meet Opposition." *New York Times*, August 7, 2010. http://www.nytimes.com/2010/08/08/us/08mosque.html?pagewanted=all&mcubz=3.

Goodwin, Jeff, James M. Jasper, and Francesca Polletta, eds. *Passionate Politics: Emotions and Social Movements*. Chicago: University of Chicago Press, 2009.

Gray, Virginia, and David Lowery. *The Population Ecology of Interest Representation*. Ann Arbor: University of Michigan Press, 1996.

Green, Emma. "What Lies Ahead for Obama's Countering Violent Extremism Program?" *Atlantic*, March 17, 2017. https://www.theatlantic.com/politics/archive/2017/03/countering-violent-extremism/519822/.

Greenwald, Glenn, and Murtaza Hussain. "Meet the Muslim American Leaders the FBI and NSA Have Been Spying On." *Intercept*, July 9, 2014. https://firstlook.org/theintercept/2014/07/09/under-surveillance/.

Grewal, Zareena. *Islam Is a Foreign Country: American Muslims and the Global Crisis of Authority*. New York: NYU Press, 2013.

Grossman, Gene, and Elhanah Helpman. *Special Interest Politics*. Cambridge, MA: MIT Press, 2002.

Haddad, Yvonne, Jane Smith, and John Esposito. *Religion and Immigration: Christian, Jewish and Muslim Experience in the United States*. Oxford: Altamira, 2003.

Haddad, Yvonne Yazbeck. *Becoming American? The Forging of Arab and Muslim Identity in Pluralist America*. Waco, TX: Baylor University Press, 2011.

———. *Not Quite American? The Shaping of Arab and Muslim Identity in the United States*. Waco, TX: Baylor University Press, 2004.

Hagerty, Barbara Bradley. "Muslims Face Risk in Giving to Charities." *Morning Edition*, NPR, June 16, 2009. http://www.npr.org/templates/story/story.php?storyId=105449968.

Hall, Stuart. "Culture, community, nations." *Cultural Studies* 7, no. 3 (1993): 349–63.
———. "The Question of Cultural Identity." In *Modernity: An Introduction to Modern Socie-ties*, edited by Stuart Hall, Don Huber, and Thomson Kenneth. Cambridge: Cam-bridge University Press, 1996.
Hammer, Julianne, and Omid Safi. *The Cambridge Companion to American Islam.* Cambridge: Cambridge University Press, 2013.
Hansen, Mark. *Gaining Access: Congress and the Farm Lobby, 1919–1981.* New York: Cam-bridge University Press, 1991.
Hawthorne, Amy, and Michele Dunne. "Remember That Historic Arab Spring Speech?" *Foreign Policy*, May 21, 2013. http://foreignpolicy.com/2013/05/21/remember-that -historic-arab-spring-speech/.
Heaney, Michael. "Multiplex Networks and Interest Group Influence Reputation: An Ex-ponential Random Graph Model." *Social Networks* 36 (2014): 66–81.
Herman, Susan. "Taking Liberties: The ACLU and the War on Terror." ACLU, June 12, 2011. https://www.aclu.org/other/taking-liberties-aclu-and-war-terror.
Hilal, Maha. "When Life Is Disposable: Muslim Bodies as Precarious in the War on Ter-ror." Amnesty International. Accessed March 20, 2020. https://www.amnestyusa.org /when-life-is-disposable-muslim-bodies-as-precarious-in-the-war-on-terror/.
Hill, Howard C. "The Americanization Movement." *American Journal of Sociology* 25, no. 6 (1919): 609–42.
Hilsman, Roger, Laura Gaughran, and Patricia A. Weitsman. *The Politics of Policy Making in Defense and Foreign Affairs: Conceptual Models and Bureaucratic Politics.* Engle-wood Cliffs, NJ: Prentice-Hall, 1987.
Hing, Bill Ong. "Beyond the Rhetoric of Assimilation and Cultural Pluralism: Addressing the Tension of Separatism and Conflict in an Immigration-Driven Multiracial So-ciety." *California Law Review* 81, no. 4 (1993): 863–925.
———. "Misusing Immigration Policies in the Name of Homeland Security." *CR: The New Centennial Review* 6, no. 1 (2006): 195–224.
———. "Vigilante Racism: The De-Americanization of Immigrant America," *Michigan Jour-nal of Race and Law* 3, no. 7 (2002).
Hirschman, Charles. "The Origins and Demise of the Concept of Race." *Population and Development Review* 30, no. 3 (2004): 6.
Holyoke, Thomas. "Interest Group Competition and Coalition Formation." *American Jour-nal of Political Science* 53 (2009): 360–75.
Huntington, Samuel. *Who Are We? The Challenges to America's National Identity.* New York: Simon and Schuster, 2004.
Irigaray, Luce. *Je, Tu, Nous: Toward a Culture of Difference.* New York: Routledge, 1993.
Islamic Circle of North America (ICNA). "Historic First National Muslim Advocacy Day." April 17, 2015. http://www.icna.org/historic-first-national-muslim-advocacy -day/.
Islamic Society of North America (ISNA). "New National ISNA Survey Finds Strong Sup-port for Climate Solutions among Muslim-Americans." October 31, 2018. http:// www.isna.net/new-national-isna-survey-finds-strong-support-for-climate -solutions-among-muslim-americans/.
Ito, Suzanne. "ACLU Lens: King Hearing Relies on False Premises, Discriminatory Atti-tudes." *Speak Freely* (blog), ACLU, March 11, 2011. https://www.aclu.org/blog /national-security/aclu-lens-king-hearing-relies-false-premises-discriminatory -attitudes.
Jachimowicz, Maia, and Ramah McKay. "'Special Registration' Program." Migration Policy Institute, April 1, 2003. http://www.migrationpolicy.org/article/special-registration -program#1.

Jamal, Amaney. "The Political Participation and Engagement of Muslim Americans: Mosque Involvement and Group Consciousness." *American Politics Research* 33, no. 4 (2005): 521–44.

Jenkins, J. Craig. "Resource Mobilization Theory and the Study of Social Movements." *Annual Review of Sociology* 9 (1983): 527–53.

Jetpac. "Liftoff! We've Launched a National Campaign for Muslims to Train, and Run, for Local Office." 2017. https://www.jet-pac.com/.

Jetten, Jolanda, Nyla R. Branscombe, Michael T. Schmitt, and Russell Spears. "Rebels with a Cause: Group Identification as a Response to Perceived Discrimination from the Mainstream." *Personality and Social Psychology Bulletin* 27, no. 9 (2001): 1204–13.

Jewish Telegraphic Agency. "Jewish Groups Join Call to Mayors to Denounce 'Anti-Sharia' Marches." June 9, 2017. https://www.jta.org/2017/06/09/news-opinion/politics /jewish-groups-join-call-to-mayors-to-denounce-anti-sharia-marches.

Johnson, Jill. *Lesbian Nation: The Feminist Solution.* New York: Simon and Schuster, 1973.

Jones-Correa, Michael A., and David L. Leal. "Political Participation: Does Religion Matter?" *Political Research Quarterly* 54, no. 4 (2001): 751–70.

Kahera, Akel Ismail. *Deconstructing the American Mosque: Space, Gender, and Aesthetics.* Austin: University of Texas Press, 2002.

Kaleem, Jaweed. "How the Orlando Attack Could Mark a Shift for Gay Muslims." *Los Angeles Times*, June 14, 2016. https://www.latimes.com/nation/la-na-gay-muslim -20160614-20160612-snap-story.html.

Kalkan, Kerem Ozan, Geoffrey C. Layman, and Eric M. Uslaner. "'Bands of Others'? Attitudes Toward Muslims in Contemporary American Society." *Journal of Politics* 71, no. 3 (July 2009): 847–62.

Kaplan, Jeffrey. "Islamophobia in America? September 11 and Islamophobic Hate." *Terrorism and Political Violence* 18, no. 1 (2007).

Karp, J. "The Influence of Elite Endorsements in Initiative Campaigns." *Citizens as Legislators* 3 (1998): 149–65.

Khalidi, Omar. "Mosques in North America." *American Studies Journal* 52 (2008). http:// www.asjournal.org/52-2008/mosques-in-north-america/.

Khan, Azmat. "Pamela Geller: 'This Is a Clash of Civilizations.'" *Frontline*, PBS, September 27, 2011. http://www.pbs.org/wgbh/frontline/article/pamela-geller-this-is-a -clash-of-civilizations/.

Kinder, Donald, and Lynn Sanders. *Divided by Color: Racial Politics and Democratic Ideals.* Chicago: University of Chicago Press, 1996.

King, David C., and Jack L. Walker. "The Provision of Benefits by Interest Groups in the United States." *Journal of Politics* 54 (1992): 394–426.

Klandermans, Bert. "Collective political action." In *Oxford Handbook of Political Psychology*, edited by D. O. Sears, L. Huddy, and R. Jervis, 670–709. Oxford: Oxford University Press, 2003.

Klein, Oliver, Russell Spears, and Stephen Reicher. "Social Identity Performance: Extending the Strategic Side of SIDE." *Personality and Social Psychology Review* 11 (2007): 28–45.

Klüver, Heike, Christine Mahoney, and Marc Opper. "Framing in Context: How Interest Groups Employ Framing to Lobby the European Commission." *Journal of European Public Policy* 22, no. 4 (2015).

Kollman, Ken. *Outside Lobbying: Public Opinion and Interest Group Strategies.* Princeton, NJ: Princeton University Press, 1998.

Koopmans, Ruud, Paul Statham, Marco Giugni, and Florence Passy. *Contested Citizenship: Immigration and Cultural Diversity in Europe.* Minneapolis: University of Minnesota Press, 2005.

Lajevardi, Nazita, and Kassra A. R. Oskooii. "Old-Fashioned Racism, Contemporary Islamophobia, and the Isolation of Muslim Americans in the Age of Trump." *Journal of Race, Ethnicity, and Politics* 3 (February 2018).

Lajevardi, Nazita, Melissa R. Michelson, and Marianne Marar Yacobian, "The Unbearable Whiteness of Being Middle Eastern: Causes and Effects of the Racialization of Middle Eastern Americans." In *Understanding Muslim Political Life in America: Contested Citizenship in the Twenty-First Century*, edited by Brian R. Calfano and Nazita Lajevardi, 52–68. Philadelphia: Temple University Press, 2019.

Laub, Zachary. "The Impact of the Iran Nuclear Agreement" (Backgrounder). Council on Foreign Relations, updated May 8, 2018. The following webpage is updated as the situation evolves: https://www.cfr.org/backgrounder/impact-iran-nuclear-agreement.

Leonard, Karen. *Muslims in the United States: The State of Research*. New York: Russell Sage Foundation, 2003.

Leslie, Katie. "Ted Cruz Strongly Backs Trump Travel Ban, While John Cornyn More Cautious." *Dallas News*, January 30, 2017. https://www.dallasnews.com/news/politics/2017/01/30/ted-cruz-strongly-backs-trump-travel-ban-john-cornyn-cautious.

Levin, Brian. *Special Status Report: Hate Crimes in the Cities and Counties of the U.S.: Compilation of Official Data (15 Jurisdictions)*. California State University, San Bernardino, Center for the Study of Hate and Extremism, 2017. https://mynewsla.com/wp-content/uploads/2017/04/Special-Status-Report-Metro-Areas-2017-Final-Draft-32517.pdf.

Levitt, Peggy. "Transnational Migrants: When 'Home' Means More Than One Country." Migration Policy Institute, October 1, 2004. https://www.migrationpolicy.org/article/transnational-migrants-when-home-means-more-one-country.

Lewis, Charles, and Mark Reading-Smith. "False Pretenses." Center for Public Integrity, January 23, 2008. https://publicintegrity.org/2008/01/23/5641/false-pretenses.

Lichtblau, Eric. "Arrests Tie Charity Group to Palestinian Terrorists." *New York Times*, July 28, 2004. https://www.nytimes.com/2004/07/28/us/arrests-tie-charity-group-to-palestinian-terrorists.html

Lima, Alvaro. "Transnationalism: A New Mode of Immigrant Integration." Paper presented at Securing the Dream: Power, Progress, Prosperity, the Statewide Latino Public Policy Conference, The Mauricio Gastón Institute, University of Massachusetts, Boston, September 17, 2010. http://www.bostonplans.org/getattachment/b5ea6e3a-e94e-451b-af08-ca9fcc3a1b5b/.

Liptak, Kevin, and Nicole Gaouette. "Trump Withdraws from Iran Nuclear Deal, Isolating Him Further from World." CNN, updated May 9, 2018. https://www.cnn.com/2018/05/08/politics/donald-trump-iran-deal-announcement-decision/index.html.

Lopez, David, and Yen Espiritu. "Panethnicity in the U.S.: A Theoretical Framework." *Ethnic and Racial Studies* 13, no. 2 (2010).

López, Gustavo, and Jynnah Radford. "2015, Foreign-Born Population in the United States Statistical Portrait." Hispanic Trends, Pew Research Center, May 3, 2017. http://www.pewhispanic.org/2017/05/03/facts-on-u-s-immigrants-current-data/.

Love, Erik. *Islamophobia and Racism in America*. New York: NYU Press, 2015.

Lowery, David. "Why Do Organized Interests Lobby? A Multi-Goal, Multi-Context Theory of Lobbying." *Polity* 39 (2007): 29–54.

Magnusson, Paul. "FBI Reveals FBI Tapping of Sirhan Lawyer's Calls." *Washington Post*, August 3, 1997. https://www.washingtonpost.com/archive/politics/1977/08/03/fbi-reveals-nsa-tapping-of-sirhan-lawyers-calls/044c120f-a22f-449a-b175-62f424a06378/.

Mandaville, Peter. "Reimagining Islam in Diaspora: The Politics of Mediated Community." *International Communication Gazette*, 2001.

McClurg, Scott, and Jeremy Philips. "A Social Network Analysis of Interest Group Contributions and Partisan Behavior in the 2006 House of Representatives." Proceedings of the Political Network Summer Conference, Southern Illinois University Carbondale, 2011.

McCormick, Ty. "Could Lindsay Graham's Terrorism Amendment Target Immigrants from Ireland?" *Foreign Policy*, May 22, 2013. https://foreignpolicy.com/2013/05/22/could-lindsey-grahams-terrorism-amendment-target-immigrants-from-ireland/.

Menjívar, Cecilia. "Liminal Legality: Salvadoran and Guatemalan Immigrants' Lives in the United States," *American Journal of Sociology* 111, no. 4 (January 2006): 999–1037.

Meyer, Stephen. "Adapting the Immigrant to the Line: Americanization in the Ford Factory, 1914–1921." *Journal of Social History* 14, no. 1 (1980): 67–82.

Minnite, Lorraine C. "Outside the Circle: The Impact of Post-9/11 Responses on Immigrant Communities in New York City." In *Contentious City: The Politics of Recovery in New York City*, edited by John H. Mollenkopf, 165–204. New York: Russell Sage Foundation, 2005.

Mitchell, Katharyne. "Education for Democratic Citizenship: Transnationalism, Multiculturalism, and the Limits of Liberalism." *Harvard Educational Review* 71, no. 1 (2001): 51–79.

Mogahed, Dalia. "Islamophobia Is Made Up." *Islamic Monthly*, September 25, 2013. http://www.theislamicmonthly.com/islamophobia-is-made-up/.

Moghul, Haroon. *How to Be a Muslim: An American Story*. Boston: Beacon Press, 2017.

Mohamed, Besheer. "New Estimates Show U.S. Muslim Population Continues to Grow." Pew Research Center, January 3, 2018. https://www.pewresearch.org/fact-tank/2018/01/03/new-estimates-show-u-s-muslim-population-continues-to-grow/.

Morales, Laura, and Miruna Morariu. "Is 'Home' a Distraction? The Role of Migrants' Transnational Practices in Their Political Integration into Receiving-Country Politics." In *Social Capital, Political Participation and Migration in Europe: Making Multicultural Democracy Work?* edited by Laura Morales and Marco Giugni, 140–71. London: Palgrave Macmillan, 2011.

Morawska, Ewa. "Immigrant Transnationalism and Assimilation: A Variety of Combination and the Analytic Strategy It Suggests." In *Toward Assimilation and Citizenship: Immigrants in Liberal Nation-States*, edited by Christian Joppe and Ewa Morawska, 133–76. Basingstoke, UK: Palgrave-Macmillan, 2003.

Mosquera, Patricia M. Rodriguez, Tasmiha Khan, and Arielle Selya. "American Muslims' Anger and Sadness about In-Group Social Image." *Frontiers in Psychology* 7 (2017).

MPAC (@mpac_national). "#ISpeakOutBecause." Twitter, August 13, 2014, 11:41 a.m. https://twitter.com/mpac_national/status/499626778718380034.

Muslim Justice League. "Contacted by the FBI?" Accessed March 26, 2020. https://www.muslimjusticeleague.org/when-the-fbi-knocks/.

——. "What Is 'Countering Violent Extremism' (CVE)?" Accessed March 26, 2020. https://www.muslimjusticeleague.org/cve/.

Muslim Legal Fund of America. "Impact." Accessed March 25, 2020. https://app.mobilecause.com/vf/MLFA.

——. "Muslim Leaders Convene in Dallas for National Leadership Conference." October 6, 2017. https://www.mlfa.org/news/muslims-leaders-convene-in-dallas-for-national-leadership-conference/.

Muslim Public Affairs Council (MPAC). "Action Alert: Say Yes to Diplomacy, No to War with Iran." February 20, 2012. https://www.mpac.org/take-action/action-alert-say-yes-to-diplomacy-no-to-war-with-iran.php.

——. "Burma's Rohingya: A Slow Genocide." September 14, 2017. https://www.mpac.org/blog/policy-analysis/burmas-rohingya-a-slow-genocide.php.

——. *Counterproductive Counterterrorism: How Anti-Islamic Rhetoric Is Impeding America's Homeland Security.* December 2004. http://www.mpac.org/assets/docs/publications/counterproductive-counterterrorism.pdf.

——. "Envisioning Peace: The MPAC Perspective on the Israeli-Palestinian Conflict." June 8, 2007. https://www.mpac.org/assets/docs/publications/MPAC-Envisioning-Peace.pdf.

——. "I Am Change: Civic Leadership Program." 2014. https://www.mpac.org/programs/i-am-change/mpac-hosts-i-am-change-leadership-program.php.

——. "Interfaith Coalition Decries Hate Group Leader's Appearance at L.A. Jewish Federation." June 23, 2012. https://www.mpac.org/issues/islamophobia/interfaith-coalition-decries-hate-group-leaders-appearance-at-l.a.-jewish-federation.php.

——. *An Islamic Perspective on Giving Zakat to the MPAC Foundation.* July 10, 2015. https://www.mpac.org/old-images/zakat-brochure.pdf.

——. *MPAC Congressional Report Card: Grading our 113th Congress.* 2014. https://www.mpac.org/assets/docs/publications/MPAC-Congressional-Reportcard-2014.pdf.

——. "MPAC Coordinates Meeting with FBI on Surveillance Reports." December 29, 2005. https://www.mpac.org/programs/anti-terrorism-campaign/mpac-coordinates-meeting-with-fbi-on-surveillance-reports.php.

——. "MPAC Launches #ISpeakOutBecause Campaign." August 7, 2014. http://www.mpac.org/issues/civil-rights/mpac-launches-ispeakoutbecause-campaign1.php.

——. "MPAC Statement on CVE Act of 2015." July 15, 2015. https://www.mpac.org/blog/updates/speaking-out-on-cve-act-of-2015.php.

——. "MPAC Urges Senate to Oppose Sanctions on Iran." January 14, 2014. https://www.mpac.org/issues/foreign-policy/mpac-urges-senate-to-oppose-sanctions-on-iran.php.

——. "A Nation of Immigrants: Realizing a Comprehensive Immigration Reform." September 17, 2013. https://www.mpac.org/publications/policy-papers/a-nation-of-immigrants.php.

——. "Our Approach to Government Engagement." http://www.mpac.org/programs/government-relations.php.

——. "Position Paper: On Intervention in Syria." September 6, 2013. http://www.mpac.org/assets/docs/publications/MPAC-Intervention-in-Syria-Position-Paper.pdf.

——. *A Review of U.S. Counterterrorism Policy: American Muslim Critique & Recommendations.* September 2003. http://www.mpac.org/assets/docs/publications/counterterrorism-policy-paper.pdf.

——. *Safe Spaces Initiative: Tools for Developing Healthy Communities.* Accessed April 2, 2020. https://www.dhs.gov/sites/default/files/publications/Tools%20for%20Developing%20Healthy%20Communities-MPAC%20Toolkit%20Report.pdf.

——. *Selecting 'Options on the Table' Carefully: The Consequences of a Military Strike on Iran.* January 30, 2012. https://www.mpac.org/assets/docs/publications/MPAC_Paper--Selecting_Options_on_the_Table_Carefully__The_Consequences_of_a_Military_Strike_on_Iran.pdf.

——. "Statement of Fall of Saddam Hussein & Post-War Iraq." April 10, 2003. http://www.mpac.org/issues/foreign-policy/statement-of-fall-of-saddam-hussein-post-war-iraq.php.

——. "Trump's tweets at #Iran could trigger WWIII." Facebook, July 17, 2019. https://www.facebook.com/mpacnational/photos/a.456754193393/10157600175398394/?type=3&theater.

——. "Unprecedented Violence Erupts in Jammu and Kashmir." September 22, 2016. https://www.mpac.org/blog/policy-analysis/unprecedented-violence-erupts-in-jammu-and-kashmir.php.

——. "U.S. Should Support Kashmiri Call for Self-Determination." September 5, 2008. https://www.mpac.org/issues/foreign-policy/u.s.-should-support-kashmiri-call -for-self-determination.php.

——. "Welcome Palestine? MPAC's Analysis on the UN Resolution for Palestinian State-hood." September 21, 2011.

——. "Young Leaders Summits." Accessed March 25, 2020. https://www.mpac.org /programs/young-leaders/summits.php.

Naber, Nadine. "'Look, Mohammed the Terrorist Is Coming!' Cultural Racism, Nation-Based Racism, and the Intersectionality of Oppressions after 9/11." *Race and Arab Americans before and after 9/11: From Invisible Citizens to Visible Subjects*, edited by Amaney Jamal and Nadine Naber, 276–304. Syracuse, NY: Syracuse University Press, 2007.

Nacos, Brigitte Lebens, and Oscar Torres-Reyna. *Fueling Our Fears: Stereotyping, Media Coverage, and Public Opinion of Muslim Americans*. Lanham, MD: Rowman & Lit-tlefield, 2007.

——. "Muslim Americans in the News before and after 9/11." Paper prepared for the Harvard Symposium "Restless Searchlight: The Media and Terrorism," cospon-sored by the APSA Communication Section and the Shorenstein Center at John F. Kennedy School, Harvard University, 2002.

Nadwi, Syed Abul Hassan Ali. *Muslims in the West: The Message and Mission*. Leicester, UK: The Islamic Foundation, 1983.

Nagel, Caroline R., and Lynn A. Staeheli. "'We're Just Like the Irish': Narratives of Assimi-lation, Belonging and Citizenship amongst Arab-American Activists." *Citizenship Studies* 9, no. 5 (2005): 485–98.

Najarro, Ileana. "Man Who Threatened Muslim Is Sentenced to 13 Months." *New York Times*, July 7, 2015. https://www.nytimes.com/2015/07/08/nyregion/no-jail-term -for-threats-against-a-muslim-man.html?_r=0.

Neal, Caren. "A Social Movement Online Community." *Media Movements and Political Change* 33 (2012): 163–93. https://sociology.unc.edu/files/2016/12/Gaby-SMOC -Caren-Et-al.pdf.

Newport, Frank. "Seventy-Two Percent of Americans Support War Against Iraq." Gallup, March 24, 2003. http://news.gallup.com/poll/8038/seventytwo-percent-americans -support-war-against-iraq.aspx.

Nisbet, Erik, and James Shanahan. *MSRG Special Report: Restrictions on Civil Liberties, Views of Islam, and Muslim Americans*. December 2004. Ithaca, NY: Media and So-ciety Research Group, Cornell University. http://arabsandterrorism.com/resources /Restrictions_on_Civil_Libe.pdf.

Nixon, Richard. "Memorandum Establishing a Cabinet Committee to Combat Terror-ism." September 25, 1972. Available at The American Presidency Project, UC Santa Barbara, https://www.presidency.ucsb.edu/documents/memorandum-estab lishing-cabinet-committee-combat-terrorism.

Noakes, Greg. "Coalition Criticizes Terrorism Bill." *Washington Report on Middle East Af-fairs*. April/May 1995. https://www.wrmea.org/1995-april-may/american-muslim -activism-coalition-criticizes-terrorism-bill.html.

Nownes, Anthony J. "The Population Ecology of Interest Group Formation: Mobilizing for Gay and Lesbian Rights in the United States." *British Journal of Political Science* 34 (2003): 49–67.

Nownes, Anthony J., and Patricia Freeman. "Interest Group Activity in the States." *Jour-nal of Politics* 60 (1998): 86–112.

NPR, July 18, 2018. https://www.npr.org/2018/07/18/630132952/muslim-americans -running-for-office-in-highest-numbers-since-2001.

O'Connor, Patrick, and Julian E. Barnes. "Gingrich Calls for Regime Change in Iran." *Wall Street Journal*, November 24, 2011. http://online.wsj.com/article/SB100014240529 70204531404577054911628578368.html.

Okamoto, Dina G. "Toward a Theory of Panethnicity: Explaining Asian American Collective Action." *American Sociological Review* 68, no. 6 (November 2003): 811–42.

Olson, Mancur. *The Logic of Collective Action: Public Goods and the Theory of Groups*. Cambridge, MA: Harvard University Press, 1971 [1965].

Omi, Michael, and Howard Winat. *Racial Formations in the United States*. 3rd ed. New York: Routledge, 2015.

Padgett, Tim. "Why So Many Latinos Are Becoming Muslims." WLRN Public Radio, October 9, 2013. http://wlrn.org/post/why-so-many-latinos-are-becoming-muslims.

Padilla, Felix. *Latino Ethnic Consciousness: The Case of Mexican Americans and Puerto Ricans in Chicago*. Notre Dame, IN: Notre Dame University Press, 1985.

Page, Benjamin, and Robert Shapiro. *The Rational Public: Fifty Years of Trends in American Policy Preferences*. Chicago: University of Chicago Press, 1992.

Pantoja, Adrian, and Gary Segura. "Fear and Loathing in California: Contextual Threat and Political Sophistication among Latino Voters." *Political Behavior* 25, no. 3 (2003).

Patel, Faiza, and Meghan Koushik. "Countering Violent Extremism." Brennan Center for Justice, New York School of Law, March 16, 2017. https://www.brennancenter.org /publication/countering-violent-extremism.

Paul, David, and Rachel Paul. *Ethnic Lobbies and US Foreign Policy*. Boulder, CO: Lynne Rienner, 2008.

Pavlenko, Aneta. "'We Have Room for But One Language Here': Language and National Identity in the US at the Turn of the 20th Century." *Multilingua* 21 (2002): 163–96.

Peek, Lori. "Becoming Muslim: The Development of a Religious Identity." *Sociology of Religion* 66, no. 3 (2005): 215–232.

——. *Behind the Backlash: Muslim Americans after 9/11*. Philadelphia: Temple University Press, 2006.

"Peter King's Obsession." *New York Times*, March 7, 2011. http://www.nytimes.com/2011 /03/08/opinion/08tue1.html.

Pew Research Center. "Black Voter Turnout Fell in 2016, Even as a Record Number of Americans Cast Ballots." May 12, 2017, https://www.pewresearch.org/fact-tank /2017/05/12/black-voter-turnout-fell-in-2016-even-as-a-record-number-of -americans-cast-ballots/.

——. "Controversies over Mosques and Islamic Centers Across the U.S." *Religion & Public Life*, September 27, 2012. http://www.pewforum.org/2012/09/27/controversies -over-mosques-and-islamic-centers-across-the-u-s-2/.

——. "Fact on U.S. Immigrants: Statistical Portrait of the Foreign-Born U.S. Population in the United States." June 3, 2019. http://www.pewhispanic.org/2016/04/19 /statistical-portrait-of-the-foreign-born-population-in-the-united-states-2014-key -charts.

——. "Most Muslim Americans Are U.S. Citizens, But Many Are Not Registered or Did Not Vote in 2016 Election." *U.S. Muslims Concerned about Their Place in Society, but Continue to Believe in the American Dream: Findings from Pew Research Center's 2017 Survey of U.S. Muslims*. July 26, 2017. http://www.pewforum.org/2017/07/26 /political-and-social-views/pf_2017-06-26_muslimamericans-04new-02/.

——. *Muslim Americans: Middle Class and Mostly Mainstream*. May 22, 2007. https://www .pewresearch.org/wp-content/uploads/2007/05/muslim-americans.pdf.

——. *Muslim Americans: No Signs of Growth in Alienation or Support for Extremism*. August 2011. http://www.pewforum.org/2011/08/30/muslim-americans-no-signs-of -growth-in-alienation-or-support-for-extremism/.

———. "Section 6: Terrorism, Concerns about Extremism & Foreign Policy." August 30, 2011. http://www.people-press.org/2011/08/30/section-6-terrorism-concerns-about -extremism-foreign-policy/.

———. *United in Remembrance, Divided over Policies: Ten Years after 9/11.* U.S. Politics & Policy, September 1, 2011. http://www.people-press.org/2011/09/01/united-in -remembrance-divided-over-policies/.

———. "U.S. Muslims Concerned about Their Place in Society, But Continue to Believe in the American Dream: Findings from Pew Research Center's 2017 Survey of U.S. Muslims." July 26, 2017. http://www.pewforum.org/2017/07/26/findings-from-pew -research-centers-2017-survey-of-us-muslims/.

———. *U.S. Muslims Concerned about Their Place in Society, But Continue to Believe in the American Dream: Findings from Pew Research Center's 2017 Survey of U.S. Muslims.* July 26, 2017. https://www.pewresearch.org/wp-content/uploads/sites/7/2017/07/U .S.-MUSLIMS-FULL-REPORT.pdf.

———. "Views of Islam and Violence." September 9, 2009. http://www.pewforum.org/2009 /09/09/publicationpage-aspxid1398-3/.

Phalet, Karen, and Maykel Verkuyten. "Political Mobilization of Dutch Muslims: Religious Identity Salience, Goal Framing and Normative Constraints." *Journal of Social Issues* 66, no. 4 (2010): 759–79.

Phillip, Abby, and Abigail Hauslohner. "Trump on the Future of Proposed Muslim Ban, Registry: 'You Know My Plans.'" *Washington Post*, December 22, 2016. https://www .washingtonpost.com/news/post-politics/wp/2016/12/21/trump-on-the-future-of -proposed-muslim-ban-registry-you-know-my-plans/.

Portes, Alejandro, and Rubén Lambaut. *Immigrant America: A Portrait.* Berkeley: University of California Press, 2006.

Poston, Larry. *Islamic Da'wah in the West: Muslim Missionary Activity and the Dynamics of Conversion to Islam.* New York: Oxford University Press, 1992.

Potok, Mark. "DOJ Study: More Than 250,000 Hate Crimes a Year, Most Unreported." Southern Poverty Law Center, March 26, 2013. https://www.splcenter.org/hatewatch /2013/03/26/doj-study-more-250000-hate-crimes-year-most-unreported.

Putnam, Robert. *Bowling Alone: The Collapse and Revival of American Community.* New York: Simon and Schuster, 2000.

Raphelson, Samantha. "Muslim Americans Running for Office in Highest Numbers since 2001."

Read, Jen'nan Ghazal. "Discrimination and Identity Formation in a Post-9/11 Era." In *Race and Arab Americans Before and After 9/11: From Invisible Citizens to Visible Subjects*, edited by Amaney Jamal and Nadine Christine Naber, 305–17. Syracuse, NY: Syracuse University Press, 2004.

Read, Jen'nan Ghazal, and John P. Bartkowski. "To Veil or Not to Veil? A Case Study of Identity Negotiation among Muslim Women in Austin, Texas." *Gender & Society* 14, no. 3 (2000): 395–417.

Reilly, Daniel W. "Rep. Peter King: There Are 'Too Many Mosques in This Country.'" *Politico Now* (blog), Politico, September 19, 2007. https://www.politico.com/blogs /politico-now/2007/09/rep-peter-king-there-are-too-many-mosques-in-this -country-003213.

Reny, Reny, Ali Valenzuela, and Loren Collingwood. "'No, You're Playing the Race Card': Testing the Effects of Anti-Black, Anti-Latino and Anti-Immigrant Appeals in the Post-Obama Era." *Journal of Political Psychology* 42, no. 2 (2020): 283–302.

Ricoeur, Paul. *Time and Narrative.* Translated by Kathleen Blamey and David Pellauer. Chicago: Chicago University Press, 1988.

Robbins, John. "CAIR Brief on Countering Violent Extremism (CVE)." CAIR-MA, July 9, 2015. http://www.cairma.org/cair-brief-on-countering-violent-extremism -cve/.

Rubenzer, Trevor, and Steven Redd. "Ethnic Minority Groups and US Foreign Policy: Examining Congressional Decision Making and Economic Sanctions." *International Studies Quarterly* 54, no. 3 (2010): 755–77.

Rucht, Dieter. "German Unification, Democratization and the Role of Social Movements: A Missed Opportunity?" *Mobilization: An International Quarterly* 1, no. 1 (1996): 35–62.

Sachedina, Abdulaziz. *The Islamic Roots of Democratic Pluralism.* New York: Oxford University Press, 2001.

Said, Edward W. *Covering Islam: How the Media and the Experts Determine How We See the Rest of the World.* New York: Vintage, 1981.

——. *Culture and Imperialism.* New York: Random House, 1983.

——. *Orientalism.* New York: Vintage, 1978.

Salisbury, Robert. "An Exchange Theory of Interest Groups." *Midwest Journal of Political Science* 13 (1969): 1–32.

Salisbury, Robert, John Heinz, Edward Laumann, and Rovert Nelson. "Who Is at War with Whom? Interest Group Alliances and Opposition." *American Political Science Review* 81 (1987): 1217–34.

Sanders, Sam. "Ted Cruz Criticized after Suggesting Law Enforcement Patrol Muslim Areas." NPR, March 23, 2016. https://www.npr.org/2016/03/23/471600823/ted-cruz -faces-criticism-after-suggesting-law-enforcement-patrol-muslim-areas.

Sarder, Sarah. "Dallas Muslim Leader Omar Suleiman Arrested during DACA Protest on Capitol Hill." *Dallas Morning News*, March 6, 2018. https://www.dallasnews.com /news/immigration/2018/03/06/dallas-muslim-leaderarrested-daca-protest -capitol-hill.

Sarsour, Linda. "Salam Al-Marayati wrote this on my status." Facebook, August 22, 2015. https://www.facebook.com/linda.sarsour/posts/10153688511010572.

Saylor, Corey. "Is Sharia Compatible with Democracy?" Speech delivered at the University of Maine, March 24, 2014.

Sayyid, Bobby S. *A Fundamental Fear: Eurocentrism and the Emergence of Islamism.* London: Zed Books, 2003.

Schleifer, Theodore. "Ted Cruz: Muslim Refugees from Syria Should Go to Other Islamic Countries." CNN, November 17, 2015. https://www.cnn.com/2015/11/17/politics /ted-cruz-refugees-syria/index.html.

Schmitt, Gary, and Peter Skerry. "On the Peter King Hearing and Islamism in America." Brookings, March 10, 2011. https://www.brookings.edu/opinions/on-the-peter-king -hearing-and-islamism-in-america.

Schmitt, Michael T., Russell Spears, and Nyla R. Branscombe. "Constructing a Minority Group Identity out of Shared Rejection: The Case of International Students." *European Journal of Social Psychology* 33, no. 1 (2003): 1–12.

Schmitter, Philippe C., and Wolfgang Streeck. "The Organization of Business Interests: Studying the Associative Action of Business in Advanced Industrial Societies." Max-Planck-Institut für Gesellschaftsforschung (MPIfG) Discussion Paper 99/1, March 1999.

Schneider, Elizabeth M. "The Dialectics of Rights and Politics: Perspectives from the Women's Movement." *NYU Law Review* 5, no. 89 (1986).

Schumann, Christoph. "A Muslim Diaspora in the United States?" *Muslim World* 97, no. 11 (2007): 11–32.

Schwandt, Kimberly. "President Obama Doesn't Rule Out Military Option in Iran." *Fox News*, November 14, 2011. https://www.foxnews.com/politics/president-obama -doesnt-rule-out-military-option-in-iran.

Sekhon, Vijay. "The Civil Rights of 'Others': Antiterrorism, The Patriot Act, and Arab and South Asian American Rights in Post-9/11 American Society." *Texas Forum on Civil Liberties & Civil Rights* 8 (2003).

Selod, Saher, and David Embrick. "Racialization and Muslims: Situating the Muslim Experience in Race Studies." *Social Compass* 7, no. 8 (2013).

Shaikh, Ahmed. "MPAC, Countering Violent Extremism and American Muslim Astroturf—A Critical Review." *Altmuslim* (blog), Patheos, June 9, 2015. https://www .patheos.com/blogs/altmuslim/2015/06/mpac-countering-violent-extremism-and -american-muslim-astroturf-a-critical-review/.

Shain, Yossi. "Jewish Kinship at a Crossroads: Lessons for Homelands and Diasporas." *Political Science Quarterly* 117, no. 2 (2002): 279–304.

Shakir, Zaid. "Let Them Fly: Ode to a Little Dreamer." Facebook, March 6, 2018. https:// www.facebook.com/imamzaidshakir/photos/a.10151919830963359/10155345 424068359/?type=1&theater.

Silber, Mitchell D., and Arvin Bhatt. *Radicalization in the West: The Homegrown Threat.* Intelligence Division, New York Police Department (NYPD), 2007. https://info .publicintelligence.net/NYPDradicalization.pdf.

Sinno, Aulkader, ed. *Muslims in Western Politics.* Bloomington: Indiana University Press, 2009.

Skocpol, Theda. *Social Policy in the United States.* Princeton, NJ: Princeton University Press, 1995.

Smith, Caroline, and James M. Lindsay. "Rally 'Round the Flag: Opinion in the United States before and after the Iraq War." Brookings, June 1, 2003. https://www.brookings .edu/articles/rally-round-the-flag-opinion-in-the-united-states-before-and-after -the-iraq-war.

Soehl, Thomas, and Roger Waldinger. "Inheriting the Homeland? Intergenerational Transmission of Cross-Border Ties in Migrant Families." *American Journal of Sociology* 118, no. 3 (2012): 778–813.

Sorkin, Amy Davidson. "The N.S.A.'s Spying on American Muslims." *New Yorker*, July 10, 2014. https://www.newyorker.com/news/amy-davidson/the-n-s-a-s-spying -on-muslim-americans.

Southern Poverty Law Center (SPLC). "ACT for America." Extremist Files. Accessed March 27, 2020. https://www.splcenter.org/fighting-hate/extremist-files/group/act -america.

——. "David Yerushalmi." Extremist Files. Accessed March 23, 2020. https://www.splcenter .org/fighting-hate/extremist-files/individual/david-yerushalmi#.UalaAKVfmCI.

——. "Live-Blog: ACT for America's 'March against Sharia' Rallies." June 10, 2017. https:// www.splcenter.org/hatewatch/2017/06/10/live-blog-act-americas-march-against -sharia-rallies.

——. "Nation of Islam." Extremist Files. Accessed March 18, 2020. https://www.splcenter .org/fighting-hate/extremist-files/group/nation-islam.

Strickland, Patrick. "US: Are 'Anti-Sharia" Bills Legalising Islamophobia?" *Al Jazeera*, October 1, 2017. http://www.aljazeera.com/news/2017/09/anti-sharia-bills-legalising -islamophobia-170928150835240.html.

Strolovitch, Dara. "Do Interest Groups Represent the Disadvantaged? Advocacy at the Intersection of Race, Class, and Gender." *Journal of Politics* 68, no. 4 (2006): 894–910.

Sunstein, Cass R. "Interest Groups in American Public Law." *Stanford Law Review* 38, no. 1 (1985): 29–87.

Tajfel, Henri. "Social psychology of intergroup relations." *Annual Review of Psychology* 33, no. 1 (1982): 1–39.

Tajfel, Henri, ed. *Social Identity and Intergroup Relations*. Vol. 7. Cambridge: Cambridge University Press, 2010.

Tajfel, Henri, and John C. Turner. "An Integrative Theory of Intergroup Conflict." *Social Psychology of Intergroup Relations* 33, no. 47 (1979): 74–89.

Telhami, Shibley. *The World Through Arab Eyes: Arab Public Opinion and the Reshaping of the Middle East*. New York: Basic Books, 2013.

Tesler, Michael. "The Conditions Ripe for Racial Spillover Effect." *Political Psychology* 36 (2015): 101–17.

Thelen, Kathleen. "Historical Institutionalism in Comparative Politics." *Annual Review of Political Science* 2 (1999): 369–404.

Truman, David. *The Governmental Process*. 2nd ed. New York: Knopf, 1971.

Tyler, Tom R., Stephen Schulhofer, and Aziz Z. Huq. "Legitimacy and Deterrence Effects in Counterterrorism Policing: A Study of Muslim Americans." *Law & Society Review* 44 (2010): 365–402.

Uddin, Asma T. *When Islam Is Not a Religion: Inside America's Fight for Religious Freedom*. New York: Pegasus Books, 2018.

United Nations. "UN Human Rights Chief Points to 'Textbook Example of Ethnic Cleansing' in Myanmar." UN News, September 11, 2017. http://www.un.org/apps/news/story.asp?NewsID=57490.

United States Congress. BRIDGE Act. H.R. 496. 115th Cong. (2017). https://www.congress.gov/115/bills/hr496/BILLS-115hr496ih.pdf.

——. Freedom of Religion Act of 2017. H.R. 852. 115th Cong. (2017). https://www.congress.gov/115/bills/hr852/BILLS-115hr852ih.pdf.

——. No Religious Registry Act of 2017. H.R. 489. 115th Cong. (2017). https://www.congress.gov/115/bills/hr489/BILLS-115hr489ih.pdf.

——. Uniting and Strengthening America by Providing Appropriate Tools Required to Intercept and Obstruct Terrorism Act of 2001 (USA PATRIOT Act). Pub. L. No. 107–56, 115 Stat. 272. (2001). http://www.gpo.gov/fdsys/pkg/PLAW-107publ56/pdf/PLAW-107publ56.pdf.

United States Department of Justice, Federal Bureau of Investigation (FBI). "2017 Hate Crime Statistics." Uniform Crime Reporting (UCR), November 13, 2018. https://ucr.fbi.gov/hate-crime/2017.

——. *Decade in Review: Self-Selecting US Persons Drive Post-2006 Increase in Anti-US Plotting*. March 7, 2011. https://d3gn0r3afghep.cloudfront.net/foia_files/2016/09/13/Decade_in_Review__March_7-2011__.pdf.

——. *Domestic Investigations and Operations Guide*. December 16, 2008. https://vault.fbi.gov/FBI%20Domestic%20Investigations%20and%20Operations%20Guide%20(DIOG).

——. *Hate Crime Statistics, 2001*. Uniform Crime Reporting (UCR). Accessed March 23, 2020. https://ucr.fbi.gov/hate-crime/2001.

——. "Response to Media Reporting Regarding Counterterrorism Training." FBI National Press Office, September 15, 2011. https://archives.fbi.gov/archives/news/pressrel/press-releases/response-to-media-reporting-regarding-counterterrorism-training.

United States Department of Justice, Immigration and Naturalization Service. "Department of Justice Proposes New Rule for Nonimmigrant Aliens." June 13, 2002. Available at US Department of State Archive, http://2001-2009.state.gov/s/ct/rls/fs/2002/11409.htm.

United States Department of Justice, Office of the Inspector General. *The September 11 Detainees: A Review of the Treatment of Aliens Held on Immigration Charges in*

Connection with the Investigation of the September 11 Attacks. June 2003. https://oig.justice.gov/special/0306/chapter2.htm#II.

United States Government Printing Office (GPO). *Compilation of Hearings on Islamist Radicalization—Volume I.* Washington, DC: GPO, 2012. https://www.gpo.gov/fdsys/pkg/CHRG-112hhrg72541/pdf/CHRG-112hhrg72541.pdf.

United States of America v. Holy Land Foundation for Relief and Development et al. North American Islamic Trust (5th Cir. October 20, 2010). http://caselaw.findlaw.com/us-5th-circuit/1541982.html.

US Council of Muslim Organizations (USCMO). "Muslim Council Adopts Points on Countering Violent Extremism." February 17, 2015.

——. "Statement on President Trump's Recognition of Jerusalem as the Capital of Israel." December 17, 2017. https://uscmo.org/index.php/2017/12/07/statement-of-the-us-council-of muslim-organizations-on-president-trumps-recognition-of-jerusalem-as-the-capital-of-israel/.

——. "USCMO Calls to Stop Genocide in Aleppo and to Immediately Protect Civilians." December 14, 2016. https://www.muslimamericansociety.org/humanitarian-crisis-in-aleppo-syria/.

——. "USCMO Meets with Myanmar, OIC, Turkish Ambassador Demanding Halt to Rohingya Ethnic Cleansing." September 15, 2017. https://uscmo.org/index.php/2017/09/15/4998/.

Uslaner, Eric. "Does Diversity Drive Trust?" FEEM working paper, May 22, 2006.

Teun, A. Van Dijk. "Principles of Critical Discourse Analysis." *Discourse & Society* 4, no. 3 (1993): 249–83.

Van Nuys, Frank. *Americanizing the West: Race, Immigrants, and Citizenship, 1890–1930.* Lawrence: University Press of Kansas, 2002.

Verba, Sidney, Kay Lehman Schlozman, and Henry E. Brady. *Voice and Equality: Civic Voluntarism in American Politics.* Vol. 4. Cambridge, MA: Harvard University Press, 1995.

Vertovec, Steven. "Migration and Other Modes of Transnationalism: Towards Conceptual Cross-Fertilization." *International Migration Review* 37, no. 3 (2003): 951–73.

Volpp, Leti. "The Citizen and the Terrorist." *UCLA Law Review* 49 (2001): 1576–601.

Wahiba, Abu-Ras, and Zulema Suarez. "Muslim Men and Women's Perception of Discrimination, Hate Crimes and PTSD Symptoms Post 9/11." *Traumatology* 15, no. 3 (September 1, 2009).

Walker, Jack L. *Mobilizing Interest Groups in America: Patrons, Professions and Social Movements.* Ann Arbor: University of Michigan Press, 1991.

——. "The Origins and Maintenance of Interest Groups in America." *American Political Science Review* 77, no. 2 (1983): 390–406.

Whitehead, John W., and Steven H. Aden. "Forfeiting Enduring Freedom for Homeland Security: A Constitutional Analysis of the USA Patriot Act and the Justice Department's Anti-Terrorism Initiatives." *American University Law Review* 51 (2002): 1081.

White House Office of the Press Secretary. "Fact Sheet: The White House Summit on Countering Violent Extremism." February 18, 2015. https://obamawhitehouse.archives.gov/the-press-office/2015/02/18/fact-sheet-white-house-summit-countering-violent-extremism.

——. "President Says Saddam Hussein Must Leave Iraq within 48 Hours." March 17, 2003. http://georgewbush-whitehouse.archives.gov/news/releases/2003/03/20030317-7.html.

——. "Remarks by the President on the Middle East and North Africa." May 19, 2011. https://obamawhitehouse.archives.gov/the-press-office/2011/05/19/remarks-president-middle-east-and-north-africa.

Winter, Jana. "Welcome to the Quiet Skies." *Boston Globe*, July 28, 2018. http://apps
.bostonglobe.com/news/nation/graphics/2018/07/tsa-quiet-skies/?p1=HP
_SpecialTSA.

Wodak, Ruth. "Critical Discourse Analysis: History, Agenda, Theory, and Methodology."
In *Methods of Critical Discourse Analysis*, edited by Ruth Wodak and Michael Meyer.
London: Sage, 2001.

——. "The Discourse-Historical Approach." In *Methods of Critical Discourse Analysis*, edited by Ruth Wodak and Michael Meyer. London: Sage, 2001.

Women's Mosque of America. "FAQ." Accessed March 19, 2020. http://womensmosque
.com/faq/.

Wood, Elisabeth Jean. *Insurgent Collective Action and Civil War in El Salvador*. Cambridge:
Cambridge University Press, 2003.

WorldNetDaily (WND). "Congressman: Muslims 'Enemy amongst Us.'" February 13,
2004. http://www.wnd.com/2004/02/23257/.

Young, Stephen. "Abbott Signs Bill Tightening Up Texas' Anti-BDS Statute." *Dallas Observer*, May 10, 2019. https://www.dallasobserver.com/news/texas-tightens-up-anti
-bds-law-11661667.

Zaller, John. *The Nature and Origins of Mass Opinion*. New York: Cambridge University
Press, 1992.

Ziglar v. Abbasi, 582 U.S. ___ (2017). https://supreme.justia.com/cases/federal/us/582/15
-1358/opinion3.html.

Zinn, Howard, and Anthony Arnove, eds. *Voices of a People's History of the United States*,
2nd ed. New York: Seven Stories Press, 2009.

Zionist Organization of America (ZOA). "ZOA Criticizes ADL, AJC, Reform, for Joining
Anti-Israel CAIR, MPAC, Presby. in Letter Supporting Syrian Refugees." December 8, 2015. https://zoa.org/2015/12/10306402-zoa-dont-bring-isisterrorist
-infiltrated-hamas-supporting-jew-hating-syrian-muslims-into-the-u-s/.

Index

Note: Page numbers in *italics* refer to figures.

CPSIA information can be obtained
at www.ICGtesting.com
Printed in the USA
LVHW031004120221
679143LV00001B/95

9 781501 754005